asury off ??

operations

Mastering
treasury office
operations

A practical guide for the
back office professional

DENIS NOLAN AND GORDON AMOS

FINANCIAL TIMES

Prentice Hall

An imprint of **Pearson Education**

London • New York • San Francisco • Toronto • Sydney • Tokyo • Singapore
Hong Kong • Cape Town • Madrid • Amsterdam • Munich • Paris • Milan

PEARSON EDUCATION LIMITED

Head Office:
Edinburgh Gate
Harlow CM20 2JE
Tel: +44 (0)1279 623623
Fax: +44 (0)1279 431059

London Office:
128 Long Acre
London WC2E 9AN
Tel: +44 (0)20 7447 2000
Fax: +44 (0)20 7240 5771
Website: www.business-minds.com

First published in Great Britain 2001

© Pearson Education Limited 2001

The right of Denis Nolan and Gordon Amos to be identified as Authors
of this work has been asserted by them in accordance
with the Copyright, Designs and Patents Act 1988.

ISBN 0 273 63579 4

British Library Cataloguing in Publication Data
A CIP catalogue record for this book can be obtained from the British Library

10 9 8 7 6 5 4 3 2 1

Typeset by Northern Phototypesetting Co Ltd, Bolton
Printed and bound in Great Britain by Redwood Books, Trowbridge, Wiltshire

The Publishers' policy is to use paper manufactured from sustainable forests.

About the authors

Denis Nolan, Director of ArbiTrain Ltd, is a well-known market practitioner with over thirty years' experience in the global exchange, money and derivatives markets.

As a chief dealer and treasurer in London, the Middle East and Japan during the 1970s and 1980s, he was among the very first treasurers of international financial institutions to embrace financial futures and derivatives as a logical extension of money and exchange dealing strategies.

A founder member of LIFFE and a visiting lecturer at the City University Business School London, he has written extensively on foreign exchange and addressed conferences and seminars on financial markets' instruments, derivatives, arbitrage, back office and Code of Conduct, in Europe, USA, the Middle East and Japan.

With a wide training background and as an internationally recognized expert on the subject he was commissioned by ACI–The Financial Markets Association in December 1998 to write a global 'Model Code of Conduct' for its 70 member countries, covering treasury OTC financial markets. The work was completed in March of this year and has recently been published.

Gordon Amos FAIBF FCIB is an international banking consultant, business advisor and lecturer with over thirty-five years' experience, particularly in treasury, capital markets, risk management and operations.

Formerly a senior international banker, he has many years' knowledge of a wide range of banking which he gained in the UK and in nine years abroad in Australia, Germany and India.

Experience with ANZ Banking Group and previously National Westminster includes trade and international finance business, syndicated lending, equity and fixed interest investment and portfolio management after formative years in retail banking.

A fellow of both the Australian Institute of Banking and Finance, Melbourne, and the Chartered Institute of Bankers, London, he is the appointed Moderator for the Banking Operation Regulation, Market Practice and Treasury Management subject of the Chartered Institute of Bankers/UMIST associateship degree link examinations.

Currently, he is a managing consultant at M86 Limited, which is the UK arm of SMS Consulting, an Australian-based group specializing in project management and technology in the financial services industry.

CONTENTS

FOREWORD

Traditionally, much of the knowledge and skills of professionals in the wholesale financial markets has been learned on the job. This approach has varied from the simple 'sit, watch and learn' approach to the sophisticated mentoring systems used by some large financial institutions. It is true that such training has always been supplemented by formal training programmes, nevertheless, until recently the traditional approach was dominant. A side effect of this emphasis on 'on-the-job training' has been the difficulty experienced by outsiders understanding what insiders do.

The ratio of 'on-the-job' training to other training techniques is now declining. The reason is that the markets have changed drastically over the last 20 years: increased use of new technology (computers and communication systems) and new theoretical ideas (option pricing) have increased the number of products, many of them highly complex, and increased the linkages markets. To communicate knowledge and skills in this new world every educational tool and technique needs to be used.

This is where the work of ACI Education becomes important. ACI Education (formerly the ACI Institute) is the educational division of ACI–The Financial Markets Association. This is the primary international professional body for the international financial markets, founded in 1955 and now represented in over 80 countries internationally with an excess of 24 000 members.

The task of ACI Education is simple to state and is embodied in the charter of ACI. It is to ensure that educational programmes that reflect the constantly changing nature of the industry are made available to both new entrants to the profession and seasoned professionals and to set professional standards for the industry globally. This task is both challenging and exciting. Recent innovations include the decision to convert the examinations to an electronically delivered format, a change that facilitates the availability of ACI's professional examination programme on a daily basis, via a network of over 5000 test centres globally.

ACI also, as part of its educational programmes, encourages authors, publishers and tutors to provide a wide variety of routes to its examinations as possible. For this reason it is delighted that Gordon Amos, Denis Nolan and FT Prentice Hall have produced *Mastering Treasury Office Operations*. It captures in text the core professional knowledge necessary to pass the ACI Settlements

Certificate. In recent years the treasury settlements areas of the major financial institutions have been increasingly in the spotlight. Once considered a 'starting point' for young professionals hoping to progress to positions in trading rooms today they are attracting a new breed of bankers seeking to make their careers in the settlements of middle office areas. This book covers, in great detail, the increasingly complex world of settlements and will be appreciated as a source of information, not only by the professionals in this field but also by a wider audience.

Heering Ligthart
President
ACI–The Financial Markets Association

INTRODUCTION

When the ACI–The Financial Markets Association first suggested during 1998 that we should write a book for one of its core syllabus subjects, Treasury Operations and Settlements, we had one immediate concern – the timing. While it was true that improvization and changes in business processing and settlement practice, prompted mostly by new technology, had been a feature of the financial markets for decades, the end of that year would herald the beginnings of a new operational era.

First, a new currency, the euro was about to be launched, replacing ten of the convertible EC currencies, which would be relegated and consigned to 'legacy' status. Second, new clearing systems were scheduled to come on stream, which would facilitate the change. There had already been considerable delays and technical problems with the essential cross-border co-operation and state of readiness of the various parties involved with TARGET to such an extent that at times the project appeared to be singularly inappropriately named. A guide to back office administration launched at such a time would have been a rather speculative attempt on what was aspired to rather than what is.

However, after some early problems, the new regime has settled into a smooth operational mode, which in turn opened the way for completion of the work. In changing markets there is no 'perfect' time. Indeed, as we go to press, the new ACI international Model Code of Conduct is also being published which will undoubtedly have an impact on back office practice: appropriate extracts have therefore been included in this book with the permission of the ACI.

Clearly a textbook such as this, particularly one written for an international student base, must be generic in character although we have drawn on examples from specific countries where appropriate. Also, in the interest of the student trying to gain a basic understanding of the subject, we have simplified in numerous instances to try and present a coherent picture based on the axiom of Occam's Razor which may be neatly coined as 'do not subdivide unnecessarily'. However, to achieve this primary aim we must therefore add the caveat that there are always exceptions to the general rule and rely on the old adage of 'when we say never, we mean hardly ever'!

Today, treasury operations and settlements is a wide-ranging subject and it would be impossible to write exhaustively on all the issues involved. Within our brief, which was essentially to meet the general requirements of the subject syllabus for bank dealers, we have attempted to alert the back office professional to particular aspects on an issue and where to go to find out more as required. Also for this reason, we have taken the view of the banks in the various markets covered while acknowledging the role of other participants.

ACKNOWLEDGEMENTS

We have taken all reasonable steps to ensure that information is as up to date as possible. In an increasingly fluid business world however changes come by the day and any action taken based on information in this book should therefore be checked for current validity.

In our endeavours to keep pace with and anticipate the various changes and issues we are grateful to many people for their support and assistance.

Initially, our gratitude must go to David Foreman for having the idea of bringing the authors together, to Ann McGoff of the ACI for her unending support and to Richard Stagg and Jonathan Agbenyega of Financial Times Prentice Hall for the renowned publisher's patience. We also like to thank Peter Witte of West LB, the Chief Examiner for the ACI Settlements subject, for reading the manuscript and making helpful suggestions.

A debt of gratitude is due to Graham Bright and Shelagh Ashley of SWIFT for their help with the SWIFT documentation and to Nigel Brigden, Chief Examiner of ACIB/BSc Banking Operations: Regulation, Market Practice and Treasury Management subject CIB for his valuable technical assistance on clearing and security.

A special word of thanks is also due to Alastair Mirlees of CLS for his advice and updating on the state of the multilateral payments netting industry, to Guy Milnthorpe and Rudi Schiffer of ANZ Bank for their assistance with documentation and payments systems respectively and also to Graham Oakeby and Malcolm Heywood for aspects of regulatory reporting. Paul Mason was of invaluable help on derivatives processing and settlement procedures.

We would like to thank ACI–The Financial Markets Association, the Financial Services Authority, the Bank of England, the Chartered Institute of Bankers, the Bank for International Settlements, the European Central Bank, SWIFT, City Networks, ISDA and Reuters for permission to reproduce extracts from their publications.

Finally, we are both profoundly grateful to Liz Amos for her encouragement, enthusiasm and invaluable help with the editing.

Denis Nolan
Gordon Amos
London, September 2000

Defining treasury operations

This chapter introduces the core processing functions of treasury operations, and also shows that a wide-ranging scope of activities is necessary in order to provide a full support role to the trading room.

AN OVERVIEW

Until quite recently, it was common among international bankers to say that beyond the trading or dealing room was treasury operations, usually called the back office by treasury professionals. This slightly deprecating phrase reflected the misleading view that the complicated work was done by dealers or traders in the front office while the work of the back office in processing and settling deals was painstaking but relatively simple and could be done by clerks sited anywhere. But this also disguised the fact that many dealers did not actually know what was done in treasury operations, while staff in the latter felt that dealing was a mysterious art form that only caused them problems.

Indeed, the back office is usually located behind the trading room, but the work that is performed there has changed considerably, evolving far beyond just processing into a total support role for the dealing functions. Coupled with this has come the realization that front and back offices are interdependent and need to understand each other's work. Neither has a future role without the other.

Increasing regulation and compliance requirements, risk management needs and interactive systems development, have combined to make 'back office efficiency' one of the most critical factors in ensuring the well-being of an international bank today. This is certain to continue as the work of the back offices becomes more onerous while financial products become increasingly complex, despite streamlining of processing systems.

Today, treasury operations has grown into one of the key administrative areas of a financial institution, responsible for the processing of all financial market transactions and usually much more, including a crucial role in the control of risk. Modern international banks have a large daily turnover in numerous currencies from treasury transactions, which result in high value payments and receipts in many centres. This has only been partly reduced through netting arrangements and systems. Errors can be expensive, so there is strong emphasis on early discovery and fast rectification of mistakes: this means that stringent cross-checking systems and procedures need to be in place.

An important development in the back office has been the advent of straight-through processing (STP), also called 'hands-off' or exception processing. This has been made possible through system advances of real time on line input in the trading room, which in turn has meant that the back office can recall deals input in the trading room to verify from an external source. In practice this is done automatically, comparing incoming data from brokers and counterparties and investigating exceptions. Indeed, with the introduction of full trading systems the deal is 'confirmed' as it is done, allowing the back office to concentrate principally on exception reporting, settlement and risk control. This is a completely different approach to the old style input and checking of written paper-based deals that represented only a dealer's version of what the deal was before external verification could even commence.

One of the basic tenets for a treasury area in a bank is the strict segregation of duties and location between the front and back office, the latter controlling confirmations and settlement transactions. Further, the separation of reporting lines up to senior management level between those responsible for these basic functions is clearly laid out in regulatory guidelines and is the subject of strong recommendations in the Model Code. These rulings are even more important in an era of straight-through processing where the checks are fewer and must essentially be independent. However, while this is straightforward for the processing functions, the independent monitoring and management of complex trading risks can be much more problematical, requiring the ability and market knowledge to understand how the trades and hedges in the dealer's book are structured.

Flexible control

A key concept for the head of a treasury operations unit is that of 'flexible control'. There are two perspectives on this. The first is summed up by saying, 'the bottom line is that the bank has to do business otherwise it is out of business.' The challenge in treasury is that it is a fast moving area where financial innovation is the lifeblood of the markets. Back office professionals must anticipate market developments as efficiently as the traders and work closely with them. However, at some stage, they must take a view as to whether, for example, a new product will 'fly' and start to gather what will be by definition scarce resources – both people and systems – to meet the new demand. This husbanding can be as challenging in its own way as working out the accounting required for the new product. Of course, there is a point at which it is necessary to say, 'We are not ready: we should not do

> **Back office professionals must anticipate market developments as efficiently as the traders and work closely with them.**

this business yet.' But that point is a subjective one that needs to be based on a careful look at the facts and the collective experience of the senior treasury management group. It is usually possible to cope with a few deals of the new product; several hundred will cause chaos if all is not properly in place.

A second perspective on flexible control is making sure that the right amount of attention and response is given in proportion to what is *really* required. Two obvious priorities are:

- good on-going control of payments authorization, ensuring prompt follow-up to confirmation and reconciliation exceptions;
- efficient housekeeping for the standing data tables in the database of the various systems, which may be in use in any given bank.

But attention must also be paid to factors that do not necessarily impact on the day-to-day running of the unit, and which, if neglected, will ultimately introduce problems that may become intractable over the longer term. One critical rule is to ensure that the accounting treatment for treasury products is correct and understood by staff. Even though the prime accounting control responsibility will probably lie with a separate finance unit, it is important that operations understand what and why entries are being passed in the bank's books. A corollary to this is that the operations head is firmly in the chain for the approval of accounting, systems and procedures for new products and product variations.

An important accounting-related priority is the protection of the integrity of the systems in use by making sure that staff report systems problems through a formal procedure to the support unit via treasury operations line management. The cumulative effect of constant attention to this facet of keeping systems up to date and problem free can be just as important in efficiency terms as an upgrade of a system. However, large treasuries usually have complex systems configurations, which have evolved over time. This can mean these and the interfaces to other systems can be difficult to change quickly to meet the needs of the business. The issues of 'buying in' package solutions and building interfaces to existing systems versus in-house developments to meet these demands are discussed later in the book.

Also in the larger treasury banks, the current approach to the organization of the back office is to cluster the processing units around the front office business units. For example, the money market business unit will have a back office support unit within treasury operations processing the deals for that area. There are several good reasons for this, which are explored later, but the main one is that it works for the traders and the support staff.

Cash reconciliation is another function where the head of the back office must keep the tightest control. This is the point at which money leaves the bank, rendering it vulnerable to fraud if this area is neglected or behind schedule. It is very much the bank's last line of defence and must be efficient at all times. If the head of the back office does not have the reconciliation unit under their direct control they should negotiate and enforce a service contract to ensure that, for example, the back office has a New York reconciliation by say 9.30 am the following day. Only in this way can they, in turn, provide a dependable service to the traders, and indeed, to the bank.

But this is not all. Such is the complexity of a large modern treasury with a wide product range that each back office becomes unique in the functions, procedures, systems and controls that it adopts over time. This means that the staff and management must be largely self-motivated in finding new ways to improve efficiency and keep up to date in a fast developing industry. It is not advisable to wait until the next audit to be told that this or that can be improved: it may be too late by then – the next business processing problem or new product will be upon you!

Modern technology may have removed the input and routine checking role from the back office, allowing more focus on efficiency, quality of service and reduction in costs, but this has been more than offset by increased complexity in day-to-day operations. These include compliance in various forms, risk control and the need to keep up to date with systems develop-ments in the dealing room and back office. Such developments include screen-based trading and input, links externally for confirmations, brokers, netting, payments and reporting. It all adds up to a challenging environment demanding its own high quality people who understand the overall picture and who seek rigorous solutions to practical banking problems. For the budding office manager these and other topics are explored in the chapters that follow.

> **Staff and management must be largely self-motivated in finding new ways to improve efficiency and keep up to date in a fast developing industry.**

INTRODUCING THE CORE FUNCTIONS

The mainstream role of the back office is in direct support of the trading room or front office. Traditionally, this included the input of deals written and autho-rized by traders, checking of input, verification by confirmation, settlement and reconciliation of nostro accounts as soon as possible. However, with the advent of online data capture systems and, more importantly, online trading systems the input of deals has progressively moved to the trading floor.

Input and completion

The first core function for the back office is to recall the deal through the input system and decide what has to be done to complete the details of the deal. Deals input through front-end data capture or agreed on one of the proprietary trading systems will have already been subjected to numerous system checks to ensure that the transaction is technically correct. Some deals will require settlement instructions to be added, but for straightforward foreign exchange and money market deals done with other banks and large corporates, standard settlement instructions (SSIs) may have already been added from the SSI database file. This could also be true for derivatives trans-actions in the larger treasuries. However, these types of transactions generally need more checking and manual intervention because of the wide variety of their use. At this stage the bank is able to release its own confirmation to the counterparty, particularly OTC.

Verification by confirmation

Input by traders directly into data-capture systems has brought its own rewards. Provided the input is accurate, the traders immediately benefit from online positions and maturity ladders. This is further enhanced by the facility to manipulate/interpolate the outstanding book with many charting and analytical tools. Conversely, this has allowed the back office to concentrate on exception reporting rather than on input.

Thus, the second core function for the processing support unit is to verify the deal from an external source as soon as possible after the transaction has been done. For bank-to-bank trading, the verification can take the form of a confirmation of a deal done through Reuters 2000 or EBS trading systems, or a broker's confirmation via Barts 3 if the deal has been done through a broker. It can also be a confirmation from the counterparty, normally via SWIFT (see page 29), which will be matched automatically using Accord or a similar in-house matching system such as TRAM (transaction matching system). This enables unmatched items to be investigated quickly. Telephone confirmation can also be sought. Additionally, the widespread use of SSIs, now actively encouraged by the regulators, has reduced the need for swapping settlement instructions. However, some banks still do this as a security measure for value today/done today deals, even where SSIs are held. Deals done with customers (non-banks) will normally be confirmed by telex or mail, with instructions swapped on the telephone, depending on the arrangements. Increasingly, however, corporate customers are using automatic confirmation-matching services.

The procedures we have described so far are based mainly on foreign exchange and money market transactions. Other more specialized transactions, such as financial futures or bond trades, must be matched by the back office online with the centralized exchange or market regulatory body within a set time. It is essential that the deal is confirmed independently of the trader before any kind of value is given or payment is made.

Settlement

The third core function in the processing chain is that of settlement. This can take the form of a clean currency payment/receipt at the bank's agency accounts. Other transactions cause different payment messages, depending on the event triggered in the 'lifecycle', for example, a payment made against the receipt of bond or other securities at Euroclear or Clearstream, two of the major securities clearing houses. Normally, agents will be instructed to pay or receive via a SWIFT message. As this is in a standardized format it is easily fed into accounting, reporting and other systems at the agent bank.

Likewise, at the initiating bank, accounting entries and reporting are created from the one common events file. An important corollary to the payment process is that the deal may be one included in a netting arrangement with the counterparty. Although there are several legal concepts and methods of netting, the basic idea is that payments and receipts are set off against one another each day and only one net amount is paid or received for each currency. Default clauses in swap agreements are frequently cited in this way. The underlying concept is designed to reduce credit and payment exposure risk (this is explained in Chapter 6).

Reconciliation

Operations areas are typically involved in a number of reconciliation processes, including the agreement of traders' overnight positions, nostro accounts and brokerage. This can also mean agreeing positions for margin calls in futures trading or agreeing custody accounts to the underlying securities in securities trading. However, the basic reconciliation function is to agree or reconcile the entries that have passed over an account with an agent bank against those that have been passed internally in the books of the bank to a nostro account. (The word 'nostro' simply means 'our account with them'.) After reconciliation, the unmatched items in both accounts then represent those that have not been responded to in either the books of the bank or its agent and should therefore be investigated immediately.

In summary, the core functions of the back office are :
- input (where necessary) and completion of details of deal;
- verification of deal by both inward and outward confirmations;
- settlement of the deal depending on the event which may also include netting;
- reconciliation of nostros, positions, books.

These functions are vital to the on-going viability of the bank.

THE BACK OFFICE CAN ALSO INCLUDE ...

Although the phrase 'the back office' was originally synonymous with the processing functions of input, confirmation, settlement and reconciliation, this has progressively broadened to include many other aspects supporting the trading room. In some banks this includes 'middle office', risk management, immediate responsibility for treasury accounting, documentation of various types, producing the financial results, analysis and budget forecasts for the treasury business unit, input into regulatory reporting, and systems development (including telecommunications), both for the support areas and the trading room itself. The bigger the treasury unit, the more likely it will have some or more of these functions, depending on the level of expertise within the area (see Fig 1.1). These are dealt with in more detail later in the book.

Risk management

This is a function that can sit well in the back office provided it is properly staffed by officers who understand fully the business and risks involved – which usually means ex-market practitioners! It can range from agreeing overnight cash positions for the trading room through to full-risk modelling associated with derivatives trading and hedging. In between can come monitoring of counterparty, country, dealer and market-related limits that have been set and approved in other areas of the bank such as the credit department.

Treasury accounting

This unit acts as an intermediary between the treasury business unit and the finance department to ensure that the accounting of treasury products is accurate and correct. Unit heads should be in the accounting approval chain for new and changed products, as well as for operations and systems. It also enables treasury operations people to understand the accounting that is peculiar to treasury, such as the 'trading account' and 'base currency' concepts. This can be vital when much of the accounting is 'hidden' by being automatically systems generated as a result of deal input of various types. Indeed, this problem is self-perpetuating as the more complex the deals become the more likely a bank will be to automate to prevent errors.

Documentation

This can range from simple customer mandates through to full legal documentation with both banks and customers. Although now considered the norm, standard documentation (at least in the interbank market) was rare and generally deemed to be unnecessary until the advent of derivatives, starting with the swap and options market in the early 1980s. Now a full range of regulatory legal agreements is available, depending on what types of business are being conducted and, crucially, whether the counterparties intend to net payments at settlement. This is covered in more detail in Chapter 8.

Organizationally, this area can be viewed in a similar way to the accounting function. If documentation forms part of the back office then the business will be more understood by management and better controlled as a result. Many investment banks now locate 'documentation' with lawyers, if the complexity demands this, in their back offices or even in the trading room itself, to ensure that the unit co-ordinates the paperwork with the trading room.

Financials, analysis, budgets, regulatory reporting

Depending on the size of the business unit, a small financials section allows the treasury business head to have a 'hands-on' role for all financial aspects of the business. These include not only the income stream from the product mix for a particular bank, but also the cost base supporting each type of product. Many products overlap, both in terms of use (for example, swaps done as trades and hedges) and in terms of processing – including systems. For instance, one back office system may be used to process all derivatives executed. This can make it difficult to isolate the income stream (and the proportion of people committed in producing it) and the corresponding processing costs, unless the full structure of the business is thoroughly understood. Moreover, most treasuries form part of a larger bank and therefore have group business directives or requirements of which to take notice. This may mean that a specific product is continued with as a service to customers or even a 'loss leader' because of an overall bank view that it should be in a particular market. In short, the product portfolio must be properly costed and accounting staff dedicated to treasury can have a vital role in this area.

In an ideal world, the suite of reports required by the regulators would be entirely system generated and require no intervention. In practice, treasury is a rapidly evolving area with systems tending to lag behind the business and there needs to be liaison with the unit responsible for submitting returns (usually the finance area) to keep it informed of developments.

As a minimum requirement, senior management of treasury should vet the reports showing treasury business, such as the open positions report called the S3 (in London) to ensure agreement.

Systems and telecommunications

This is possibly the most problematical area for the treasury back office. Over the last ten years there has been a rapid convergence of telecommunications and systems functions in the industry. In the treasury environment the trading room and the back office quite often use different parts of the same system, allowing various forms of straight-through processing with telecommunications ports in the dealing room for doing the deals and in the back office for reporting, confirmations and settlement. Many of these specialized requirements are unique to an international bank treasury in each country in which it operates. Further, a bank will probably wish to standardize its trading rooms and back offices in each country to meet global requirements. All this means that each treasury unit needs to have a degree of autonomy for this critical function with its own dedicated resources and specialists, subject to overall bank or group requirements.

> **It is still necessary for one area to be accountable for the total system requirements for a treasury unit to function efficiently.**

Although rapid technological change and straight-through processing have cut through traditional boundaries of responsibility, it is still necessary for one area to be accountable for the total system requirements for a treasury unit to function efficiently and indeed to avoid chaos on the network or switching system supporting the traders. These days, as everyone either wants to be or is an expert on systems, a line must be drawn in terms of what is allowed and what is not. This is often best done in operations or the back office, with the primary control seen as another support function for the trading room, alleviating the latter of this burden and allowing it to concentrate on business.

Fig 1.1   **The treasury back office**

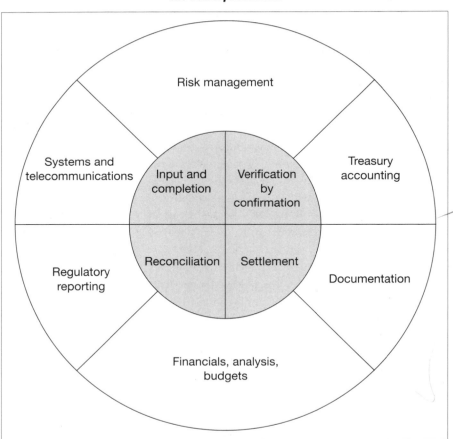

However, traders must be allowed sufficient freedom to experiment with new ideas and software within this controlled environment – on a 'loose rein' basis – but of course completely segregated from the real books of the bank. These and other such issues are explored in more depth later in the book.

RESOURCES

An overview of operations would not be complete without mention of the people that make it all work. Traditionally, traders were regarded as highly specialized staff, supported by competent personnel in the back office. Indeed, the back office was seen as a training ground for the dealing room, with bright clerks vying with each other to gain access as telex clerk or positionkeeper in the room. This arrangement was advantageous in that they already understood how the back office worked and would cause the minimum disruption to the bank's work as dealing room skills were learnt. At the same time, ageing traders found that their skills were being applied to a risk management job or possibly to less stressful processing work.

Nowadays, as complexity has increased, high quality, specialized people are needed in both the dealing room and the back office. The operations manager has become a specialist in his or her own right, requiring a mix of international banking and treasury business knowledge, as well as the ability to use systems and telecommunications to deliver best practice. To this must be added a sound accounting knowledge and a legal background to meet the demands of this critical role. The manager must also lead and enthuse a team of specialized staff, who are no longer in any sense the 'poor relation' of the dealers, to provide a full dealing room service. Recent bank failures (see Table 1.1) have reinforced this trend, emphasizing the need for high quality staff throughout the treasury unit.

Heads of operations should ensure that their staff are qualified to use the varied systems that are critical to the treasury. Without them it cannot operate at all in a modern high value, high volume business, never mind efficiently. Internal and external training courses are invaluable and must be on-going, particularly for confirmations and settlement systems, such as those provided by SWIFT and Euroclear that are constantly being upgraded.

It is important that the unit heads have an adequate budget for this purpose so that they can plan the training schedule for the area: piecemeal ad hoc on-the-job training is no longer a viable option.

Finally, it should be realized that the key human resource factor in treasury in the last 30 years has been the accelerating shift of the input function in its various forms from the back office to the dealing room. This has turned the organizational structure of the treasury function on its head and is producing the all-rounder in the organization: someone who is 'squaring the circle' by understanding fully both front and back office requirements while pursuing profitable business in an increasingly complex market.

Table 1.1

The treasury back office: what can go wrong?

Date	Name	Cause	Lesson
1974	Bankhaus Herstatt, Cologne	Losses in foreign exchange	Delivery or settlement time zone risk[1]
1986	Hammersmith and Fulham local authority, London	Interest rate swaps losses	Dealing ultra vires/documentation[2]
1995	Barings Bank, Singapore	Futures and options index trading losses	Segregation of duties/management control[3]

1 In June 1974 Bankhaus ID Herstatt, Cologne, a small but very active bank in foreign exchange (FX) dealing, failed following substantial losses from FX speculation. The suspension announcement was made early/mid-afternoon European time by the German Central Bank (the Bundesbank) after European currency settlement for that day had been completed. However, the corresponding US dollar countervalue payments had not been executed and were suspended, thus triggering the unlikely but real delivery/time zone risk in foreign exchange deals resulting in a 100% loss of contract amount (up to USD20 million). This involved several counterparty banks who had already paid the European currency equivalent in settlement of Herstatt's purchases maturing on that day, but who did not receive their own US dollar purchase amount. Rather suprisingly, it subsequently emerged that many large FX market participants were not even aware that such a risk existed. Although the Herstatt phenomenon was riddled with malpractice, poor management and lack of control, the dramatic timing of the Bundesbank announcement highlighted the settlement risk to such an extent that it is often referred to today as the 'Herstatt Risk' (*see also* Chapter 6 on netting).
2 The Hammersmith and Fulham local authority issue highlighted the need for adequate documentation evidencing authentication and authorization to trade in specific financial markets and instruments.
3 Lack of segregation of duties between front and back offices was clearly the main contributing factor in the Barings débâcle where poor overall control was a critical issue.

SUMMARY

Key points
- Back office defined
- Core functions:
  - input and verification
  - confirmation
  - settlement
  - reconciliation
- Other functions
- Input function 'shift'

We have looked at a range of functions that may be included in treasury operations or back office, depending on the size of the bank's treasury and the degree of autonomy required or desired. At the centre are four core processing functions that a bank needs to do to complete its work each day.

The life of a deal

This chapter explains the various instruments traded in a typical treasury and gives an overview of the processing function.

TYPES OF DEALS

The remaining chapters of this book cover in detail the various processes in the life of a treasury deal from input through to reconciliation. In between come verification, confirmation and settlement with netting where applicable. Additionally, an outline of treasury accounting is provided to complete an understanding of the total process. From a back office management viewpoint, comprehension of both the operational and financial risks involved at various stages of the cycle is also essential.

It is therefore a useful exercise, at this stage, to look at the workflow or life of a typical deal from the moment of completion in the treasury dealing room through to final maturity. All deals contain a series of steps in their lifecycles, many of which are common, such as passing of accounting entries. However, before we can understand the back office route of a particular trade we must decide on which type of deal is involved, some of which are more complex than the traditional foreign exchange (FX) and money market transaction.

Up to the early 1980s most treasuries traded the same basic instruments or products, such as FX and domestic money market deposits, plus certificates of deposit (CDs), bills and (sometimes) bonds and Euromarket paper (similar to domestic instruments but in foreign currency). These markets had usually developed as the complementary transaction to the international trade between individuals and companies and eventually countries. For example, the FX market originated to meet the need to buy or sell foreign currency as a result of the sale or purchase of goods abroad. Over time, arbitrage and speculative transactions have come to account for a greater percentage of the market, overtaking payment flows to meet international settlement of debt.

From about 1981 onwards a new range of instruments strategies and products came on-stream, beginning with financial futures that had originally been launched in Chicago in 1972. Many of the new products, discussed in more detail later, were complementary 'off-balance-sheet' versions of existing money or cash market instruments from which they were derived, hence the name 'derivatives'. They allowed a greater range of hedging against underlying or physical transactions than had been possible before, but also opened the door to an array of speculative strategies and opportunities.

From the back office viewpoint this presents immediate difficulties depending on a particular bank's systems configuration. Hedge transactions (for example, loans or deposits hedged by a swap) need to be identified and linked. This is usually straightforward, using a common systems reference. 'Package' transactions involving, for example, a loan/deposit, with a related swap and/or option, can be processed and settled adequately through a bank's systems on a component basis.

However, when shown in the bank's books separately, they will not necessarily represent the 'true' picture, particularly in the older legacy systems. They may have to be tracked independently as a package for profit and loss and risk management purposes, with appropriate adjustments made to correct initial systems reporting. These issues are discussed in a later chapter.

Although varying considerably in scope, structure and use, derivative instruments have three basic properties as follows:

- the accounting for the instruments is off balance sheet;
- delivery is normally 'cash settlement' basis;
- they represent an efficient method of hedging interest rate risk or exchange rate risk, though the primary use is for arbitrage and speculation.

Table 2.1 compares in outline the main instrument groups and their characteristics including derivatives, traded in a broadly based treasury of a typical international bank.

PROCESSING OVERVIEW

All deals – whether an FX deal, money market loan or deposit, derivative transaction or repo – have certain common characteristics. All require input to the bank's system to be recorded for verification, confirmation, settlement and reconciliation. This process ensures transactions are properly recorded and enables correct accounting in the books of a bank and accurate risk management measurement. Fig 2.1 shows the process for an FX deal.

Strict control at each stage of the processing cycle is critical as a wrongly recorded trade will not only corrupt the remainder of the processing cycle (for example, a wrong confirmation or payment message will be sent), but the error may eventually prove costly to correct, as well as taking up valuable back office rescue time. In this scenario, the controls and checks in straight-through processing (STP) become even more critical as they are driven by exception and therefore fewer in number.

Strict control at each stage of the processing cycle is critical.

But before examining STP later in the book we should first look at the workflow overview of a typical deal, including the main standard aspects of processing and the points to watch for. These can be summarized as follows.

Input

- Deal capture for all transaction types is usually on a screen-based system, which can be manual input or a live trading system.
- For the major participants most deals in the FX market are completed on screen-based trading systems such as Reuters or EBS.

Table 2.1

Treasury products and their characteristics

Product	Description	Treasury uses/purpose	Balance sheet	Credit risk	Where traded	Settlement/delivery	Amount	Date(s)
Foreign exchange	Exchange of one currency for another	Hedging/speculation in FX	Off balance sheet	Delivery risk; replacement risk	OTC	Usually full delivery	Any agreed amount	Spot (two days) or forward
Deposits	Borrowing/lending, usually interbank	Obtain/place funds unsecured, usually short term up to one year	On balance sheet	100% for depositor	OTC	Full delivery	Any agreed amount	Various periods, usually from spot
Certificates of deposit	Negotiable receipts for fixed periods	Investment/liquidity	On balance sheet	100% risk for the holder with the issuer	OTC	Full delivery of proceeds	Variable minimum. Usually any agreed amount	Usually fixed periods up to five years
FRAs	Forward/forward interest rate contract for a notional amount	Hedging/speculation in forward interest rates and arbitrage	Off balance sheet	Small/marginal (replacement)	OTC	Non-deliverable, cash settlement for interest rate differential on notional amount	Any agreed amount	Two (forward/forward) dates
Currency options	Contracts giving holder the right to buy or sell FX at an agreed rate	Hedging/speculation in FX	Off balance sheet	Marginal (replacement risk for holder (buyer))	OTC and some central exchanges	OTC: usually full delivery on exercise/value date; exchange traded are variable	Any agreed amount: exchange traded standardized	OTC: European; fixed date, American period
Interest rate options	Contracts giving holder the right of interest rate protection for an amount/period	Hedging/speculation in interest rates	Off balance sheet	Marginal/replacement risk for option holder	OTC and some central exchanges	Usually cash settlement	Any agreed amount; OTC: exchange traded – standardized	Agreed period
Interest rate swaps	Agreements to swap interest rate commitments	Interest rate exposure management/hedging arbitrage	Off balance sheet	Variable credit risk for both counterparties	OTC; recently exchange traded	Cash settled, non-deliverable	Any agreed amount; OTC: exchange traded – standardized	Usually up to ten years
Bonds	Negotiable borrowers certificate for term periods of over seven years	Investment, liquidity arbitrage	On balance sheet	Full credit risk for holder of proceeds	OTC	Full delivery	Any agreed amount	Fixed floating period, usually over seven years
Repos	Purchase/resale agreements	Liquidity/cashflow	On balance sheet	Very small	OTC	Full delivery	Any agreed amount	Usually short date
Financial futures	Financial transactions for set future date	Risk transfer/hedge (speculation)	Off balance sheet	Virtually nil	Exchange traded	Generally cash settled, some deliverable	Standard/fixed amounts	Set periods, long and short

- Most banks have interactive screen-based input by dealers for all FX, money market and derivatives transactions, to enable dealers to analyze their own positions quickly. The dealer knows what he/she has done and is less likely to make an error of fact on input.

- Away from the main trading centres, input based on paper deal slips completed by dealers is still encountered. This may be where a bank is dealing with a corporate or private customer who is likely to use an in-house account to settle a transaction. Timely and regular frequent collection from the dealing room is essential and time stamping of tickets is still common practice.

- If paper based, encoding of the deal slip will be necessary by back office clerks, usually using SWIFT or SWIFT-similar codes for the name of the counterparty. Other fields may also need encoding prior to input, such as the instructions for settlement if standard settlement instructions are not in place (such as on corporate deals where payment may need to be made to a third party beneficiary).

- In some less sophisticated banks or in developing countries it is still possible to encounter older limited interactive screen or even mask input, with input being done by either the dealers directly into the system or by the back office based on paper-based deal slips completed by dealers. In the latter case, the input clerk can make additional errors when inputting the deal, creating a further risk if the subsequent checking procedures do not pick up these errors. Once the norm in all input systems, these processes are rapidly disappearing worldwide, as automated trading systems remove this double potential for error.

- Data input is system checked on input against known conditions or requirements and exceptions, such as the calculation of a value on an FX deal not agreeing with the exchange rate or interest calculation not agreeing with interest rate. These are reported on the screen, with the transaction unable to progress until the problem is resolved.

- The use of standard settlement instructions (SSIs) is now the norm and is encouraged by the regulatory authorities as an important factor in reducing errors and streamlining the settlement process. Indeed, for straight-through processing (STP) to be viable, SSIs are essential for the majority of deals input, otherwise the volume of exception reporting significantly reduces the cost benefits inherent in STP.

- The basic concept means that a bank will hold on file within its system the agent bank for settlement of a counterparty. This will automatically be used without further reference *unless* countermanded by the counterparty for a specific transaction. This change may be agreed when the deal is done, or later in the back office when instructions are exchanged.

- SSIs are almost invariably used where they are in place. To assist in reconciliation procedures some banks have separate agents for FX, money market and derivatives transactions. However, this can mean that when a settlement problem occurs one account can be in credit while another in debit. In practical terms it can be more efficient to have all the problems in one basket.

Fig 2.1

The FX process flow

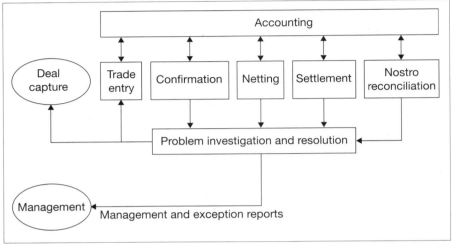

Source: New York FX Committee

Verification and confirmations

- Once the deal has been accepted by the system in its entirety the checking can begin.
- Typically, this will be screen based, whether input has been paper based or direct.
- It is possible to check the input details but perpetuate an error of fact. For example, if the dealer erroneously recorded the counterparty name as Nat West Antwerp instead of Amsterdam, nothing will highlight or draw attention to the mistake until the incoming confirmation is matched or mismatched.
- The advent of screen-based trading systems has eliminated most of this potential problem where the essential elements of the deal are matched when the deal is done.
- However, for other deals it is essential that an external verification is applied to the deal before it is settled. This can take the form of a broker or counterparty confirmation, which are typically incoming feeds matched automatically to the outstanding deals file of the bank with exceptions reported and investigated. (Systems-driven matching of confirmations is covered in detail in the next chapter.)

- Some banks reserve the right to obtain telephone confirmation of 'value today–done today' deals as an extra security check, even where deals have been agreed over a screen-based system.

- Just as a bank will expect a confirmation from its counterparty to use in its matching process, so it will send a confirmation itself. A complete range of SWIFT confirmations required for each product event is examined in the next chapter.

- Confirmations form the 300 series in SWIFT, starting with a simple MT 300 for an FX transaction through to money markets and derivatives. They form another building block in the full automation of the processing environment.

- The essential generic information included in a confirmation for all deals consists of: reference number, type of transaction, name and location of counterparty, price dealt, amount(s) and currency(ies) involved, and details of transaction, including action and value dates and settlement instructions.

Settlement and netting

- Once confirmed, a deal is ready for the settlement process to begin. Depending on the transaction, this can take many forms. It can range from settlement of an FX deal on value date, cash settlement of difference for many derivatives, through to delivery against payment for bonds or securities.

- Most products have several events during their life. For example, a loan may be paid away at start date, have interim interest payments, reprice interest if on a floating-rate basis and finally be repaid with interest at maturity.

- Bank treasury systems have been developed to produce the required SWIFT message to meet the event on the required date using the 200 'payment' message series via its 'gateway' into the SWIFT system. Thus a message will be generated to, for example, its correspondent agent bank, national payments clearer, Euroclear or other custodian, to effect settlement. Of course, other means are also used, such as telex or proprietary software links.

- The concept of STP may mean only one check in the settlement process. At present, many banks effect a final check of payments before releasing their payments file, to ensure that everything is correct.

- To meet growing concern about fraud and money laundering, banks should also perform a second check at a senior independent level for third party payments (where the ultimate beneficiary or recipient of the funds being paid away is not the deal counterparty).

- For outward payments to be effected in a timely manner, strict adherence to the cut-off times for payments on a worldwide basis is essential.

- Netting in its various forms (payment or close-out, bilateral or multilateral) has grown quickly over the last ten years, with the intention to reduce settlement risks and exposures. The advent of continuous linked settlement (CLS) reinforces netting as a viable concept by effectively providing on-going multilateral netting on a continuous basis.

- Modern systems-driven deal processing is based on the concept of constant monitoring and exception reporting, which is progressively hands-off. This allows back office staff to concentrate on the identified problems instead of having to search for and uncover them.

Reconciliations

- Cash reconciliations fall into two categories: internally (positions) and externally (nostro accounts representing agents' correspondents accounts).

- Modern trading systems have mostly replaced the need for the position-keeper who kept the running balance of the nostro for each currency. However most banks still need this function to a limited extent because of the deals that are done outside the trading systems.

- Like much of the processing procedure, reconciliation is based on exception reporting. Typically, an incoming SWIFT file will be matched to an outstanding deals file using a proprietary software package. Matched, probable match or unmatched reports are produced, based on key fields such as value date, value, counterparty etc.

- Problems are investigated and resolved as quickly as possible, usually taking the highest value first, as this is where the greatest potential loss is likely to be.

- Ultimately, a late payment will result in an interest amount to be claimed or paid. Resolution of the dispute will depend on the circumstances surrounding the deal. This may include whether confirmations were properly sent/received and instructions followed. As processing becomes more automated, the incidence of this type of error has decreased, but this tends to be compensated for by increasing complexity in the deals themselves.

- The compensation rules at the clearing houses worldwide are different and a treasury operations manager needs to have a working knowledge of the various clearing houses to negotiate competently in the case of a dispute with a counterparty.

Accounting

- Treasury accounting includes such concepts as the 'trading' or 'exchange dealing account' and 'trade dating' found in most treasury systems. Accounting entries are usually generated based on a code profile held for each product type on a time event basis.

- A second important point concerns the 'base currency' approach. Its purpose is to provide the 'base' or 'shadow' currency in which all transactions in other currencies will be tracked historically and revalued. This has no relevance for settlement purposes, but is a vital tool for revaluation and hence profit or loss determination for transactions.

- Forward books of outstanding items in the portfolio will normally be revalued on a marked to market basis.

- As noted earlier in the chapter, some complex transactions with a mix of products need to be accounted for and risk evaluated as a whole to obtain a true picture.

- Accounting aspects are discussed in more detail in Chapter 9.

SUMMARY

We have looked at the types of deals in the treasury environment and their characteristics, analyzing the lifecycle of a deal and presenting a processing overview.

Key points

- Input
- Verification
- Confirmation
- Settlement
- Netting
- Reconciliations
- Accounting

3

Input, verification and confirmations

This chapter covers the progress of our deal through the input, verification and confirmation stages of the processing chain. At the end of this it is ready for settlement. Good quality control at these early stages is a sound priority, as the early rectification of errors may cost but a fraction of the eventual expense, should the problem comes to light at a late stage.

INPUT

Traditional input systems

In many ways 'input' is the most important part of the processing procedure. An error made at this stage of the process will, at some stage, need to be rectified, and this means the use of valuable time and resources that could be more profitably used elsewhere. Even worse, until the problem is rectified, the remaining elements of processing, such as settlement, accounting and risk management, may be affected. This could lead to wrong settlement details, corrupted accounting entries and misleading 'value at risk' when positions are revalued. Of course, it all depends on the error and how serious the resulting problem is.

Traditional input systems using paper-based or screen input depended initially on what the dealer's instant record of the deal was when it was concluded. This was always a flaw in the system as it meant that even the highest quality input checking by the back office would not uncover an incorrect deal input or written error by the dealer until the confirmation from the broker or counterparty was received. Nevertheless, for dealing with non-trading system counterparties, good quality checking is still essential, since it reveals errors that can be corrected quickly before settlement date is reached.

Quality checking was and remains essential for all treasury business, including foreign exchange (FX), money markets and derivatives, whether exchange traded or over-the-counter. However, as we shall see, the basis of the checking has developed dramatically from 'error' checking to 'exception' checking, due to a rapidly changing systems environment.

The arrival of computer-based FX and money market trading systems solved this problem for both the dealers and back office at a stroke. It meant that, for the first time, dealers were responsible for the direct input to the computer system and had no one to blame if the data was incorrect. For the back office the impact was even more profound, allowing resources to be concentrated on resolving already identified problems instead of having to find them.

Thus online direct trading systems represent a watershed in the processing chain, ensuring that the deal initially recorded by the dealer is correct. The advent of trading systems such as Reuters 2000 and EBS changed the old procedures completely.

What happens now

Most major international banks have built interfaces between their trading and back office systems. After the trade is done on one of these trading systems it is passed automatically to the back office system. Other trades will also be arriving from different sources, such as telephone trades done with customers, which will be input by dealers through a 'front-end' data capture system. Trading done on the internet will also have an automatic feed into the back office.

The trade or deal will probably not be complete at this stage, requiring addition rather than amendment to complete the data required for further progression through the processing chain to risk management, settlement, accounting and reconciliation. This support role will be carried out by the back office staff, either adding data that is known to them, such as a reference or base currency rate, or obtained by contact with the settlement unit of the counter-party. For banks, the settlement agent for FX and money market deals will usually already be held on record through the bilateral use of standing settlement instructions (SSIs), which allow banks to handle large volumes of transactions on an automated basis. The use of SSIs is explained below.

Corporate customers are still more likely to swap instructions, particularly for FX deals, as these may be in settlement of trade and other commercial transactions that require special instructions (notably the addition of a reference for a bill or invoice if the proceeds are paid to a third party).

Use of SSIs

Encouraged by the Bank of England and other regulators, the use of SSIs has increased steadily over the last decade. SSIs clearly reduce the number of errors that used to occur by paying or receiving at the wrong agent. This was a common problem when instructions were exchanged with a counterparty each time a deal was done. Of course, the telephonic exchange of settlement instructions also enabled details of the deal itself to be confirmed before the advent of online trading systems (in which the essentials of the deal could be matched automatically within the dealing room). Some banks in the London market still prefer the practice of telephoning to confirm value today–done today deals as a final check before funds are released, irrespective of the mechanism of trading that has been used.

> SSIs clearly reduce the number of errors that used to occur by paying or receiving at the wrong agent.

Thus banks and major corporates bilaterally swap standard agents for each currency in which deals are to be transacted and these standing instructions are used unless they are countermanded in a particular instance. For many banks this involves the creation of a special file on which these instructions can be held so that data can be accessed either by the relevant input applications or directly linked to 'front-end' trading systems. Some banks, usually with large volumes, keep separate agent banks for each type of business. For example, FX, money market and derivatives transactions may each have a separate nostro account (the term given to these accounts in the books of the principal bank).

SWIFT (*see* Chapter 4) provides for the standardized exchange of SSIs using a special message type (MT 293) that allows banks to automate the maintenance process. It is also possible to exchange these instructions by mail or fax, but these are relatively slow and non-standardized. By using SWIFT with a proprietary storage application, it is possible to automate the installation and maintenance of quite large databases in a cost-effective way, ready for use in in-house processing systems.

This automation has been particularly useful with the introduction of the euro since a large number of changes were necessary to prepare for the conversion to the euro as addition to the existing legacy currencies. Other aspects that proprietary applications manage is the ability to cater for forward-dated changes to SSIs and the passing of outgoing SSIs to other banks. The automation of these functions has reduced operational risks considerably, particularly 'wrong agent' errors with associated costs, and has improved the quality of data held while allowing quick and efficient investigation of any problems.

At this stage we may regard the input of the deal as being complete. As explained earlier, there was traditionally a clear separation between the largely manual 'input' and 'checking' functions. Today, many input tasks have become self-checking, either on trading or by in-house systems, or even the input itself has become a check of previously assumed data. Straight through processing concepts allow for no manual checking at all in the traditional sense, provided the integrity of the initial data is assured.

But the deal still needs a check from an external source, be it the broker or counterparty. This function is 'verification'. Conversely, an outgoing confirmation from the bank to the other counterparty will act as their external check on the deal in their books. These actions need to be done urgently or as soon as possible to catch errors early and quickly; this in turn translates into online systems generation and matching.

VERIFICATION

Exception checking

Automation has removed much of the routine of checking for errors on input. This allows resources to be focused on correcting problems identified by those automated processes, thereby reducing the cost of both the errors themselves and resources used in resolving them. This has become known as the principle of exception checking and plays a vital role in most banks where high volumes are the norm. It does not mean that transactions are not checked; rather, the reverse is true, as all items are system checked to a known standard and the exceptions reported.

The prime requirement is to apply an external verification to a deal as quickly as possible after being struck in the dealing room. This may take the form of an automatic matching of the details of the deal with an incoming automated brokers note, or counterparty confirmation using an online application that matches these to the outstanding deals file at the bank.

> **The prime requirement is to apply an external verification to a deal as quickly as possible after being struck in the dealing room.**

The automatic process is typically dependent on a series of graded matches on a field-by-field basis. Thus messages are classified into categories depending on how successful the match has been overall. Some fields will be mandatory to match (for example, counterparty name code) before any sort of match can be made. Categories could consist of:

- **total match**: all fields match based on set criteria and no further action is required;
- **probable match**: most fields (including the mandatory ones) agree but there are some discrepancies (in an online system these will be highlighted to allow experienced checking staff to verify visually or overrule the system proposal);
- **possible match**: some fields match, but up to one mandatory field does not match (again visual checking will allow messages to be matched manually and the deal will be tagged with the code of the authorizing checker for future reference);
- **no match**: this is where the system has been unable to find a match; possible causes can include duplicate messages (which can also be checked automatically) or a delay by the counterparty or broker sending their messages.

Software vendors usually develop proprietary systems on a modular basis for applications of this type with, for example, separate monitoring systems for FX, money market, derivatives and securities. This allows banks to mix and match according to their business mix.

A leading example of electronic matching systems available is the SWIFT Accord confirmation matching system, which can also be enhanced to provide a level of bilateral payment netting. Another market leader is City Networks which, among other related products, supplies TRAM for counterparty confirmation matching. BART is a system set up in London by money brokers to send and match confirmations electronically.

Once matched or confirmed in this way by an external source, the deal can be transferred from the outstanding deals file to the matched deals file and proceed to the next stage of the process, which is settlement. Also the deal can now pass accounting entries into the books of the bank, depending on the type of transaction involved. Chaser letters are generated for deals not confirmed. Normally this would be a SWIFT message to the counterparty stating that a confirmation is awaited by next day or correcting an error.

Any deals caught by netting agreements need to be clearly identified so that an accurate picture can be built up during the day of the net position for a particular counterparty. Final confirmation of net positions by currency will also be exchanged before payments are effected. There can be a quite complex situation where netting occurs across a number of instruments, with different systems for a counterparty, which needs close monitoring.

Third party payments

Transactions involving third parties, such as those mentioned earlier for corporates, do require additional checking. This is partly because they are more complex, but also to guard against the bank becoming party to fraud or money laundering activity. The deals involved are identified, extracted and reported automatically by the third party field on the transaction. Each should be recalled and subjected to an additional authorization by an experienced officer familiar with the type of business involved. Any problems or anomalies identified should be reported urgently to a senior officer immediately for attention.

CONFIRMATIONS
Why are confirmations necessary?

Confirmations are the workhorse messengers of a bank's back office unit and must be sent as soon as possible after a deal is done. Similarly, incoming confirmations must be matched as soon as possible after receipt. Although the term 'confirmation' is usually taken to mean those sent to and received from the counterparty to a deal, in practice several sources can 'confirm' a deal for back office purposes. These include brokers' notes in electronic form as already discussed, a confirm from a trading system (if this has been involved) or a conventional taped telephone confirmation made in the settlements unit.

Nevertheless, the most valuable confirmation remains the message from the counterparty acting as principal to a transaction. It is often the non-matching of a counterparty confirmation that first indicates the existence of a problem warranting investigation.

Why are confirmations necessary? After all, the actual deal is completed as a simple contract in the dealing room. The answer is that the confirmation authenticates the transaction to officers independent of the dealing room, as well as providing essential information regarding settlement, as not all of this is necessarily exchanged when the deal is done. Both the London Code of Conduct (LCC) (previously issued by the Bank of England and more recently the Financial Services Authority) and the Model Code together with similar guidelines of other regulatory bodies of the world's financial markets, reinforce this approach, setting clear standards of best practice to be followed by all participants (*see* Chapter 10).

Some simple principles of best practice can therefore be applied to this part of the processing cycle:

- confirmations should be generated within two to three hours of a deal being struck; the release of the confirmations message file to SWIFT should be arranged accordingly;

- the issue and checking of confirmations is a back office responsibility that should be carried out independently from those who initiate deals;

> **Confirmation authenticates the transaction to officers independent of the dealing room, as well as providing essential information regarding settlement.**

- confirmations should be dispatched and checked carefully and promptly, even when oral deal checks have been undertaken;

- wherever possible, the confirmation should show both where payment is to be made from and to and where payment is to be received, depending on what is applicable to a particular transaction;

- confirmations for internal deals done within an organization should be treated in the same way as external deals and matched with instructions received and chased up if a response is not forthcoming.

Methods of confirmation

Traditional

Up to the 1970s the normal method of confirming an FX or money market deal was by post. The golden rule was that all confirmations had to leave the same day as the day the deal was done. In some circumstances, for non-urgent business in some countries, this is still the most efficient cost-effective way of confirming a transaction.

For mainstream dealing in highly sophisticated 24-hour trading room environments this has been superseded first, by the SWIFT suite of confirmation messages and, more recently, trading systems that 'confirm' the deal immediately, subject to follow-up as explained above. Additionally, some trading environments, such as those for bonds or exchange-traded instruments, have set deadlines by which trades must be matched.

SWIFT Category 3 message type

With the development of true international markets from the 1960s, the need for a secure standardized messaging system became vital. This resulted in the formation of SWIFT, which has become the benchmark for revising existing messages and creating new ones to meet innovation in the marketplace. As explained in more detail in the next chapter, the standardization of messages in the critical area of confirming transactions, has been the key in enabling the automatic matching messages between banks.

This message type is called Category 3 and is essentially all confirmations of one sort or another covering the range of financial instruments traded. Each field of a message is strictly standardized with rules regarding usage.

A list of Category 3 messages is shown in Table 3.1. Table 3.2 shows the scope of MT300 foreign exchange confirmation. The scope of Category 3 messages is then described. Figures 3.1–3.4 outline usage rules. Figure 3.5 gives an example of the use of the MT300 to confirm a foreign exchange spot deal. (The SWIFT payment messages for this deal are shown in Chapter 4.)

Table 3.1 lists all message types defined in Category 3: 'For each message type, there is a short description, an indicator whether the message type requires authentication (Y/N), the maximum message length on input (2,000 or 10,000 characters) and whether the use of the message requires registration with SWIFT for use in a message user group (MUG) (Y/N)' (*SWIFT User Handbook*).

Table 3.1

Category 3 message types

MT	MT name	Purpose	Authen.	Max. length	MUG
300	Foreign Exchange Confirmation	Confirms information agreed to in the buying/selling of two currencies	N	10,000	N
303	Forex/Currency Option Allocation Instruction	Instructs the allocation of a block trade (forex or currency foreign exchange deal)	N	10,000	Y
304	Advice/Instruction of a Third Party Deal	Advises of or instructs settlement of a third party foreign exchange deal	Y	10,000	Y
305	Foreign Currency Option Confirmation	Confirms information agreed to in the buying and selling of options on currencies	N	2,000	N
320	Fixed Loan/Deposit Confirmation	Confirms the terms of a contract relative to a fixed loan/deposit transaction	N	2,000	N
324	Liquidation Notice for Fixed Loan/Deposit	Confirms the liquidation of a fixed loan/deposit transaction	N	2,000	N
330	Call/Notice Loan/Deposit Confirmation	Confirms the terms of a contract relative to a call/notice loan/deposit transaction	N	2,000	N
335	Advice of a Call/Notice Loan/Deposit Interest Rate Change	Advises/confirms an interest rate change relative to a call/notice loan/deposit	N	2,000	N
340	Forward Rate Agreement Confirmation	Confirms the details of a forward rate agreement	N	2,000	N
341	Forward Rate Agreement Settlement Confirmation	Confirms the settlement details of a forward rate agreement	N	2,000	N
350	Advice of Loan/Deposit Interest Payment	Advises of a loan/deposit interest payment	N	2,000	N
360	Single Currency Interest Rate Derivative Confirmation	Confirms the details of a single currency interest rate derivative transaction	N	10,000	N
361	Cross Currency Interest Rate Swap Confirmation	Confirms the details of a cross currency interest rate swap transaction	N	10,000	N
362	Interest Rate Reset/ Advice of Payment	Confirms or advises the reset rates of the floating interest rate(s) in a single or cross-currency interest rate derivative transaction and/or the payment of interest at the end of an interest period	N	2,000	N
364	Single Currency Interest Rate Derivative Termination/Recouponing Confirmation	Confirms the details of the partial or full termination or recouponing of a single currency interest rate swap, cap, collar, floor or FRA	N	10,000	N
365	Cross Currency Interest Rate Swap Termination/ Recouponing Confirmation	Confirms the details of the partial or full recouponing of termination or a cross currency interest rate swap	N	10,000	N
390	Advice of Charges, Interest and Other Adjustments	Advises an account owner of charges, interest or other adjustments	N	2,000	N
391	Request for Payment of Charges, Interest and Other Expenses	Requests payment of charges, interest or other expenses	N	2,000	N
392	Request for Cancellation	Requests the Receiver to consider cancellation of the message identified in the request	N	2,000	N
395	Queries	Requests, information relating to a previous message or amendment to a previous message	N	2,000	N
396	Answers	Responds to an MT 395 Queries or an MT 392 Request for Cancellation or other message where no specific message type has been provided for a response	N	2,000	N
398	Proprietary Message	Contains formats defined and agreed to between users and for those messages not yet live	N	10,000	N

Source: SWIFT User Handbook

Table 3.2 **Scope of MT 300 foreign exchange confirmation**

1   This message is exchanged by or on behalf of the institutions or corporates, party A and party B, which have agreed to a foreign exchange contract.

2   This message may also be sent by a money broker to the two parties (party A and party B) for which the broker arranged the deal.

3   Where there are two money brokers involved in arranging a deal between party A and party B, this message is also exchanged between these money brokers.

4   This message is also used when one of the trading parties is a fund manager as the fund manager has to specify the fund for which he is dealing.

5   The message allows split settlements where the amount is too big to be settled as a whole. It allows:

   • the specification of the legal counterparties

   • the inclusion of a beneficiary

   • a split settlement

   • the inclusion of the underlying legal agreement.

6   The message may be used to:

   • confirm the details of a new contract between the parties

   • confirm an exercised foreign currency option

   • confirm the details of an amendment to a previously sent confirmation

   • cancel a previously sent confirmation.

Source: SWIFT User Handbook

MT 300 usage rules

The MT 300 is used to confirm a deal between two parties, A and B (Fig 3.1).

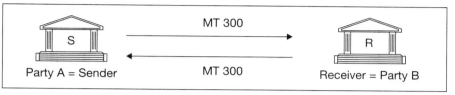

Fig 3.1

Source: SWIFT User Handbook

It can also be exchanged on behalf of an institution or corporate (Fig 3.2).

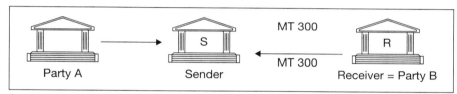

Fig 3.2

Source: SWIFT User Handbook

The MT 300 can also be used as a unilateral confirmation from a money broker to the parties A and B (Fig 3.3).

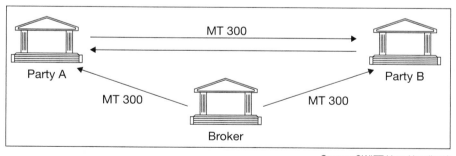

Fig 3.3

Source: SWIFT User Handbook

Or, when two money brokers are involved, the MT 300 can be exchanged by the money brokers (Fig 3.4).

Fig 3.4

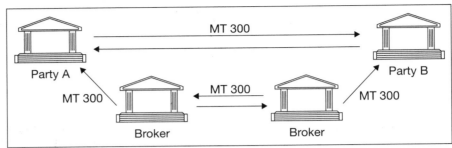

Source: SWIFT User Handbook

MT 300 example

Spot deal

On 22 January 1996, Crédit Suisse, Zürich buys 100,000 GBP against USD from Berliner Bank, Berlin. The rate is 1,6632. The deal is agreed via telephone.

On 24 January 1996, Berliner Bank will transfer the pounds to Crédit Suisse's account with Midland Bank, London.

Crédit Suisse will transfer the dollars to Berliner Bank's account with Chase Manhattan Bank. (Figure 3.5)

Fig 3.5

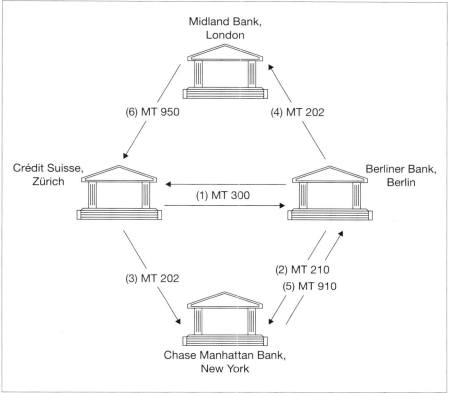

Midland Bank,
London

(6) MT 950

(4) MT 202

Crédit Suisse,
Zürich

(1) MT 300

Berliner Bank,
Berlin

(3) MT 202

(2) MT 210
(5) MT 910

Chase Manhattan Bank,
New York

Source: SWIFT User Handbook

Message 1 FX confirmation(s) by Crédit Suisse

Crédit Suisse sends a message to Berliner bank confirming the deal.

Explanation	Format
Sender	CRESCHZZ
Receiver	BEBEDEBB
Message type	300
General information	:15A
Sender's reference	:20:REFIA
Type of operation	:22A:NEWT
Common reference	:22C:BEBEBB6632CRESZZ
Transaction details	:15B
Trade date	:30T:19960122
Value date	:30V:19960124
Exchange rate	:36:1,6632
Currency, amount bought	:32B:GBP100000,00
Receiving agent	:57A:MIDLGB22
Currency, amount sold	:33B:USD166320,00
Receiving agent	:57A:CHASUS33
Optional general information	:15C
Dealing method	:24D:PHON

Source: SWIFT User Handbook

Berliner Bank sends a message to Crédit Suisse confirmiing the deal.

Explanation	Format
Sender	BEBEDEBB
Receiver	CRESCHZZ
Message type	300
General information	:15A
Sender's reference	:20:REFIB
Type of operation	:22A:NEWT
Common reference	:22C:BEBEBB6632CRESZZ
Transaction details	:15B
Trade date	:30T:19960122
Value date	:30V:19960124
Exchange rate	:36:1,6632
Currency, amount bought	:32B:USD166320,00
Receiving agent	:53A:CHASUS33
Currency, amount sold	:33B:GBP100000,00
Receiving agent	:57A:MIDLGB22
Optional general information	:15C
Dealing method	:24D:PHON

Source: SWIFT User Handbook

Securities transactions

SWIFT provides a separate category of message transactions in securities to allow prompt matching before settlement at a clearing house such as Euroclear or Clearstream, as described in Chapter 5.

Other methods of confirmation

There was a time when the ability to match confirmations automatically within a day was regarded as 'cutting edge'. The advent of exchanges such as the CME in USA and LIFFE in the UK brought the requirement (enforced by regulators) to match within 30 minutes of a financial futures trade being struck. There is also the TRAX/AIBD requirement to register a bond trade within 20 minutes of dealing. Much of this type of matching has been or is being swept away as online trading systems make these deadlines redundant.

Progressive automation has brought with it the ability to confirm trades of all types very quickly. Screen-based trading, such as on the DTB in Germany or Reuters FX trading systems, has brought instantaneous matching, so reducing errors and costs in the back office.

Straight-through processing (STP)

Thus the three key factors in streamlining this part of the processing function are:

- front-end data capture
- SSIs
- immediate matching of confirmations.

Together with automated payment systems, these have become the building blocks that have taken the concept of STP from theory to practice. It is now possible to go from when the deal is struck to payment and reconciliation without any manual intervention, relying on exception reporting alone, provided the integrity of data at initial input is assured.

SUMMARY

Key points

- Front-end input from trading systems
- Use of standard settlement instructions (SSIs)
- Automatic matching of confirmations
- Building blocks to straight-through processing (STP)

We have covered the main aspects of input, verification and confirmation of a 'generic' deal in this part of the processing cycle.

Clearing and payment systems

This chapter investigates what good settlement value is and the ways of achieving this in an international environment through payment carriers and national clearing systems.

WHAT IS GOOD SETTLEMENT VALUE ?

As we saw in the previous chapter, having recorded the deal in the books of the bank and confirmed or verified the transaction with the counterparty in one or more ways, the next step is that of settlement. This can be either a payment or receipt of funds, or both, where an exchange of currencies is involved. It can also be subject to a netting agreement where this is in place. There are various ways in which settlement can take place and these are explained below.

All treasury transactions have a contracted settlement value date. This is the date on which settlement must be made for either the contracted amount, or, in the case of non-deliverable transactions such as some derivatives, for the differential amount. These payments are transmitted by various means, discussed in the next section, to the nostro account of the beneficiary or receiving institution. (A bank that has a foreign currency account with another bank, usually in the main centre of the country of that currency, is said to have their 'nostro' account in that currency with that bank. Conversely, the overseas bank holding the account is said to have a 'vostro' account. The terms come from the Latin – nostro literally means 'our' (our account with you). Vostro means 'your' (your account with us).) The delivering or remitting party is bound to make the payment for 'good value' on the date stipulated in the contract.

This effectively means that the funds must be in the nostro account of the beneficiary institution by close of business on the agreed value date. In order to achieve this, the funds must be received by the nostro account holder by a stipulated time, generally known as the 'cut-off' time, after which the payment can only be accepted for value the next banking day, on which day the beneficiary's account will be credited.

Cut-off times

Cut-off times vary depending on the centre and the clearing system in place locally, but are usually between 8.00 am and 1.00 pm local time, to ensure value worldwide. But what exactly constitutes 'good value' in a settlement context? That is to say by when or what time must messages be despatched through a payment carrier, such as by tested telex or more usually SWIFT, to *ensure* that they reach the agent banks in good time for payment to be made? This really depends on the currencies being paid and received and can conveniently be grouped under four headings representing the major time zones around the world:

- Far Eastern and Pacific currencies
- European (now including the euro)
- sterling
- US dollar.

Sterling is still shown separately because UK times do not always correspond with Europe throughout the year. Effectively the first group of currencies, including those for Japan and Australia, are a full day ahead of London and New York and this means that the release of payments must be carefully managed, including allowing for national bank holidays, to ensure cut-off times are met.

Aspects of settlement risk, including a trade's status at any given time and the position regarding payments and receipts of currencies, are discussed in Chapter 7.

Failure to pay, amendment and cancellation

Given the large amounts traded, should a payment miss the cut-off time resulting in a one-day-late delivery, the consequences can be quite serious. They include expensive overdraft charges or, in extreme cases, a chain of failed or cancelled payments, which for credit risk or other reasons might have been conditional upon receipt of funds. This in turn could involve other costs, with the resultant cost and legal implications. It is therefore important that a bank has in place a sound procedure to ensure that all payments are made in good time to guarantee 'good value' for the beneficiary.

> It is important that a bank has in place a sound procedure to ensure that all payments are made in good time to guarantee 'good value' for the beneficiary.

The response to payment amendment or cancellation requests also varies between centres. Such requests are often accepted on a 'best endeavours' basis and usually depend on timing, payment execution and prior payment advice. A selected group of 15 countries, including the EMU members, from a general information list compiled by SWIFT on international cut-off times, cancellation stipulations and value dates is shown in Table 4.1.

- Australia
- Belgium
- Canada
- France
- Germany
- India
- Ireland
- Italy

- Japan
- Netherlands
- Portugal
- Spain
- Switzerland
- UK
- USA

Table 4.1

SWIFT cut-off times

AUSTRALIA

General Information
Cut-off Time: 14.00 local time for payments in AUD
Currency: Australia dollar   AUD
Cancellation
Payment instructions are revocable on authorized request provided the request is received as an urgent priority message and that the receiving bank has not already advised or credited the beneficiary.
Stop Payment of Cheques
Properly authorized requests for stop payment of cheques, including MT111, are acceptable and a response will be given.
Value Date(s)
Bank Transfers and Customer Transfers received before cut-off time of the nominated value date will be paid on such date under the following conditions:

If payment is to be made or reimbursement obtained outside the state or territory in which the recipient of the payment instruction is located, the cut-off time will be that applicable to the area to which the funds are directed or from which reimbursement is obtained.

However, if received after cut-off time, payment may not be effected until the next working day.

BELGIUM

General Information
Cut-off Time: 08.30. It is recommended to use URGENT PRIORITY for orders to be executed under same day value.
Currency: Euro   EUR   Belgian Franc   BEF
Cancellation
The Belgian banks will try to satisfy the requests for cancellation in the most co-operative way.
Stop Payment of Cheques
Belgian banks will try to satisfy the requests in the most co-operative way.
Value Date(s)
It is recommended to use URGENT PRIORITY for orders to be executed under the same day value.
Note
Bank branches will be closed on Friday 31 December 1999 and Monday 3 January 2000. All electronic channels (ATMs, telebanking, etc.) will be in operation as usual.
   Central financial systems, such as the CEC (retail clearing system), ELLIPS (Belgian RTGS system), TARGET, the securities clearing system of the National Bank of Belgium, the Brussels Exchanges (Bourse, Belfox, and CIK), the Easdaq and regulated OTC markets will be closed on Friday 31 December 1999 and open on Monday s January 2000.

CANADA

General Information
Cut-off Time: The cut-off time for all payments within Canada is 18.00 EST (Eastern Standard Time). Normal practice is to request all payments to be received one (1) hour ahead of cut-off time, to allow for processing. Individual bank practice may vary in accordance with their own correspondent bank terms and conditions.
Currency: Canadian dollar   CAD

Cancellation

The request for the cancellation or amendment of a payment order can be considered only if:
(a) the payment order has not yet been executed, or if
(b) the beneficiary assents to such cancellation or amendment, and to the return of funds.

Stop Payment of Cheques

No information available. Please contact your correspondents for further details.

Value Date(s)

No information available. Please contact your correspondents for further details.

Note

(1) From April 04 to October 30, 2000, the province of Saskatchewan (in the Central Time Zone) remains at GMT –6. From January 01 to April 03, 2000, and from October 31 to December 31, 1999, the province of Saskatchewan (in the Mountain Time Zone) remains at GMT –6.

(2) Although the Civic Holiday (first Monday in August) is a bank holiday in most of the country, our Large Value Transfer System will still be operational.

FRANCE

General Information

Cut-off Time: There are no formal country agreements. Individual bank practice varies in accordance with their correspondent terms and conditions.

For same day funds: funds are available for transfer today in like funds or withdrawal in cash, subject to the settlement of the transaction through the payment systems used.
– Financial institution holidays for high value payment follow the TARGET calendar.
– For other payments, please refer to your correspondent.

Currency: From 01/01/1999: Euro   EUR

As a national denomination French Franc   FRF

National payment systems, whether they exchange payments in euro or in national denomination, settle same day value payments in euro. All payment systems convey ERI or similar. Access to European payment systems is available from France either in euro or in national denomination.

Cancellation

The request for the cancellation of a payment order, irrespective of its value date, can be granted only if:
– the payment has not yet been executed or advised by the receiving bank, or if
– the beneficiary assents to such cancellation in case the payment order has already been executed or advised.

Stop Payment of Cheques

No information available. Please contact your correspondents for further details.

Value Date(s)

There are no formal country agreements. Individual bank practice varies in accordance with their correspondent terms and conditions. European Banking Federations' recommendations related to funds disposal are supported.

Euro reciprocal accounts

European Banking Federations' recommendation is also supported: the ordering bank should authorize the executing bank to register the transaction on the nostro account maintained with that executing bank.

GERMANY

General Information

Cut-off Time: There are no formal country agreements. Individual bank practice varies in accordance with their correspondents terms and conditions.

Currency: Euro   EUR   Deutsche Mark   DEM

Cancellation

The request for the cancellatin of a payment order, irrespective of its value date, can be granted only if:
(a) the payment order has not yet been executed or advised by the receiving bank, or if
(b) the beneficiary assents to such cancellation in case the payment order has already been executed or advised.

Stop Payment of Cheques

No information available. Please contact your correspondents for further details.

Value Date(s)

There are no formal country agreements. Individual bank practice varies in accordance with their correspondents' terms and conditions. High Value and Urgent Payments may be settled on national holidays, except 01.01 and 25.12. For details please contact your correspondent directly.

Field 53/54

In case of direct payment orders being sent to a bank quoting the account maintaining/holding office of the same bank in the same country in field 53 respectively 54 if present, no additional cover-payment should be sent to that bank.

IRELAND

General Information

Cut-off Time: The banks will not guarantee to give same day value for payments received from abroad after 8.00 a.m.
Currency: Euro   EUR   Irish Pound   IEP
Interest on IEP balances is calculated on 365 day basis.
(For Northern Ireland see United Kingdom

Cancellation

A request for the cancellation of a payment order, irrespective of its value, can be granted only if:
(a) the payment order has not yet been executed or advised by the receiving bank, or if:
(b) the beneficiary assents to such cancellation in case the payment order has already been executed or advised.

Stop Payment of Cheques

No information available. Please contact your correspondents for further details.

Value Date(s)

No information available. Please contact your correspondents for further details.

Currency

Interest on IEP balances is calculated on 365 day basis.

INDIA

General Information

Cut-off Time: 09.30 a.m. The banks will not guarantee to give same day value for payments received from abroad after 09.30 a.m.
Currency: Indian Rupee   INR

Cancellation

Revocation of payment instructions will normally be accepted on a best endeavour basis and provided the receiving bank has not already advised the payment or credited the beneficiary.

Stop Payment of Cheques

Requests to stop payment on cheques would be honoured on a best effort basis.

Value Date(s)

Messages for BIC listed branches should invariably contain the 3 character branch code, failing which banks will bear no responsibility for value dating.
Cut-off time and value dates are binding only on SWIFT BIC branches located in Mumbai. Messages meant for destinations and branches not listed in the BIC DIrectory should be sent through Telex etc. as before and not via the SWIFT system.

Bank Transfers
Same day value will be effected provided
(a) the instructions are received by the banks before the cut-off time and
(b) both banks listed in fields 53A and 58A are located at Mumbai.
Instructions received after cut-off time will be acted upon at the earliest, value first normal following working day.
Customer Transfers
Customer transfers will be effected as per the normal practice of the receiving bank.
Note
The financial institution holidays 2000 were not received at press time.

ITALY

General Information
Cut-off Time: 08.00 a.m.
Currency: Euro   EUR   Italian Lira   ITL
Cancellation
As the receiving bank can execute the payment orders also before the value date specified for the crediting of funds, the revocation of a payment order will be effective only if it reaches the bank before the execution of the payment order. If the execution of revoking payment instructions involves a retransfer of funds to the transmitting bank, the value applicable to this transfer will follow the rules foreseen for a new operation.
Stop Payment of Cheques
No information available. Please contact your correspondents for further details.
Value Date(s)
Cut-off time is extended to 09.00H for properly formatted SWIFT messages. If the required value date falls on a day where banks observe a half-day holiday (Dec. 24, Dec. 31) then cut-off time is advanced to 14.00H (extended to 15.00H for properly formatted SWIFT messages) on the working day immediately preceding that of the required value date.
By way of exception, whenever the payment is to be made through or in favour of the Banca d'Italia (field 56, 57 or 58 of the message) the foreign bank must arrange for the order to reach its Italian paying agent not later than 13.00H on the working day immediately preceding that of the required value date, if the latter is a day on which Italian banks are closed in the afternoon, then the cut-off time is further advanced to 11.00H on the working day immediately preceding that of the required value date.
Customer Transfers
The orders will be executed in accordance with the banking practice of the receiving bank as soon as possible after the receipt of instructions.

JAPAN

General Information
Cut-off Time: 10.30 a.m.
Currency: Yen   JPY
Cancellation
Revocation of payment instructions will be accepted on a best endeavours basis and provided the receiving bank has not yet advised or credited the beneficiary.
Stop Payment of Cheques
No information available. Please contact your correspondents for further details.
Value Date(s)
(1) Bank transfers:
Instructions received on the value date before the cut-off time will be effected by the receiving bank with the value of the same day.
(2) Customer transfers:
Instructions will be effected as soon as possible in accordance with the normal practice of the receiving bank.

(3) Forward value transactions:
The value date should be within three business days after the date of transmission.
(4) Back value transactions:
Instructions received with a value date before the date of receipt will normally be effected with value of the latter date.

NETHERLANDS

General Information
Cut-off Time: 08.00
Currency: Euro   EUR   Netherlands Guilder   NLG

Cancellation
The receiving bank can advise or execute the payment order before the value date specified for the crediting of funds. Therefore, the revocation of a payment order will be effective only if it reaches the receiving bank before the advising or the execution of the payment order. If the execution of revoking payment instruction involves a retransfer of funds to the transmitting bank, the value applicable to this transfer will follow the rules foreseen for a new operation.

Stop Payment of Cheques
No information available. Please contact your correspondents for further details.

Value Date(s)
(a) For bank transfers the rule is that for instructions received by the receiving bank before cut-off time, payment shall be effected the same day, while instructions received after this time payment shall be effected the first business day after receipt.
(b) For customer transfers to the beneficiary's bank the beneficiary will, under normal circumstances, be credited not later than two business days after the date started in field 32 of the message.

PORTUGAL

General Information
Cut-off Time: 08.00 a.m.
Currency: Euro   EUR   Portuguese Escudo   PTE

Cancellation
Payment instructions are revocable by request provided the receiving bank has not already advised or credited the beneficiary.

Stop Payment of Cheques
No information available. Please contact your correspondents for further details.

Value Date(s)
Bank Transfers
For instructions received on the value date by the receiving bank before cut-off time, payment will be effected the same day. While for payment instructions received after this time will be effected the first business day after receipt.
Customer Transfers
These will be executed in accordance with the banking practice of the receiving bank as soon as possible after the receipt of the instructions.

SPAIN

General Information
Cut-off Time: 8.00 a.m.
Currency: Euro   EUR   Spanish Peseta   ESP

Cancellation
All financial instructions received in Spain are irrevocable. The request for cancellation of a payment order can be granted only if:

(a) the request has been received by SWIFT message MTn92
(b) the payment order has not yet been executed or advised by the receiving bank.

Stop Payment of Cheques

The request for Stop Payment of Cheques can be granted only under the following conditions:

(a) The request has been received by SWIFT message MT-111
(b) The reason for the Stop Payment request is included in message MT-111
(c) The only acceptable reasons are:
– lost cheque
– stolen cheque

Stop Payment requests for any other reason, or failing to comply with the above conditions, may not be granted by Drawee Bank.

Value Date(s)

Bank Transfers

For instructions received on value date by the receiving bank before cut-off time, payment will be effected the same day, while for instructions received after this time payment will be effected the first business day after receipt.

Customer Transfers

These will be executed in accordance with the banking practice of the receiving bank as soon as possible after the receipt of the instructions.

Note

The financial institution holiday dates listed for 2000 are transmitted on a provisional basis.

SWITZERLAND

General Information

Cut-off Time: The general cut-off time for Swiss franc payment orders with same-day value is 8.00 a.m. (CET). Individual bank practice varies in accordance with their own terms and conditions.

Currency: Swiss Franc   CHF

Cancellation

It is common practice in Switzerland to accept cancellations on a best effort basis with time or amount sensitive payment orders given top priority.

Stop Payment of Cheques

Stop payment requests will be executed, provided the cheque has not been honoured. The stop payment request is valid for a period of six months.

Value Date(s)

It is common practice in Switzerland that funds in Swiss francs are made available to the beneficiary with same-day value, provided the payment order has been received prior to the cut-off time.

Note

Standards

For foreign currency conversions into Swiss francs, it is common practice in Switzerland to round the fractional remainders of Swiss franc amount to the nearest five rappen (cents). For example CHF 10.88 would become CHF 10.90. In order to improve the automatic processing of payment orders and to implement differrent pricing scheme options, some banks may request payment orders to conform to specific formatting rules. However, it should be noted that none of these preferences violate SWIFT standards, they are merely suggested regulations. Please contact your Swiss correspondent for information as to how these specific regulations can positively impact you.

In addition to generally recognized holidays there are a number of bank holidays which are only observed in some cantons or even only in some communes.

UNITED KINGDOM

General Information
Cut-off Time: Applies to Sterling inter-bank payment instructions. The participating UK banks will apply a normal cut-off time of 12.00 noon (London time) to instructions received from abroad to make payments in Sterling which indicate that payment is to be made on the day on which those instructions are received in the United Kingdom.
Currency: Pound Sterling   GBP

Cancellation
Revocation of payment instructions will normally be accepted on a best endeavours basis and provided the receiving bank has not already effected payment.

Stop Payment of Cheques
No information available. Please contact your Clearer for guidance.

Value Date(s)
The value date contained within a payment instruction would, according to London practice, indicate the date on which payment should be made by the receiving bank if that is possible, bearing in mind cut-off times.

UNITED STATES

General Information
Cut-off Time: There are no formal country agreements. Individual bank practice varies in accordance with their correspondent terms and conditions.
Currency: US Dollar same day funds   USD   US Dollar next day funds   USN
USD – Same Day Funds – Signifies funds available for transfer today in like funds or withdrawal in cash, subject to the settlement of the transaction through the payment system(s) used (see definition of settlement).
USN – Next Day Funds – Signifies funds available for transfer today in like funds, and available the next business day for same day funds transfer or withdrawal in cash, subject to the settlement of the transaction through the payment system(s) used (see definition of settlement).
Settlement: refers to the balance amounts – which result from payments drawn on, and made to banks through a payment system – that are presented to the Federal Reserve System for debiting or crediting the Lawful Reserve Accounts of the banks on the payment system that settle in this manner. Settlement is completed when all of the appropriate debit or credit entries have been made across the Lawful Reserve Accounts.

Cancellation
All financial instructions received in the United States are irrevocable. Requests for cancellation(s) are subject to prior agreement(s) which the sender has with the receiver.

Stop Payment of Cheques
There are no formal country agreements. Individual bank practice varies in accordance with their own correspondent terms and conditions.

Value Date(s)
There are no formal country agreements. Individual bank practice varies in accordance with their own correspondent terms and conditions.

Field 53/54
Field 53 (sender's correspondent bank) and Field 54 (receiver's correspondent bank)
Under normal banking practice, banks in the United States will effect a Transfer only on instructions of the owner or one of its designated offices. Individual bank practice varies in accordance with their own correspondent terms and conditions.

Note
Each State has jurisdiction over its holidays, which are designated by legislative enactment or executive proclamation. It is important to consult your correspondent for complete information about holidays in individual states. Time zone Arizona (in region US5) remains –7 GMT.

Source: SWIFT

Nostro accounts with correspondent banks

In order to make or receive foreign currency payments, either on their own behalf or on behalf of their customers, all banks hold currency accounts with correspondent banks in various centres. The payment or settlement of currency transactions is executed through these nostro accounts. Large international banking groups often use their own branches for this purpose, where it is practical, or where local practice permits or encourages such activity.

Nostro account relationships between international banks are often a reciprocal arrangement and the turnover, conduct and management of these accounts are important factors in the overall correspondent banking relationship between the institutions. An active nostro account, well conducted with efficiency and co-operation on both sides, can often be the catalyst for more lucrative reciprocal business between the institutions.

Basic settlement process and risks

There are four 'players' in the settlement process. These are the counterparty banks that have concluded the transaction between each other followed by the correspondent banks in the country of the currencies involved in the transaction, which we have reviewed above. We will now examine the mechanisms that we have termed 'payment carriers' used to instruct the correspondent banks and finally the domestic settlement systems used to pass value from payer to beneficiary. These four elements form the basis of all settlement processes and are represented diagrammatically in Fig. 4.1.

Risks

Any amount that is due to be received under a contract should be regarded as settlement risk until final confirmation of receipt is confirmed. Typically this will be either during or at the end of the business day, depending on the local settlement system (*see* below). When a counterparty defaults there may be one or more types of settlement risk involved ranging from internal failings through to the time zones where settlement is taking place. The latter is particularly true of FX deals where one side may be paid away before receipt of the counter-value. This type of risk, commonly called settlement or 'Herstatt' risk, is explained in Chapter 6.

INTERNATIONAL PAYMENT CARRIERS

The first step in the process of settlement is to instruct the correspondent of a foreign bank to pay and/or receive the agreed amounts, depending on the trans-

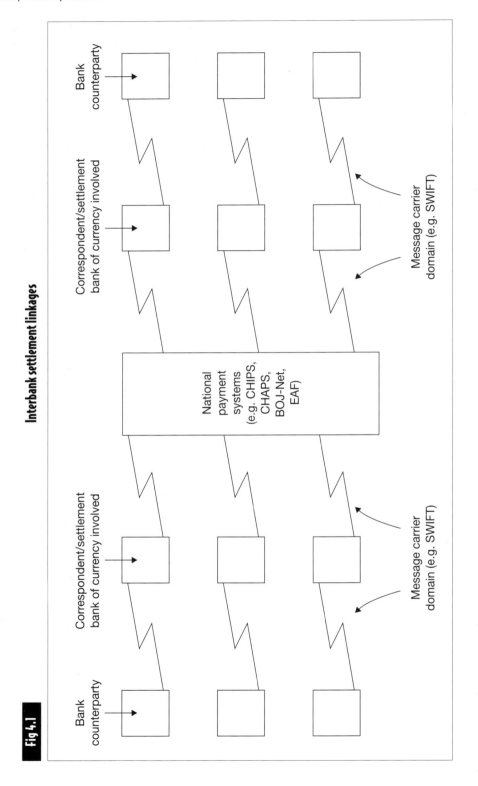

Interbank settlement linkages

Fig 4.1

action involved, through the domestic payment system of the relevant country. These instructions may be transmitted by tested telex, but more likely in today's global markets by SWIFT (*see* below), which is now the major international payment carrier and supplier of other telecommunication services such as confirmations (as we saw in the last chapter).

Tested telex method with authentication by test keys

In order to make a payment from a nostro account to the counterparty's correspondent in favour of the beneficiary, it is necessary for the paying bank to authenticate the instructions. The traditionally accepted method for this was by mutually pre-agreed authenticated signatures on a bank remittance form or letter. Later, as the scale of the business increased, telegraphic payments (TT transfers) evolved as a necessity. In order to facilitate TT payments, a method of authentication called 'tested telex' became the accepted system. This involves the use of test keys: a bilateral secret code set up between the two institutions to authenticate the payment order.

The code or test key usually has at least three or more dimensions to it, with strict security and normally dual access constraints, with further controls where the ultimate beneficiary is a third party or not a financial institution. Typically, the essential parts of the message containing the value data are encoded (for example, currency, amount, value date). Under no circumstances should dealing room personnel be allowed access to these codes or the procedures for the control of such items.

SWIFT

By the early 1970s the test key system proved too cumbersome and expensive for the ever increasing volumes and size of payments of cross-border traffic. A more efficient and cost-effective approach was required. Following a feasibility study commissioned by 60 European and North American banks, the Society for Worldwide Interbank Financial Telecommunication (SWIFT) formed in 1973 by 239 banks from 15 countries.

SWIFT is a Brussels-based non-profit co-operative, which is owned, financed and directed by its member banks. Over 6700 financial institutions are involved in 189 countries (as at 2000). Corporates (non-banks) cannot make payments on SWIFT directly, but a service has been introduced to enable them to interchange certain types of confirmations (*see* Chapter 3).

> A standardized message system has enabled banks to build automatic interfaces to their own systems.

Most importantly, a standardized message system has enabled banks to build automatic interfaces to their own systems, thus enabling other related functions such as reconciliations to be automated. In addition to currency payments, new technology has enabled SWIFT to expand its services to automated FX confirmation matching and payments netting. Throughout this book there are frequent references to SWIFT services and procedures. SWIFT is now the predominant system for most international currency payments, whereas the tested telex method is very infrequently used by market participants. SWIFT annual message volume reached 113 million in 1997 for FX, money market and derivatives alone, representing a 20 per cent increase in traffic compared with 1996.

Current operations

SWIFT interacts with its members at several levels. It produces:

- A general manual – setting out its articles of association, general terms and conditions including tariff policy and service description;
- *User handbook* – setting out terminal interface specifications, security, billing, connection and training procedures and, most importantly, message standards and examples (all continually upgraded and added to);
- A newsletter – advising new developments to members;
- *International Bank Identifier Code (BIC) Directory* (updated quarterly) – providing a list of all members classified in various ways (by country, SWIFT code etc.), together with essential information on each country and currency codes (this is also available as a database called BIC Database Plus).

The BIC standard

The universal method of identifying financial institutions is based on the use of bank identifier codes (BICs). These facilitate automated processing of telecommunications messages in banking and related financial institutions. The codes contain eight or eleven characters comprising the following: bank (four), country (two), location (two), branch (three). The location is generally the city involved and the branch the office within the city. This is one of the key codes used in all messages sent through SWIFT.

Terminology

A distinct terminology is used within SWIFT and the accompanying technology. A list is given in Table 4.2 of some of the most frequently used abbreviations, together with their definitions. The *User Handbook* should be consulted for more detailed information.

Typical SWIFT abbreviations and what they mean

Table 4.2

ACK	A message sent that is accepted by SWIFT will be positively acknowledged with a short message, an ACK. It is printed together with the original message.
NAK	A message sent that is not accepted by SWIFT will be negatively acknowledged with a different message, a NAK. Error codes contained in the NAK message indicate why the message sent has not been accepted. (See the *User Handbook* for the meaning of the error code.)
LAK	This is the ACK for a log-in message.
LNK	This is the NAK for a log-in message.
ISN	Input sequence number. There is a sequence number in the header of each message sent. The SWIFT system always checks this number. If it is not the one expected, the message will be rejected.
OSN	Output sequence number. Every message received from SWIFT (originating from another bank or from SWIFT itself) also contains a sequence number. The systems keeps a record of the OSN sequence and if an unexpected OSN is received a warning is printed. The user must, in this case, first check for output message with a PDM (possible duplicate message) trailer. If there are no PDMs, the user must retrieve the missing message(s) in any OSN-gap with an 020 system message.
PDE	Possible duplicate emission. This will be added into the trailer by the system whenever a message has to be retransmitted due to failure to receive an Acknowledgement. A banking message received from another bank may also contain a PDE. This will be clearly marked as such on the printout. This means 'Take care! You may have already received another copy of this message.'
PDM	Possible duplicate message. This is added b SWIFT to a message of which prior delivery is dubious and will only appear in received messages. As with the PDE, this means 'Take care! You may have already received another copy of this message.'

Source: SWIFT User Handbook

Security procedures

The principal security features on SWIFT are set out in the policy and operational volumes of the *User Handbook*. These cover the member banks' responsibilities in using the system and, conversely, the responsibilities and limits of liability of SWIFT itself. Important points covered are the restriction of access to authorized users, protection against mutilated or fraudulent messages, encryption on circuits to provide privacy, authentication of messages, and other procedures.

The SWIFT authenticator is an improved and automated version of the telegraphic test keys traditionally used for the authentication of, and confirmation of amounts in, messages between banks. It is automatically calculated on the entire message text, instead of only on selected data as with test keys. This ensures that any change in the message text is detected. As for test keys, the controls and procedures for the use of such authenticators must be strictly segregated from the dealing room.

Message types

The essence of SWIFT is the ability to provide *standard* messages according to set rules and procedures depending on the transaction involved. The SWIFT *User Handbook* details the principles that govern the message-type construction and outlines the main concepts of the checking arrangement for each message to ensure that it conforms to text standards.

Settlement process

The automation of the payment process by international banks has improved efficiency by reducing manual intervention to a minimum. By improving accuracy it has also reduced costs. Thus once the trade has been captured and confirmed by exchanging and matching MT 300 messages, the automated payment transmission of messages (with some important checks, such as whether a netting agreement is in place) can proceed. As we saw in the last chapter, the use of standard settlement instructions (SSIs) makes this process even more straightforward.

Let us assume that Bank X has sold AUD against USD to Bank Y at spot. Typically, Bank X will now generate an MT 202 message via its main computer instructing its AUD correspondent bank to pay the required amount to the correspondent bank of Bank Y for value on the spot settlement date. Conversely, Bank Y will instruct its correspondent bank to pay USD to the correspondent bank of Bank X. These payments messages may match with 'receive' messages (MT 210) sent to the correspondent banks. However, some banks no longer send MT 210s, preferring to rely on a fast and efficient nostro account reconciliation process to pick up 'non-received' payments.

A typical example of how SWIFT messages work for the confirmation and settlement of a spot foreign exchange deal is shown in Fig. 4.2, continuing the example started in Chapter 3.

However, if the currency traded is the domestic or home currency for either counterparty then the payment instructions may be transmitted direct to the domestic clearing system (if the bank concerned is a clearing member) and not through SWIFT. Note the confirmation will flow through SWIFT whatever the currency involved.

Corporate settlements can also follow a different path to that of interbank trades, with additional instructions to credit a third party (as is common in

This is the example from Chapter 3 where the confirmations are shown. This section continues the messages through to settlement. Message 1, confirmation(s) is shown in Chapter 3.

- On 22 January 1996 Crédit Suisse, Zürich, buys GBP100,000 against USD from Berliner Bank, Berlin. The rate is 1.6632. The deal is agreed via telephone.
- On 24 January 1996 Berliner Bank will transfer the pounds to Crédit Suisse's account with Midland Bank, London.
- Crédit Suisse will transfer the dollars to Berliner Bank's account with Chase Manhattan Bank.

Confirmation and settlement of a spot FX deal

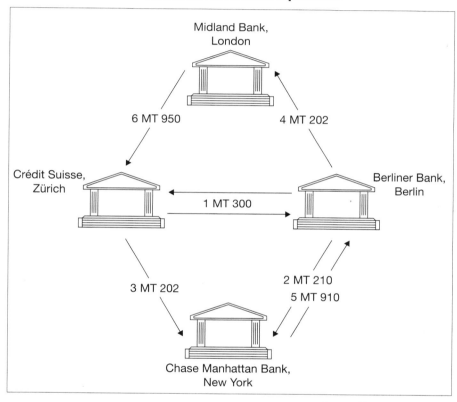

Fig 4.2

Source: SWIFT User Handbook

Message 2 Notice to receive

Berliner Bank sends an MT 210 Notice to Receive to Chase Manhattan Bank, providing notification of the amount that is to be received from Crédit Suisse in settlement of the deal.

Explanation	Format
Sender	BEBEDEBB
Receiver	CHASUS33
Message type	210

Sender's reference	:20:REF2
Value date	:30:960124
Related reference	:21:BEBEBB6632CRESZZ
Currency and amount	:32B:USD166320,00
Ordering institution	:52A:CRESCHZZ

Source: SWIFT User Handbook

Message 3 General financial institution transfer

Crédit Suisse will request Chase Manhattan Bank to credit Berliner Bank with the funds, value 24 January 1996.

Explanation	*Format*
Sender	CRESCHZZ
Receiver	CHASUS33
Message type	202

Sender's reference	:20:REF3
Related reference	:21:BEBEBB6632CRESZZ
Value date, currency and amount	:32A:960124USD166320,00
Beneficiary institution	:58A:BEBEDEBB

Source: SWIFT User Handbook

Message 4 General financial institution transfer

Berliner Bank will request Midland Bank to credit Crédit Suisse with the funds, value 24 January 1996.

Explanation	*Format*
Sender	BEBEDEBB
Receiver	MIDLGB22
Message type	202

Sender's reference	:20:REF4
Related reference	:21:BEBEBB6632CRESZZ
Value date, currency and amount	:32A:960124GBP100000,00
Beneficiary institution	:58A:CRESCHEZZ

Source: SWIFT User Handbook

Message 5 Statement of account/confirmation of credit

On 24 January 1996, Chase Manhattan Bank credits Berliner Bank with the funds. This transaction will appear as follows on the MT 950 Statement Message for the account:
:61:960124C166320.00S910BEBEBB6632CRESZZ//36836522A

In addition, Chase Manhattan Bank, prior to the statement, may send an MT 910 Confirmation of Credit, as shown below:

Explanation	Format
Sender	CHASUS33
Receiver	BEBEDEBB
Message type	910

Sender's reference	:20:REF5
Related reference	:21:BEBEBB6632CRESZZ
Account identification	:25:3458245-223
Value date, currency and amount	:32A:960124USD166320,00
Ordering institution	:52A:CRESCHZZ

Source: SWIFT User Handbook

Message 6 Statement of account/confirmation of credit

On 24 January 1996 Midland Bank credits Crédit Suisse with the funds. This transaction will appear as follows on the MT 950 Statement Message for the account:
:61:960124C100000,00S910BEBEBB6632CRESZZ//356739MM

In addition, Midland Bank, prior to the statement, may send an MT 910 Confirmation of Credit, as shown below:

Explanation	Format
Sender	MIDLGB22
Receiver	CRESCHZZ
Message type	910

Sender's reference	:20:REF6
Related reference	:21:BEBEBB6632CRESZZ
Account identification	:25:H4736-11234
Value date, currency and amount	:32A:960124GBP100000,00
Ordering institution	:52A:BEBEDEBB

Source: SWIFT User Handbook

settlement of a bill or trade transaction), which will be added to the SWIFT message. Instructions may also already be in place to debit or credit a currency account held with the bank with which the corporate has dealt. This is, of course, normal practice where a corporate has dealt with its house or main bankers. But the lack of direct access into SWIFT has encouraged the opening of currency accounts where frequent deals are done with a particular bank. However, this practice can lead to unnecessary accounts being opened. Banks also sometimes maintain currency accounts with each other, to simplify the settlement process on a variety of transactions.

A list of the main message Category 2 types (payments) used for treasury business is given in Table 4.3.

Table 4.3

SWIFT Category 2 treasury-related message types

MT 200 Financial institution transfer for its own account
MT 201 Multiple financial institution transfer for its own account
MT 202 Multiple financial institution
MT 203 Multiple general financial institution transfer
MT 204 Financial markets direct debit message
MT 205 Financial institution transfer execution
MT210 Notice to receive
MT 290 Advice of charges, interest and other adjustments
MT 291 Request for payment of charges, interest and other expenses
MT 292 Request for cancellation
MT 293 Information service message
MT 295 Queries
MT 296 Answers
MT 298 Proprietary message
MT 299 Free format message

Source: Swift User Handbook

In addition to currency payments, SWIFT provides a number of other what it calls operational information services, including deal confirmation/matching via the Accord system, standard settlement instructions (*see* Chapter 3) and various forms of payment netting as an extension of the Accord service. It was selected as the network provider for the European Union TARGET system, which enables the various national real-time gross settlement (RTGS) systems to be linked for euro payments.

> **A good working knowledge of the overall system has become vital for supervisors and management.**

SWIFT has become such an integral part of the back office that a good working knowledge of the overall system has become vital for supervisors and management, both technically and from a user viewpoint. This is why it is important to have on-going training to keep staff up to date with developments. Current plans include applications to develop an IP (internet protocol)-based next generation of SWIFT products and services called SWIFTNet to assist banks with straight-through processing management (*see* Chapter 11).

Euro-impact on category 2 message standards

Table 4.4

Introduction

This section contains guidelines on how to make the best use of the existing Category 2 message standards in light of the implementation of the single European currency, the euro.

In July 1996, the Standards Department circulated a proposal for country comments within the SWIFT community. The aim of the proposal was to gauge the impact of the introduction of the single European currency on SWIFT message standards.

The Standards Department felt that the country comments alone were insufficient to make a proper evaluation. The formation of an EMU Working Group was subsequently approved by the Board Operations Committee.

Work of the EMU Working Group

The EMU Working Group started by evaluating the impact of the euro on SWIFT message standards.

The working group defined testing specifications and time frames for introducing the euro currency code, EUR, on the network.

Finally, they defined scenarios and guidelines on how to best use the existing standards in this context.

Impact on SWIFT Message Types

The EMU Working Group agreed on the following:

- The impact on the message types should be minimal.

- It is essential to specify both the euro and the national currency of countries in the Economic and Monetary Union during the transition period (from 1 January 1999 to 2002 for the first group of countries).

  When the euro becomes the currency of settlement, the national or original currency may continue to be forwarded to the customer, for information purposes only.

- The need to express different denominations of the same currency must be met in a way which does not impact the actual handling of SWIFT formats by using a solution which can be removed when no longer needed.

Consequently, the EMU Working Group devised a solution whereby users could specify euro-related information (ERI) in a structured manner within free text fields of existing message formats.

Source: Swift User Handbook

NATIONAL CLEARING SYSTEMS

There are two distinct elements in interbank funds transfer systems. The first is the transfer of *information* between the payer and payee banks, in the form of a payment order or message that is processed according to pre-defined rules and operating procedures. These may include identification, reconciliation and confirmation of payment messages. The second element is *settlement* – the actual transfer of funds between the payer's bank and the payee's bank. Settlement discharges the obligation and, where irrevocable and unconditional, is described as final settlement.

Each main centre has its own domestic automated clearing systems to facilitate interbank and commercial payments in its national currency. Examples of these are Fedwire and the Clearing House Interbank Payments System (CHIPS) in the USA, Clearing House Automated Payments System (CHAPS) in the UK, Bank of Japan Financial Network System (BOJ-Net) in Japan and Eiliger Zahlungsverkehr (EIL-ZV) in Germany. However, both Japan and Germany have differing specialized arrangements for large value interbank cross-border payments, called FEYNECS and EAF respectively. These systems are explained in detail below, together with TARGET, which linked national systems for euro payments from January 1999.

Other major systems in Europe include:

- France – SAGITTAIRE, an end-of-day system for cross-border transactions; and TBF, a real-time gross settlement system for large value payments and credit transfers, which enables users to monitor cash positions with the Central Bank on a real-time basis;

- Italy – SIPS for interbank payments; and ME, a final settlement mechanism for clearing balances, mainly for banks operated by the Italian Central Bank.

Opening hours of selected G-10 payment systems are shown in Fig. 4.3. Although constructed several years ago, the chart still conveys the essential interlinking between the various payment systems.

Current or planned opening hours of selected G-10 payment systems

Fig 4.3

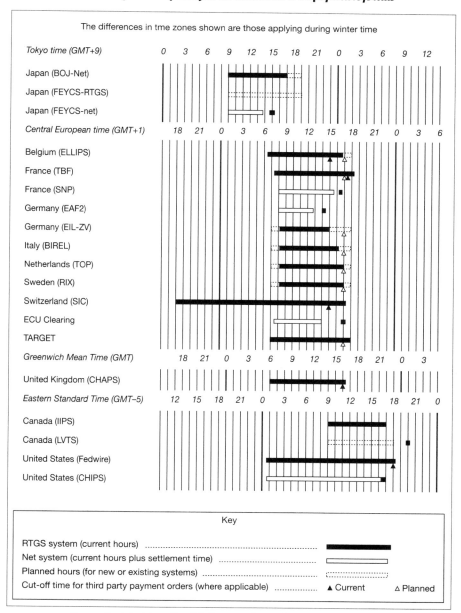

Source: Bank for International Settlements: Central Bank Payment and Settlement Services,

TYPES OF SYSTEMS

There are two basic types of payments systems.

Real-time gross settlement systems (RTGS)

RTGS puts an emphasis on the removal of delays in the payment clearing that used to build up, particularly in the older systems. Under an RTGS system, the clearing bank can issue a payment at any time during the working day and the receiving bank can receive it without recourse. In other words, processing and settlement take place in real time continuously throughout the day. Message-flow structures, queuing arrangements and management of intraday liquidity are key technical issues in the design of an RTGS system. The London CHAPS and FEDWIRE in USA are examples of an RTGS system.

The development of RTGS systems is one response to the growing awareness of the need for sound risk management in large value funds transfer systems. Because of the updating process it offers a mechanism for limiting settlement and systemic risks in the interbank process, precisely because final settlement on individual items take place on a continuous basis throughout the day.

End-of-day clearing system (EOD)

The other main type of clearing system is the end-of-day (EOD). This is so called because it operates on the basis of a net end-of-day transfer, which the clearing organization members agree for each member. This type of system, although simpler to operate (typically using bilateral limits), is not as effective in minimizing inherent intraday risks as RTGS. Examples of end-of-day systems are CHIPS in USA and BOJ-Net in Japan.

US systems

Fedwire

A credit transfer system, Fedwire is governed by the Federal Reserve Bank (Regulation J) and is a real-time gross settlement system, allowing banks that have an account with one of the reserve banks to send or receive payments. The value of payments is in excess of $200 trillion per annum.

CHIPS

CHIPS is a private-sector payment system owned and operated by the New York Clearing House Association (NYCHA). It began operation in 1971 as an electronic replacement for an existing paper-based clearing system. Like Fedwire, CHIPS is a credit transfer system; unlike Fedwire, however, CHIPS nets payment transactions multilaterally and settles the net obligations at the end of the day. It is typical of an end-of-day system in that, under the rules, no payments can be withdrawn (revoked) from the system once they have been entered, and upon receipt the funds are assumed to be cleared by the recipient bank. As a result of this, a system has evolved whereby intraday bilateral limits are imposed by each member on other members, along with cap limits on individual banks.

Liquidity risk is also closely monitored by the clearing house, which has wide powers to act quickly in a crisis. Great attention is given to back up procedures and systems to minimize the exposure that might result from operational failure. In the event of default of a member, the remaining participants would essentially share the loss based on their bilateral limits and collateral security. From a settlements viewpoint, strict rules with a penalty interest rate structure are applied with regard to compensation claims.

CHIPS participants may be commercial banks, Edge Act corporations, investment companies, or banking affiliates of a commercial banking institution with an office in New York City. A non-participant wishing to send payments must employ a CHIPS participant to act as its correspondent or agent. There are over 120 participants connected to a single network and each participant starts the business day with a zero balance, with balances calculated continuously during the day as payments are made and received. CHIPS normally operates from 7.00 am to 4.30 pm Eastern time, with settlement usually completed by 6.00 pm. (*see* Fig 4.3 for operating hours of the main large value international payment systems).

NYCHA recovers the cost of operating the system from the participants, according to usage. The pricing policy structure includes a minimum fee and a reducing charge per message as volume increases; high volume users (over 80 000 messages a month) pay USD0.13 per message. All receivers , except high volume receivers, are charged USD0.18 per message.

UK: CHAPS

CHAPS is an electronic clearing system handling credit transfers. It is designed to create, encrypt, authenticate and transmit payment messages between two settlement banks. It became a full RTGS system in 1996. There is no minimum or maximum limit to the value of each transfer, but in practice the average value at over £2 million is large. CHAPS payments are guaranteed and unconditional same-day sterling credit transfers. The sending bank gives an irrevocable undertaking to settle these transfers, once the CHAPS payment message has arrived at and been automatically acknowledged by the receiving bank. This effectively means that once a settlement member sending a payment has put their name to it, there is a commitment to that payment, even if at the end of the day the originating customer does not have the funds to meet it. This in turn means that the control of customer credit risk (member *vis-à-vis* customer) is critical.

There are 16 settlement members, including the Bank of England, that are direct members of the CHAPS clearing system, with around 400 other financial institution participants through agency agreements. Most now use SWIFT to pass payment instructions to their settlement member.

Under CHAPS rules the system closes at 4.00 pm each day. This allows 20 minutes, at the end of which settlement takes place with the Bank of England on a multilateral net basis in accounts on its books. The settlement member concerned continues to be responsible for ensuring that the Bank of England receives its final settlement figures. Full back-up facilities are in place to meet operational failure or in case settlement cannot be completed in the normal way. However, of more immediate concern are the management of credit risk – both customer and interbank and liquidity risk.

> **Once a settlement member sending a payment has put their name to it, there is a commitment to that payment.**

Each settlement bank in CHAPS can choose the nature and extent of the facilities it is prepared to grant to other participants and its own customers, in respect of the origination of payments. This in turn can depend on the ability to monitor positions of users, particularly the bilateral net positions between the settlement banks. (Prior to 1996, when CHAPS became a full RTGS system, intraday limits were needed to monitor both sender and receiver exposures.)

Liquidity risk stems from the possibility that a settling member may be unable to fund its overall debit position in all the clearings at close of business. At present, this risk is borne by the Bank of England, as there is no practical way to unwind the clearing each day.

The fee that a settlement bank charges its indirect participants is a matter of commercial negotiation between the parties concerned. Such charges may be on a per item basis or part of a negotiated package. The Bank of England charges on a per item basis in respect of each payment, and an annual fee in respect of running costs.

Japan: BOJ-Net and FEYCS

The Bank of Japan Financial Network System (BOJ-Net) is the main domestic currency online electronic funds transfer system used by the Bank of Japan and other financial institutions. Settlement is on a real-time basis as the payments are irrevocable and unconditional. Nested within this system (since 1989) is the Foreign Exchange Yen Clearing System (FEYCS), managed by the Tokyo Bankers Association (TBA), which handles Yen cross-border payments, including those for FX transactions. Over 200 banks are in the system, with a daily average clearing value equivalent to over USD200 billion.

Interbank net settlement for payment instructions entered into FEYCS before 1.45 pm local time is completed at 3.00 pm the same day and an individual instruction can only be amended if agreed to by the receiving bank. This contrasts with real-time payment transfers handled on BOJ-Net itself, which are irrevocable and unconditional (although in the case of designated-time settlement, payment instructions can be revoked before they are executed).

FEYCS is run completely electronically on BOJ-Net, with system participants having direct feeds from SWIFT for instructions received from overseas banks. All participants pay variable charges to the Bank of Japan for using BOJ-Net for FEYCS transactions and a fixed charge for linkage to the BOJ-Net centre.

Credit and liquidity risks are managed initially by the setting of bilateral net credit limits by each participant for the others. Each transaction is checked to see if it will exceed the limit and rejected if it does, as a receiving bank is exposed if it makes funds available to the payee before interbank settlement is completed. In the case of a bank failure, a loss-sharing rule is to be applied so that each bank with a credit position *vis-à-vis* the failed bank will bear a loss in proportion to the amount of credit extended to that bank.

Germany: EIL-ZV, ELS and EAF

EIL-ZV was set up in 1987 as an express electronic credit transfer system operated by the Deutsche Bundesbank, the German Central Bank. It is an RTGS system to process mainly large value credit transfers over DEM50,000 between accounts held at Central Bank branches and is used mainly for national transactions, such as money market operations or urgent payments.

ELS (Euro Link System) was established by the Central Bank in 1992 as the Express Transfer System – a forerunner of the present system – to allow Central Bank account holders to access EIL-ZV by means of an 'electronic counter'. It is an RTGS system and effectively every holder of a bank account in Germany can be reached for non-cash payments. It also has an interface into TARGET (*see* below) using SWIFT functionality.

EAF stands for 'Elektronische Abrechnung mit Filetransfer' and replaced the mainly paper arrangement prior to 1990. The EAF is used for the paperless exchange of credit transfers in Deutsche Marks between participants based in Frankfurt and is effectively the main large value cross-border treasury payments system in Germany.

Payments can normally be submitted to the Bundesbank's branch in Frankfurt continuously between 8.00 am and 12.30 pm local time. Payments not settled bilaterally by 12.45 pm are finally cleared and settled during two multilateral clearings at 1.00 pm and 2.00 pm. As a fully electronic system with a high level of technical stability, EAF combines a low-risk profile of a gross settlement system with the liquidity saving features of a net settlement system.

EAF has the highest payments traffic volume in Europe, with an average daily settling volume of DEM1.3 trillion, handling more than 160,000 transactions at peak times. More than 50 per cent of EAF users are foreign institutions, which settle their worldwide DEM transactions through the system. By international standards, EAF's user fees are quite low: the monthly basic fee is DEM500, with a cost recovery transaction fee of DEM0.40 payable by the remitter.

Following the implementation of the European Monetary Union (EMU) in 1999, the acronym EAF now also stands for Euro Access Frankfurt and only clears and settles in euros. During the transitional phase to the end of 2001 users who have not yet changed over to the euro can continue to make and receive payments in DEM, with the system performing the required conversion. EAF has also changed its operating hours to those of other cross-border payment systems within the EMU area. These, together with the holiday calendar, have been extended and synchronized with TARGET and run from 7.00 am to 5.00 pm, to overlap with the operating hours of the major payment systems in the USA and Japan.

TARGET

Trans-European Automated Real-time Gross Settlement Express Transfer (TARGET) started in January 1999 to link the national payments systems of the European Union by a message switch, called Interlinking and based at the European Central Bank. TARGET is an advanced real-time system built for the euro and a diagrammatical representation is shown in Fig. 4.4. CHAPS euro is an example of how TARGET links to national payment systems allowing euro payments to be settled between banks in London and, through the link, between banks in London and elsewhere in the European Union.

Mention should also be made of the EBA (ECU Banking Association) Euro clearing system based in France and involving 60 major banks in Europe. This system is designed primarily to provide same-day value volume commercial payments and financial clearing services throughout Europe and beyond, using SWIFT as the clearing service provider. Risk management capabilities are built into the system to cap credit and debit positions. A current development is the single obligation structure (SOS) legal concept, which allows netting of payments during the day with settlement of the net balance at an agreed cut-off time. Final daily settlement is at the ECB.

Thus, in terms of cross-border euro payments, TARGET may be viewed as the RTGS system for wholesale payments traffic, while EBA euro clearing complements this with same-day value for commercial payments.

RTGS systems concepts

Fig 4.4

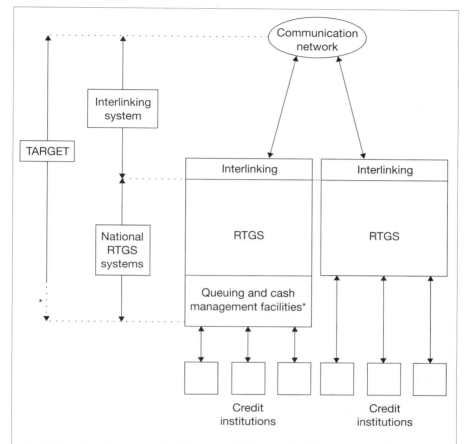

* Queuing and cash management facilities are provided on an optional basis by some RTGS systems.

A cross-border transfer through TARGET is initiated when the sending credit institution transmits a payment message to the local national central bank (the sending NCB) through the local RTGS system. Assuming the sending credit institution has sufficient funds available, the amount of the payment will be irrevocably and immediately debited from the account the sending credit institution holds at the NCB. The sending NCB will then transfer the payment message through the Interlinking network to the receiving NCB. The receiving NCB will credit the receiving credit institution's account.

Source: Bank of International Settlements: RTGS systems, March 1997

What can go wrong?

In recent years, new technology has brought about faster and more accurate payment systems. It has also helped to reduce the incidence of costly payment errors and, thereby, the number of expensive disputes. However, payment errors do occur, often resulting in late payments. Depending on the circumstances, the bank responsible for the mistake is obliged to compensate the other party for the costs involved.

Typically, payment to a wrong nostro account can result in an overdraft on one account with a 'wasted surplus balance' on another. The efficient rectification of such an error will, to a certain extent, depend on early discovery and quick corrective action. Indeed if the system highlights the error in time, it may be possible to intercept, amend or cancel the erroneous payment, depending on local cancellation procedure and cut-off times.

Where this is not possible, and there is a period of overdraft in one bank account with a surplus balance in another, the possibility or willingness of the two institutions to co-operate in minimizing the cost will depend on a number of factors.

Procedure for compensation

As an example, Bank A in London sells or lends 10 million Swiss francs (CHF) to Bank B in Paris who instructs Bank A to pay Bank X in Zürich value spot, which is Friday 15 March. Instead of paying Bank X, Zürich, for account of Bank B, Bank A erroneously pays Bank Y, Zürich, for account of Bank B, value Friday 15 March.

What develops next will depend on how quickly the error comes to light. Typically, though not necessarily, the first 'alarm' will be triggered by Bank B's overdraft at Bank X, caused by the non-receipt of CHF10 million. Depending on the nostro account advice arrangements in place, Bank X should advise Bank B electronically, by the following Monday morning at the latest, of both the non-receipt (which should have been on Bank B's pre-advised receipt list) and the extent of the overdraft, which may be somewhat less than CHF10 million.

Bank B should immediately contact Bank A to query the non-receipt. Upon investigation, Bank A quickly discovers that the funds have erroneously been paid to Bank Y instead of Bank X and advises Bank B accordingly. *As the funds have already been paid, it is Bank B who must take the initiative and instruct Bank Y to transfer CHF10 million to bank X for its account.*

As it is already some hours after the Zürich cut-off time (8.00 am) the funds can only be paid value next day, Tuesday 19 March, which effectively means a four-day overdraft interest charge for Bank B at Bank X, which it will claim from Bank A.

The extent to which this type of claim can be reduced varies considerably between centres and may depend on a number of factors. In each instance these might include the rules for compensation for the payments/clearing system in the centre concerned, with some countries more amenable to payment adjustments and, in some cases, back value than others.

Another factor is the local money market practices and conventions on short dates. Bank Y has had the 'free' use of the funds in its short-date cash flow and, depending on the relationship with Bank B, whose account it holds, may be prepared to reimburse some of the interest it may have received on the overnight surplus.

Procedure for compensation

Fig 4.5

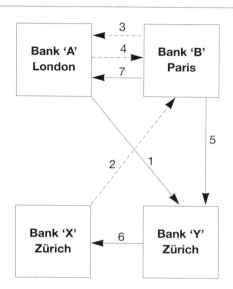

1 Bank A in London erroneously pays Bank Y instead of Bank X in Zürich for Bank B's account, value 15 March.
2 Bank X does not receive the funds pre-advised by Bank B and accordingly advises Bank B of non-receipt and resulting overdraft.
3 Bank B immediately queries non-receipt with Bank A, who investigates at once.
4 Bank A confirms that the funds have been erroneously paid to Bank Y for Bank B's account instead of to Bank X.
5 Bank B instructs Bank Y to debit its account and pay the funds to Bank X for its own account.
6 Bank Y executes Bank B's payment order.
7 Bank B claims compensation from Bank A.

Finally, the business relationship between all four institutions involved in the transaction may impact the final outcome. Where erroneous payments and overdrafts are concerned, the least expensive resolution of the problem often requires the co-operation and goodwill of all of the parties involved. For the head of treasury operations, it is frequently as much a matter of skilful negotiation and understanding the problem as knowing the rules or correct procedure – remembering that there is, for banks that deal with one another frequently, always a next time when the error may be yours!

SUMMARY

In this chapter we have looked at the process of settlement, international payment carriers and national clearing systems.

Key points

- What is meant by good settlement and the cut-off times required to achieve this
- Use of correspondent banks and nostro/vostro accounts
- How national and international payment systems work and how instructions are sent to them via SWIFT messages to settle treasury-related business
- What can go wrong, how problems are resolved and compensation agreed and paid

5

Securities delivery versus payment systems

This chapter covers securities delivery versus payments systems and the mechanics of settlement on a national and cross-border basis.

BASIC SETTLEMENT PROCESS AND RISKS

Treasury-related transactions are usually defined as FX, money market and derivatives, including repos. These transactions must eventually be settled through the nostro accounts as explained previously. However, even in this business environment a money market dealer is likely to become involved in transactions beyond straight 'vanilla' money market loans and deposits. This may mean the purchase and sale of paper-backed transactions as securities and bonds, which acknowledge the debt as a cheaper way of funding the book or as a conscious decision to allow the dealer to run a book in securities in which the bank has a particular currency and/or country interest and knowledge.

Settlement of this type of transaction is completed when delivery takes place against or versus payment (DVP) and the depositories for both domestic and international business have grown steadily in line with volumes. The accounts used in these systems have become known as custodian accounts, because securities are held by a 'custodian' pending the instructions of the beneficial owner. Each country has differing clearing and depository arrangements for domestic securities. International (cross-border) examples of these types of services are Euroclear and Clearstream, which were specifically formed for this purpose, but numerous banks also offer at the very least a custodian service for settlement of securities of their home country. Several, particularly US banks, have developed a full range of global custodian services to support investment banking operations and the industry is now one of the fastest growing in terms of fee-earning potential for international banks.

Delivery versus payment (DVP)

The settlement procedure for securities rests on the principle of delivery versus payment. The Bank for International Settlements defines a securities settlement system as providing a mechanism that *ensures* that delivery occurs if and only if payment occurs. However, within this definition, as with payment systems, there are different interpretations of the mechanics of settlement. These can be described as one of three types:

- settlement (funds being paid) on a trade-by-trade basis;
- transfer of securities intraday but net settlement at end of day;
- settlement of securities *and* funds on a net basis, with final transfers of both securities and funds occurring at the end of the processing cycle.

With most countries, separate systems exist to settle government and commercial domestic securities against assured payment. Typically, the depository holding the securities (the book transfer function) is separate from the clearing house (settlement/payment function).

The process of clearing and settling a securities trade includes a number of key steps, including matching, consequent obligations of the counterparties (clearing) and settlement by payment against delivery of securities. This can be a complicated procedure with special rules for each step and each clearing house or system having its own rules. Essentially the risks faced by the respective counterparties to securities trades are similar to those for an FX trade: failure of counterparty (settlement or liquidity risk if settlement is delayed) and replacement- cost risk representing the unrealized gain on a contract. Lack of liquidity in securities markets that may result in systemic risk (the failure of one counterparty resulting in the failure of another) in the consequent DVP systems is also of concern to central banks.

Fig. 5.1 shows the basic settlement process.

Delivery versus payment (DVP): basic settlement process

Fig 5.1

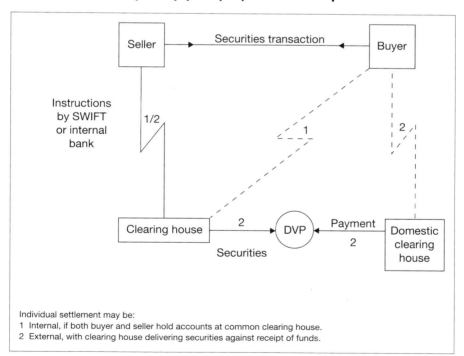

Individual settlement may be:
1 Internal, if both buyer and seller hold accounts at common clearing house.
2 External, with clearing house delivering securities against receipt of funds.

NATIONAL CUSTODIAN SYSTEMS

Domestic custodian systems and the related DVP settlement services provided for interest-related securities for the USA, UK, Japan and Germany are examined in this section, before moving on to look at the cross-border clearing houses Euroclear and Clearstream. Settlement systems for equities are beyond the scope of this book. However, Figure 5.2 shows how securities settlement systems 'link' to other settlement systems. The processing descriptions given relate to the banks' own trades, although there are a number of other types of institutions that use these systems, both for own and customers' trades. Effectively, most of the core procedures would be the same.

> **The US treasury market is the largest and most liquid government bond market in the world.**

US systems

The US treasury market is the largest and most liquid government bond market in the world. With active markets in all the main financial instruments, a national network settles transactions on a DVP basis. This can take the form of net securities against net payment, or on a transaction-for-transaction and net fund basis. Settlement of US government securities is handled separately from commercial transactions.

Fedwire (SECS) and GSCC

Set up by the 12 Federal Reserve Banks in 1967, Fedwire (Federal Reserve Book Entry System) clears USD-denominated securities of the treasury, federal and international organizations. Participants include the commercial banks and other financial organizations.

Government Securities Clearing Corporation (GSCC) compares trades between its members on a gross real time for set hours during the business day, with an extra 30 minutes to adjust for errors. Times may be extended for high volume periods. Transfers are final when processed and cannot be reversed, but will not be effected where there is an inadequate balance on account.

DTC and NSCC

The Depository Trust Company (DTC), started in 1973, has become the largest depository used for settlement processing and book transfer of securities. The main clearing houses and depositories are system linked and this allows settlement without the physical movement of securities. Transfers are trade by

Fig 5.2

Hypothetical example of linkages between settlement systems

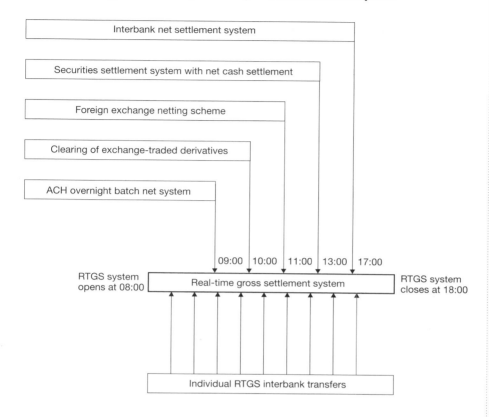

Source: BIS RTGS Systems, March 1997

trade and are provisional until payment is made by end of day. Arrangements for borrowing/lending is outside the system, as DTC provides no borrowing/lending facility itself.

Most domestic USD bond (and equity) trades are cleared through the National Securities Clearing Corporation (NSCC). There are other regional clearing centres that cover all the securities traded on the nationwide network of exchanges. Most NSCC-compared trades are eligible for continuous net settlement (CNS) service multilateral net, substituting NSCC as central counterparty to each trade.

UK systems

In the UK the government uses a variety of financial instruments to fund its budget deficit, including national savings, treasury and local authority bills and government securities. The latter are called gilts, meaning 'gilt-edged' because they come with a government repayment guarantee and form a major and distinct market. Domestic and international commercial securities, including Eurobonds and money market instruments, form a separate market. These markets are normally serviced in turn by separate settlement arrangements and systems, although recently there have been moves to bring together these functions (this is explained later). The systems as they stand now are outlined below.

CGO

The Central Gilts Office (CGO) was started in 1986 jointly by the Bank of England and the International Stock Exchange. It provides all participants in the gilts market with an online, real-time computerized book entry transfer system with assured payment. The aim was to immobilize and eventually dematerialize the underlying securities, although physical delivery can still be taken on completion of a stock transfer form (STF). Thus the stock remains registered with the Bank of England once lodged, no matter who the beneficial owner is and no STF need be completed, although the operation of the CGO is governed by the Stock Transfer Act of 1982.

In addition to handling conventional gilts, the system was enhanced in 1995 and 1997 to allow the stripping and reconstitution of gilts and the efficient processing of repos. This has removed an impediment to the growth of this market that existed before. An upgrade in January 1999 enables the CGO to handle transactions in euro or sterling-denominated securities, to accommodate a future decision on the membership of the EMU by the UK.

Participants can join the CGO service as a direct or as an indirect member through a direct member or sponsor. (A sponsor may also operate as a direct member or it may solely provide sponsorship services.) Direct members have a book entry account in the CGO in their own name and input and receive stock deliveries via a terminal located in their office, for which they are responsible. Each direct member arranges for a settlement bank to receive payments on its behalf for stock transferred from it to any other member. Conversely, the settlement bank undertakes to make payment for stock received. In return for this and to cover the exposure created, it is common practice for the settlement bank to take a floating charge over the stock held for the member.

Various formal agreements are also required between the member and the CGO and the member and its settlement bank. For example, the duties of the banks (including the Bank of England as a settlement bank) to one another are set down in a single global agreement – the CGO Assured Payment Agreement (APA). A separate APA is required for each currency (*see* below).

Direct members pay annual fees and transaction charges to the CGO. A number seek to defray the costs of the system by offering indirect membership to participants whose volume of transactions may not be substantial, on a nominee basis.

Principle of assured payments and risks

Members of the CGO have an agreement with their settlement bank, which would also be a settlement member of CHAPS, and with the Bank of England on an assured payment basis. The principle of assured payment means that whenever stock moves from one CGO account to another, an equivalent irrevocable commitment to effect payment is made in the reverse direction on the same day, which protects both the giver and taker of stock. In practice, instructions are aggregated during the day and the total amount posted against the member's CGO account at the end of the day. The corresponding movement of funds takes place on a net basis over the settlement banks' accounts at the Bank of England. Thus the settlement banks currently carry the intraday interbank credit risk inherent in the assured payment system, effectively supporting the liquidity in the market.

Processing outline

The CGO service is based on the concept of book entry transfer. Members have accounts within the CGO system that represent their holdings of securities. At any given time the balance on each account contains three elements:

- amounts earmarked for delivery (or deposit link)
- amounts held as in escrow as collateral
- balance available.

Continual processing of transfer input takes place. As soon as stock is credited to the taking member's account it is immediately available for further onward delivery. For this reason, the rules with which members must comply for the movement of stock are very strict.

Delivery is broken down into three steps and acceptance into two. Both giver and taker must agree the transaction (which is given a unique reference) positively through their terminals before processing and movement takes place. Access is only via these authorized terminals and coded security measures are used to protect the system. Additionally, normal restrictions are applied regarding physical and system access, consistent with each member's office procedures. Care should be taken to ensure that operators are of sufficient level and experience to ensure proper checking of delivery data. Authentication procedures are used to protect messages passing across the communications network.

A full range of online enquiry facilities include options to enable a member to determine their stock and payment positions at any time, to check on outstanding items and view daily reference prices for all securities, to see if the value is within predetermined bands for delivery. All deliveries are held on a sequential stock queue until there is sufficient stock available on a member's account – which may, of course, be dependent on another delivery. At 1.30 pm each day a system of 'circles processing' commences to complete deliveries and payments; the system finally closes at 7.00 pm after all payment runs, DBV (*see* below) and reconciliation routines have been completed.

> **Care should be taken to ensure that operators are of sufficient level and experience to ensure proper checking of delivery data.**

ESO

The ESO (European Settlements Office) allowed banks to settle ECU-denominated securities through Euroclear and Clearstream and/or connected systems. The system ceased operation at the end of 1997, with its functions subsumed into the CGO.

CMO

The Central Moneymarkets Office (CMO), which started in 1990, provides a central depository service for sterling money market instruments and operates an electronic book entry transfer system that eliminates the previous paper handling between members. Instruments included are treasury, local authority, trade and bank bills, bank and building society certificates of deposit and other commercial paper. Participants include discount houses, banks and brokers.

There are two methods of participation, direct and indirect membership. Essentially, a direct member will have a book entry account with the CMO in its own name and communicate directly with the CMO via a terminal in the member's office, for which they are responsible in a similar way to that for the CGO. The CMO also has an arrangement with a settlement bank to make and receive payments on its behalf for instruments transferred to or from any other member of the CMO. The CMO levies a usage-related tariff, designed to only recover the costs of the service, on each direct member but not indirect members.

Many banks do not want the involvement of direct membership, for example, where the level of activity in the sterling money market/commercial paper does not justify the cost. These institutions can become indirect members by using a nominee who is a direct member. In this case the charge for the service will be a bilateral agreement between the participants.

Risks

The CMO has no role beyond that of a depository for instruments and a payment generation facility for members. There is no assured payment scheme, as with the CGO. This means that a credit settlement risk exists for the counter-party to the transaction in the event that a settlement bank refuses or fails to meet a payment instruction given by a member. The linked transfer of securities will not be reversed by the CMO and other redress would have to be sought.

Processing outline

The normal processing day is on a continuous basis. However, deliveries against consideration cannot be accepted after 3.30 pm. Unlike the CGO, payment instructions generated by the CMO are not assured and, excep-tionally, could be rejected by the paying members' settlement bank. Securities and corresponding payments are not simultaneous. Securities are transferred on a gross basis throughout the day, with funds transfer occurring net at the end of the day.

Like the CGO, security procedures include authentication and encryption processes to protect message traffic between terminals. Members are required to show that access to the system is strictly controlled, using passwords and operators at three different levels depending on the task being performed. Thus a different operator at the appropriate level is required to verify initial input before the transaction can proceed, in a similar way to the checking standards set in SWIFT. Back-up facilities are provided, with standby terminals at the CMO available to members in an emergency.

Each member has a CMO instruments account that represents their inventory of instruments, sorted by issue type and form held (for example, collateral, outright, repurchase etc.). All instruments held within the CMO service must be payable at maturity by a CMO member. A cash memorandum account is also held for each member, reflecting the payment instructions created in respect of deliveries due, and is linked to the bank account maintained by the member with its settlement bank. The settlement process for member-to-member delivery transfers the instruments or parcels (see below) from the account of the giver to that of the taker and generates the appropriate payment instructions for the amount of the consideration.

A service of particular use to members, who pledge assets against loans from banks, is that of 'parcelling'. This allows members to create parcels of instru-ments which, when transferred, remain available for delivery as the same parcel.

Special rules apply with regard to the pledging of collateral between members, splitting and lodgement of new issues. Lodgement of securities requires authentication and validation by the CMO. It should also be noted that not all instruments are lodged with the CMO and these are dealt with by physical delivery, again requiring special procedures and conformity to the BBA published standards for London Good Delivery (covering security and printing in the case of CDs). Reference should be made to the Bank of England handbook on the CMO for these aspects.

CGO and CMO developments

From January 1999 the CGO has operated as a dual currency system using multi-currency functionality. This allows members to settle transactions against either euro or sterling consideration. It is also possible for the system to cope with securities denominated in either euro or sterling. It is envisaged that the CGO would revert to a single currency system on the date of entry of the UK joining the EMU.

Separately, the Bank of England has been conducting a review of the future development of UK securities systems, particularly the need for a full DVP mechanism in the CMO. (At present DVP means delivery against final payment in commercial bank funds for CGO transactions. It is proposed that a full DVP for the CGO and CMO would provide for simultaneous final settlement of individual transactions between accounts at the Bank of England. Settlement in central bank money takes place between settlement banks net at close of business.) With CREST software (the UK equities settlement system) in the process of modification so that it can be used by the CGO, the advantages, costs and practicalities of a CREST, CGO and CMO merger is being examined as part of this exercise, as outlined in the September 1998 Securities Settlement Priorities Review. Pan-European linkups are also being explored.

Japan

DVP-Net

This is a development of the BOJ-Net system and is designed to settle Japanese government securities (registered and book entry). The system is operated by the Bank of Japan which provides day-to-day management oversight and also acts as a settlement bank for funds. Some major securities houses with funds at the Bank of Japan may conduct principal transactions through these accounts.

Banks have full access to the system and other financial institutions have limited or indirect access. The system will not separately identify customer holdings unless they are registered holdings. Funds transferred are irrevocable once settled by the delivery of securities. There is simultaneous synchronization between final transfers of securities and funds, both on a real-time and batch basis. In the event of payment failure, a cancellation of corresponding securities deliveries would result. The Bank of Japan may extend credit facilities to banks in an emergency, but there are no formal arrangements in place.

German systems

European countries invariably have a clearing and settlement system for their own government securities, usually operated by a central bank or other centralized authority. Germany is no exception – it has developed an efficient clearing and settlement arrangement for both over-the-counter and exchange-traded futures and options, on a centralized basis.

As in other countries, German securities markets are in a period of transition, with the key driving forces being the continuing globalization of markets, EU initiatives (particularly the advent of the euro) and the increasing demand for market and operating efficiencies. This last factor, together with the requirement to maintain market integrity, has seen the concentration of clearing/custody facilities. Thus the Deutsche Börse AG (the German Stock Exchange) based in Frankfurt has progressively absorbed the Deutsche Terminbörse (DTB, the futures and options exchange) and the Deutscher Kassenverein (DKV, the central securities depository) along with other clearing/settlement facilities such as the Deutscher Auslandskassenverein (AKV, the central foreign securities depository).

> Securities markets are in a period of transition, with the key driving forces being the continuing globalization of markets, EU initiatives and the increasing demand for market and operating efficiencies.

The primary bond market dominates the equities market, due to the volumes of German government bonds. Secondary markets offer a range of facilities and instruments, including a securities lending facility for increasingly sophisticated investors. Foreign banks are active on the DTB screen-based system, progressively eroding conventional terms and national boundaries.

DKV

The Deutsche Kassenverein AG (DKV) became a DVP system in 1970 for listed fixed-interest and dividend-bearing securities, having previously been a legal arrangement only for book entries. Participants are all banks active in trading/custody of securities, securities brokers and trading firms (in respect of their own holdings). DKV is a specialized bank subject to official supervision by the Federal Banking Supervisory Office and recovers its costs from members.

Processing outline

The DKV holds and identifies securities separately or collectively for participants. It receives confirmation of trades from both counterparties and will carry out transfers for payment only if they match. Holders and recipients of securities may instruct DKV to transfer stock, free or for payment. There is no netting of trades. Transfers are not executed until cover is available for all payments, which may only be withdrawn by the DKV.

Once executed, payments cannot be reversed. No credit facilities are provided for by the securities settlement system. In theory, settlement is simultaneous, although securities account statements are delivered after payments are final and the seller cannot then stop securities transfer. If a participant were to fail, all its securities and cash transfers would be taken out of the settlement process. There is a guarantee fund that in certain circumstances may take the place of the defaulter.

DB developments

Since 1998 customers of the DB clearing, the umbrella organization, are able to settle DVP during the day, with a second processing run added for same-day settlement. Enhancements in 1999 provide for real-time settlement on individual transactions on an effectively irrevocable 24-hour basis.

CROSS-BORDER CLEARING HOUSES

Thus far we have looked at clean payment and settlement systems in Chapter 4 and domestic delivery versus payment systems in the first part of this chapter. Now we move on to examine cross-border DVP systems. In this context cross-border means the settlement for international securities (normally bearer) by institutions outside their normal resident country.

There are several distinct parts to the international securities market, including short-term Euronotes and longer dated Eurobonds, the major portion of which are denominated in USD. Typically, this paper is issued in several centres at the same time and will be exempt from withholding taxes on the interest paid. Most of the paper issued is bearer and therefore a secure system of DVP is essential as, in theory, physical delivery is the transfer of securities. To meet this need, two major depository/settlement organizations (Euroclear and Clearstream) have evolved so that transfer of ownership can take place without the need for physical movement of securities. The important role performed by these two clearing houses and the systems involved in settlement and other functions are explained below.

Two more general points need to be mentioned The first is that the securities deposited are 'fungible'. This means that the owner no longer has title to a particular security that can be identified by a certificate or registration number, but has a claim on a pool of similar securities held by the depository in its books. Secondly, the depository does not actually hold the securities at all! Instead, custodian banks in the home country of the security hold the securities to the order of Euroclear or Clearstream for delivery.

In addition to custody and settlement services, other facilities are available: trade matching and confirmation, finance and cash management, and securities lending and borrowing. For a number of years the two systems operated independently on a different settlement basis but this has been progressively overcome with a 'bridge' arrangement that now links and facilitates settlement between the two systems.

Banks are able to send settlement instructions to both clearing houses via SWIFT and additionally to Euroclear using EUCLID, the proprietary communications link of Euroclear. In this context, these systems may be regarded as the cross-border message carriers for the clearing houses. Before instructions are executed at the clearing houses, they must be validated, matched from both counterparties and proper identification of the securities made. A key point to understand is that as well as ensuring that individual transactions meet specified prerequisites, rules, which are explained below, apply to the *order or priority* in which transactions are processed, so as to minimize failures.

Basic settlement procedures for cross-border DVP systems

- Both Euroclear and Clearstream have similar processing and settlement procedures, operating a gross delivery versus payment system for an individual securities transaction.

- Basis of settlement is T+3, meaning settlement is due three days after the deal date.

- Normally, instructions must be provided to the clearing house the day before settlement takes place. This means the seller must be holding sufficient securities in its custodian account of that particular type of paper for the settlement to proceed and the buyer must provide the correct funds on a cleared basis in order for a simultaneous exchange to take place.

- Settlement takes place on a sequential basis using a prioritizing method. This is based on nominal value of the transaction and settlement dates and takes account of transfers between counterparties for the same type of paper, to reduce the number of settlements.

- Transactions can be settled with counterparties that are either internal, across the 'bridge' between Euroclear and Clearstream or external with another clearing (usually domestic) house.

- A high level of settlement efficiency is obtained by te securities lending and borrowing facilities which are integrated into the settlement process. This avoids settlement failures due to lack of available securities at a given point of time intraday.

- For the in-house accounts, net cash is settled at the end of the day to the clearing house's account, through the domestic payment system for a particular currency.

Euroclear

Originally created in 1968 by Morgan Guaranty Trust, the Euroclear Clearance System 'co-operative' was formed in 1987 from an earlier arrangement dating back to 1972 when it was sold to 120 banks. Now the number of participants is approaching 3000, with turnover of USD25 trillion settled through the system in 1995.

Morgan Guarantee Trust Company, from its Brussels office, is the appointed operator of the Euroclear System through the Euroclear Operations Centre (EOC). Morgan Guarantee Brussels is regulated by the Belgian and US Banking Authorities and in its capacity as operator of the Euroclear System is authorized as a Service Company under the UK Financial Services Act (1986).

> Access to the main securities markets to facilitate cross-border settlement at low cost has been the crucial element in the continuing success of Euroclear.

The Euroclear system clears a wide range of international fixed and floating rate paper, as well as domestic debt instruments. Participants are able to confirm, clear and settle in many currencies, on a delivery versus payment basis. Such is the extent of Euroclear in the custodian market, the majority of trades are settled internally with the transfer of securities requiring only book entries. The remainder are settled via the bridge with Clearstream and externally. Access to the main securities markets to facilitate cross-border settlement at low cost has been the crucial element in the continuing success of Euroclear, together with an ever widening range of securities that can be settled (currently numbering over 100,000).

EOC processing and settlement

The first part of the procedure, leading to DVP, is the matching process. Purchasers of securities send instructions to receive securities against payment, while sellers of securities send instructions to deliver against payment. Of course, free deliveries may also be authorized Instructions are validated immediately and rejected instructions advised to participants. After validation, the instructions are matched with counterparty instructions throughout the day on a real-time basis. Key data required to be matched include account numbers, settlement date, quantity of securities, security code of the issue traded and the currency and cash countervalue. Transactions that are not matched are recycled until matched or cancelled.

The European Monetary Institute describes the Euroclear System as achieving DVP by 'gross simultaneous settlements of securities and funds transfer' (BIS Model 1 classification). The system is based on the concept of book-entry settlement. Of the Euroclear turnover 70 per cent settles on its own books, 10 per cent via bridge transactions with Clearstream, and 20 per cent settles externally. Internal settlements are completed by book transfer against payment, provided settlement conditions are met. Delivery across the bridge

Settlement through the Euroclear system

Fig 5.3

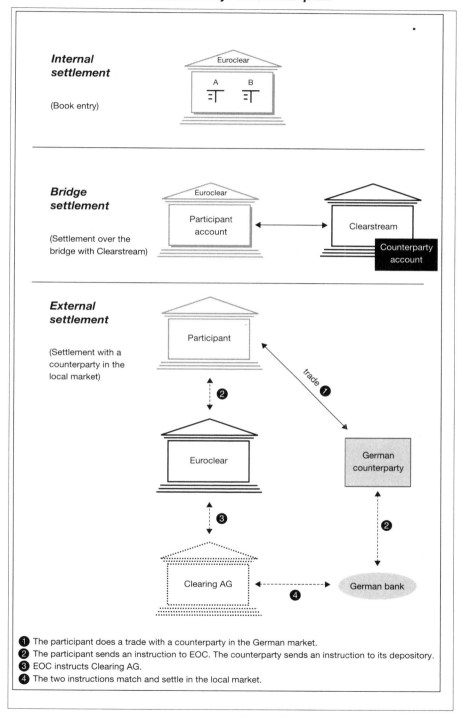

Internal settlement

(Book entry)

Bridge settlement

(Settlement over the bridge with Clearstream)

External settlement

(Settlement with a counterparty in the local market)

1 The participant does a trade with a counterparty in the German market.
2 The participant sends an instruction to EOC. The counterparty sends an instruction to its depository.
3 EOC instructs Clearing AG.
4 The two instructions match and settle in the local market.

Source: *Guide to the Euroclear System*, June 1998

requires that both Euroclear and Clearstream system settlement conditions are met. Transactions with a non-Euroclear participant are settled directly or indirectly via an agent. Final settlement in Euroclear is achieved only when a similar state is attained in the domestic market.

The actual custody operations side of EOC includes a range of services to members, with up-to-date information on individual securities. These include advance notice of income and redemption (ANIR) reports and the deadlines and corporate events (DACE) reporting and enquiry system. An additional important facility is the efficient payment of income on securities held, enabling accurate matching with generated contra-entries in a bank's accounting system.

The status of securities can be tracked through the various stages of clearance and settlement by various reports via SWIFT and EUCLID, the latter being updated several times a day. A full suite of reports is available to participants to track the functions being performed, including securities clearance and settlement, custody, lending and borrowing and money transfer via EUCLID, SWIFT, telex and mail.

Cash accounts can also be opened by participants to ease settlement operation, particularly for book transfers between participants. As Euroclear is a multi-currency system, cash operations can take place in any eligible currency. Available cash balances are updated throughout the day based on projected deliveries, with resulting cash positions the following day based on the overnight settlement process.

Input deadlines

In summary, these deadlines depend on the type of transaction (internal, external or bridge), the security involved and the medium of transmission. For daylight processing, with instruction by EUCLID or SWIFT, the cut-off time is 11.00 am. For overnight processing the deadline is 10 am for instructions by telex or mail and 7.45 pm for instructions from EUCLID or SWIFT (except for certain external transactions).

Overnight instructions for bridge and internal transactions for overnight processing must be received at EOC by the business day before settlement. Care is required for external settlement as these are dependent on a number of factors, such as time zones, local settlement rules, type of security and whether settlement is physical or book entry.

Risk

This really hinges on when the securities and cash transfers become final in each settlement method. In the case of internal trades this is on settlement, as these are on a DVP basis. Clearances across the bridge with Clearstream become final and irrevocable upon receipt of the acceptance feedback by Clearstream. Settlement of domestic trades through domestic market links with EOC will normally be on a DVP basis, where provided for in the domestic market.

Securities lending and borrowing

This service provides flexible credit facilities with Morgan Guaranty to support the securities settlement process and generally increase market liquidity. Lenders, who tend to be portfolio managers and custodians but not active traders, are able to enhance the return on their portfolios by earning fees. On the other hand, borrowers are usually active traders who require the safety net of securities in case 'trade-fails' disrupt the sequence of settlement. Lenders and borrowers have a contractual relationship with Morgan Guaranty, but not with each other. Confidentiality is ensured as the name of counterparties are not disclosed to each other, and lenders' positions are aggregated into a single pool from which securities are allocated to borrowers in a standardized way. Fees are calculated daily at an annual rate based on the value of securities borrowed/loaned, plus accrued interest.

Rebates

At the discretion of the Euroclear board, rebates are granted to participants from time to time. Rebates are based on fees paid, number of transactions, level of securities depot, lending and borrowing activity, other use of the system during the relevant period and costs incurred.

Sample EUCLID reports for securities clearance and settlement   **Table 5.1**

EUCLID		EUCLID report
Validation	Includes instructions validated, cancelled or modified	**Ra00-04**
Unexecuted securities transaction instructions	Shows all pending securities transaction instructions	**Ra70-Ra76**
Securities transaction instructions at end of life	Gives securities transaction instructions that have reached the end of their life	**Rs21**
Securities and related cash movements	Shows all securities and related cash movements resulting from participant's securities transactions and custody operations, and other debits and credits of securities:	
	• movements resulting from overnight processing	**Rs20**
	• movements resulting from daylight processing	**Rs23**
Confirmation notes	Gives confirmation notes for unexecuted instructions entered by a Euroclear or Clearstream counterparty	**RF15**
Securities balances	shows the balances in Securities Clearance Accounts	**Rs30**

Source: Guide to the Euroclear System, June 1998

Clearstream

Clearstream was started in 1970 to provide custodian management services and became a bank in 1995 to increase efficiency and effectiveness in meeting capital adequacy regulations. Like Euroclear, membership includes banks, brokers, investment and central banks and a similar wide range of security types are handled, including bonds and money market instruments on a multi-currency basis.

Settlement instructions may be sent via Clearstream Bank's own proprietary software network and communication links, SWIFT and telex. Standard communications security and authorization protocols ensure authentication. Messages are dealt with continuously in a processing cycle and allocated for completion as settlement criteria are met. These criteria are similar to Euroclear, with the system selecting transactions to settle so as to minimize failed transactions.

Processing

Settlements between Clearstream counterparties can be on a 'free of payment' basis or DVP, depending on instructions, and are handled as book transfer of securities and movement of cash between accounts of buyer and seller. Bridge settlements between customers of Clearstream and Euroclear are settled overnight via the electronic bridge on a net basis. External settlements are settled through one of Clearstream Bank's depositories depending on the market involved.

Each day, multiple-file exchanges take place between the two systems, with strict rules applied to correlate to the different settlement arrangements involved. As at present, this effectively means that Euroclear settlements are only considered during the overnight processing, but this will change as Euroclear introduces real-time same-day matching and settlement in addition to overnight batch processing.

Risk

From a back office perspective, the key risk is when does the settlement become final? By settlement we mean the transfers of cash and corresponding securities become irrevocable. Generally, this is when the transaction is booked by Clearstream in the customer's account. However, in the case of bridge transactions, settlement of proposed deliveries that have been accepted become final when the delivering system operator receives the relevant feedback transmission from the other system. The settlement remains provisional until this happens. The point at which external deliveries become final depends on the domestic system involved in the transaction for the non-Clearstream counterparty, although the Clearstream customer's account would be debited when the instruction to Clearstream's depository is generated.

Securities lending and borrowing

These credit facilities against securities are integrated into the processing function to allow optimal settlement efficiency. Three types are available:

- unconfirmed funds may be used for settlement if the customer has sufficient collateral to cover the resulting debit balance;
- the technical overdraft facility can be used for purchasing securities, but not for other purposes (normally extended for up to two days, most overdraft facilities are collaterized);
- a tripartite financing facility allows for longer term financing against securities to customers by banks.

In each case above Clearstream does not carry any credit risk merely acting as administrator and monitoring the collateral.

Euroclear and Clearstream bridge

Originally, settlement between the two systems was by physical delivery! Fortunately, in 1980 the electronic replacement (the 'bridge') was introduced, whereby each system opened an account with the other, simplifying settlement procedures. This was enhanced in 1992, allowing for multiple overnight settlement batches and file exchanges. Other improvements progressively introduced include a reduction in the time lag for settlement between the two systems, reducing the replacement cost and liquidity risks involved, back-to-back transactions, improvement in cash management and the introduction of a common deadline for settlement.

Bridge settlement

In Clearstream, as in the Euroclear system, settlement starts with several overnight processings before each settlement date. After each Euroclear or Clearstream processing, there is an electronic transmission of files to the other system. As a result, each system has two opportunities each night to receive from or to deliver to the other. Multiple processings and information exchanges ensure high settlement efficiency for bridge transactions.

Receipts from Clearstream Luxembourg

After each batch processing Euroclear informs Clearstream Luxembourg of the acceptance or refusal of each proposed delivery from Clearstream Luxembourg members to Euroclear participants. Deliveries not accepted in the first Euroclear batch processing may be proposed again by Clearstream Luxembourg for the second Euroclear batch processing.

Fig 5.4   **Exchange of settlement files with Clearstream Luxembourg**

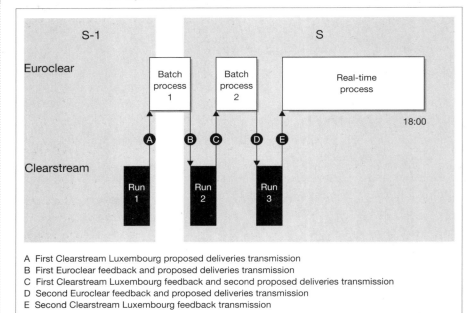

A First Clearstream Luxembourg proposed deliveries transmission
B First Euroclear feedback and proposed deliveries transmission
C First Clearstream Luxembourg feedback and second proposed deliveries transmission
D Second Euroclear feedback and proposed deliveries transmission
E Second Clearstream Luxembourg feedback transmission

Source: Quick Guide to the Euroclear System, February 2000

Triparty repos: use of Euroclear or Clearstream as agent

The explanation earlier of how the clearing houses process and settle their transactions is based primarily on that for bonds and other interest-related securities. However, we saw in Chapter 2 that most repos are also on a DVP settlement basis. A further market development has been the use of the clearing house in what are termed triparty repos. This is an agreement where the two counterparties to the repo use a third party to clear the trade. The third party, acting as agent, handles the transfer of the collateral against the cash value for a fee for both principals involved. As the underlying bonds or securities being 'repoed' may already be held by the clearing house, this improves market efficiency and reduces costs, compared to standard bilateral transactions.

Recent developments

Impact of the euro

With the introduction of the euro in January 1999, securities held in the currency of the eleven countries that have joined the EMU were converted at the permanently fixed rates against the new currency. Henceforth it would be usual to settle

DVP with euro rather than the so called 'legacy' currencies. However, as with the clean payments systems it is still possible to settle in a legacy currency instead of the euro under the interim 'no compulsion no prohibition' rule. This is likely where, say, a company has not yet adopted accounting in euros.

Real-time systems and consolidation of clearing houses

There is an increasing market trend towards 'instantaneous settlement', driven by the banks' need to reduce settlement risk and contain costs. To meet this, both Euroclear and Clearstream are planning to introduce a real-time settlement system to replace overnight batch processing for internationally traded securities, together with the expansion of custodian services and collaterized lending facilities. Competitive domestic and international clearing houses in the industry are offering an increasing number of overlapping services across the range of financial instruments, generally for equities, securities and derivative products, which in turn is leading to a consolidation of domestic and international entities. This is demonstrated by the announced plans for a pan-European securities linkup by Clearstream with the Deutsche Börse and Sicovam, the French national clearing house and a counter-proposal from Euroclear to become the 'hub' of the 'spokes' of national depositories. Obviously, banks want an efficient settlement system at the lowest cost, which will inevitably lead to consolidation in the longer term, particularly with the introduction of the euro – so highlighting how the settlement industry has evolved in a fragmented way.

SUMMARY

In this chapter we have looked at securities delivery versus payment (DVP) systems and the settlement processes involved.

Key points

- What is meant by DVP and the mechanisms involved in various systems
- Domestic custodian systems in the USA, UK, Japan and Germany
- Cross-border securities systems (for example, Euroclear and Cedel Bank)
- Other important concepts such as fungibility and assured payment
- Recent developments in the securities custodian and settlement industry

6

Netting concepts and systems

This chapter looks at the development of netting concepts and current netting settlement systems and procedures. The possibilities of continuous linked settlement (CLS) and the impact of this on settlement risk is examined in Chapter 11. Netting documentation is covered in Chapter 10.

RATIONALE OF NETTING

Background

In both value and volume terms, the daily turnover in global financial markets has shown unprecedented growth in the last few decades. For example, foreign exchange (FX) transactions have grown from a few billion US dollars in the late 1960s to over one trillion since the early 1990s. In that time, the arrangements for executing and controlling payments and receipts have been improved and streamlined, using modern technology and communications. Accordingly, there are far less serious payment and receipt errors today than 20 years ago, when both the turnover and numbers of items were only a small fraction of the present figures.

While the advent of such initiatives as SWIFT and the introduction of SSIs have improved systems and controls, they have not allayed the anxiety felt by regulators and controllers. The underlying reason for this is the huge daily movement of currencies paid on a *gross* basis, carrying with it settlement or delivery and systemic risks that could potentially affect the whole financial system. The daily movement for spot and forward FX, alone, at times exceeded USD1.5 trillion in 1998. In recent years there has been a growing concern that surfaces particularly whenever a serious crisis in confidence is triggered by the demise or collapse of an active capital markets, exchange or derivatives market participant, such as Barings bank in 1995.

The origin of this fear has its roots in a phenomenon that took place in the summer of 1974 involving a small, private but very FX-active bank in Cologne called Bankhaus ID Herstatt. It collapsed following substantial FX dealing losses from uncontrolled currency speculation. The reason why the failure of this bank had repercussions for the international markets way out of proportion to its size and activity centred on the timing of the failure and suspension announcement by the German Bundesbank.

It was early/mid-afternoon European time on 25 June 1974 when the German Central Bank announced the suspension. By this time, Deutsche Mark and European currency payments representing FX sales to Herstatt for delivery that day had been cleared, but the corresponding payments in settlement of purchases of US dollars from Herstatt had not yet been made in New York and were suspended. This effectively triggered the extremely unlikely but real 100 per cent credit risk at liquidation of FX contracts, as a result of settlement or delivery exposure (in recent years often referred to as 'Herstatt risk').

Within days, several internationally well-known banks acknowledged USD10–20 million 'losses' resulting from non-delivery of the US dollar counter-value of marks which they had already paid in Germany. Surprisingly (if not unprofessionally), some even intimated that they were unaware that such a risk existed, in the mistaken belief that the replacement or marginal risk was the only credit risk in FX dealing transactions. As an immediate result, the market turnover declined dramatically for several months thereafter.

Whilst the Herstatt failure and same-day and outstanding FX contractual defaults shocked the banking community, the scale and size of the failure was not of the order to create other significant bankruptcies as a direct result. It did however provoke a serious reappraisal of bank FX dealing limits in general, with particular reference to replacement and settlement risk. It also drew attention to the wider systemic related risk that could well materialize in the event of a sudden failure, or rumour of a failure, of a large and active international financial institution. Recent experience suggests that there is a real risk that such a development could trigger retaliatory or defensive temporary payment delays or strategic defaults, resulting in widespread payment cancellations, thus creating a 'gridlock' phenomenon and a collapse of the payments system.

Mindful of the daily turnover of up to USD1.5 trillion, the central banks and the Bank for International Settlements (BIS) have strongly recommended the implementation and use of payments netting systems (a comparatively recent development), as the most effective means of reducing the settlement risk between counterparties.

In addition to reduced risk exposure, there can be considerable savings in capital adequacy costs and substantial savings in operational costs relating to reduced messages, payments and errors. However, settlement risk is not the only credit risk in treasury dealing. There is also a potentially substantial replacement (or marginal) risk on all outstanding or unmatured transactions, which may take the form of exchange or interest rate risk. For example in FX, in the event of failure or default the extent of the risk depends not only on the exchange rate differential, but on how the outstanding transactions may or may not be fulfilled or settled.

There have been numerous attempts to introduce payment netting arrangements and systems with a sound legal basis. These were often hampered by inadequate international system mechanisms and by the many different national legal jurisdictions involved. We will look first briefly at the legal basis of netting. Next we will examine the systems that have evolved from them and the calculations involved in settlement.

Legal aspects

What is meant by the term netting? A simple example might be a situation where Bank ABC has a large volume of treasury transactions outstanding with Bank XYZ. The pay and receive volumes on a particular value date for these transactions could be large, while the difference or net balance would be much smaller. By *netting* the pay and receives, the volume of messages and value of payments necessary is much reduced. This is the basis of payment netting arrangements and systems.

There have been many attempts to implement more ambitious netting arrangements, starting with simple payment netting underpinned by a banker's lien. In certain countries this arrangement was vulnerable in the case of default to instances of legitimate 'cherry picking' by the liquidator on off balance sheet outstandings, and so proved unsatisfactory. Nevertheless, it did allow for the reduction of payments traffic and exposure on a day-to-day basis.

Netting by novation has proved the most durable of these arrangements. Simply put, a deal agreed between two counterparties is subsumed into any existing transactions, thereby creating a completely new single contract or obligation, including the new transaction. On each settlement date, each counterparty is obliged to make or receive one payment for each currency dealt. This forms the legal under-pinning of the arrangement and a first line of defence against 'cherry picking' in most national jurisdictions. Subject to other requirements, novation netting forms the basis of FXNet (*see* below).

> **For the process to work effectively, a liquidator must be precluded from 'cherry picking' the outstanding transactions.**

Other legal netting arrangements are possible, such as netting by 'close out' whereby netting is activated on a defined event such as an act of default. This is commonly found in credit and similar agreements. Another type of netting mechanism favoured by US banks is that of obligation netting for Financial Accounting Standards Board (FASB) purposes, whereby contracts with a positive mark to market are offset with those of a negative mark to market to reduce the impact on their balance sheets. However, obligation netting still requires a legally enforceable novation or close-out netting contract to meet the FASB requirements. These types of netting are outside the scope of this book

It is most important to realize that netting is a *legal* occurrence. For the process to work effectively, a liquidator must be precluded from 'cherry picking' the outstanding transactions. However, our focus is the practical use of netting mechanisms for settlement purposes and how they work (whatever the legal underpinning may be), and it is to these that we now turn.

NETTING SETTLEMENT SYSTEMS

A number of netting systems and strategies have emerged in recent years, some of which are already in regular use. Others are still in their development stages, or are operational but in the process of systems modifications to accommodate wider participation amongst market institutions. These systems vary considerably, depending on which transactions or exposures are included in the netting strategy.

A simple payment netting agreement for maturing day-to-day FX and/or other transactions between two parties is not difficult to put in place. However, a more comprehensive system that seeks additionally to net out or 'close out' all outstanding exposures in the event of default will require much more complex documentation (with all the attendant legal implications), particularly if it is a multilateral agreement involving several institutions.

This chapter will not attempt to analyze the far reaching issues that have been inhibiting the wider development of netting, but instead will outline the objectives and advantages of netting systems already in use. It will then to look at what the impact of continuous linked settlement (CLS) might have on netting arrangements for settlements.

Netting systems vary in complexity depending on what they set out to achieve. They can be set up for either *bilateral* and *multilateral* use. The main ones are summarized below.

Bilateral netting

Bilateral netting systems have individual netting with a counterparty, with a separate contract for each. They are the easiest type of netting to implement, both legally and from a systems viewpoint. However *multiple* bilateral netting can be cumbersome unless there is a market-accepted system.

Credit risk remains with original counterparty. This the most usual form of netting for the over-the-counter derivatives market using ISDA or similar documentation (*see* Chapter 10).

Individual counterparty payment netting

These are netting arrangements put in place between two individual parties for each to net 'pay' and 'receive' for each value day by currency. Remember that this type of agreement needs a legal underpinning, represented by novation or close out, to be effective should one party defaults. While payment netting reduces the number of payments required and therefore settlement risk and expense of messages, it does not reduce a bank's variable credit risk (cost of replacing outstanding contracts) or capital required under BIS guidelines.

SWIFT Accord confirmation matching and netting

This system, briefly mentioned in Chapter 3, was originally provided to match confirmations for FX and money market transactions. This service was extended by the Accord netting system to include a netting advice service based on the matched confirmations and widened to include derivatives such as forward rate agreements. Accord matches by exception, making it a cost-effective system as resources can be focused on errors.

The basic service involves matching MT Category 3 confirmations that have been generated and sent by counterparties to a deal. This is done by forcing the individual systems to produce a copy of each confirmation, which is transmitted to a central Accord system. Reports are generated back to the initiators after initial validation and eventual matching. Matching can be a complete match, mismatched or unmatched. The latter are reported at least once each day to allow investigation and correction before local cut-off times. A broker confirmation matching service is also available.

The matched confirmation is used as the basis for the bilateral netting service, resulting in a statement to both parties of net balances for relevant value dates and currencies. While SWIFT assumes no liability for the information so provided, this can still form the basis of a netting arrangement whereby only net payments are made and received by the counterparties under netting agreements that meet legal and regulatory requirements.

Fig 6.1

SWIFT Accord matching and netting

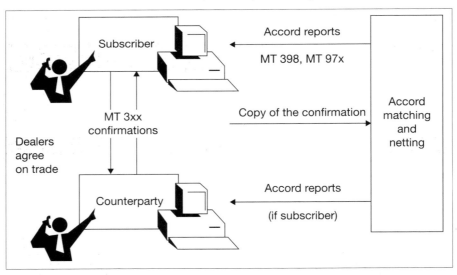

Source: SWIFT Treasury Markets Handbook

Accord work queue pairs screen

Fig 6.2

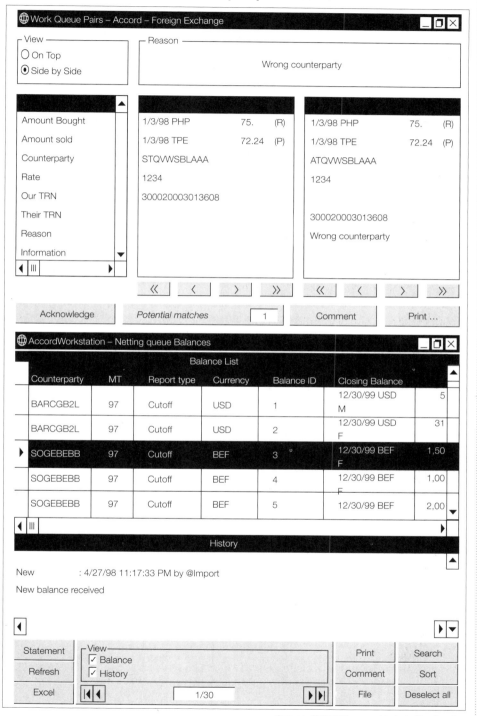

Source: SWIFT Treasury Markets Handbook

FXNet

This service was set up by a group of major FX trading banks in 1986 and provides for the netting of FX on a bilateral basis between members. By identifying a member with which it wishes to net on a bank's 'client' file, the normal MT 300 confirmation for a deal is diverted to the automated service to which each member is linked, at the same time preventing the normal automatic payment generation process. A member is not necessarily expected to net in all the currencies available for a particular member. The MT 300s received by FXNet from each counterparty is matched and at an agreed cut-off time net positions are exchanged by the counterparties and agreed for each currency. Net SWIFT messages MT 202 (pay) and MT 210 (receive) are generated by FXNet to the counterparties, allowing instructions to be passed to SWIFT after reconciliation. The message MT 950 is used to advise a statement of deals making up the net position for reconciliation purposes, which is usually done on an automatic basis using a proprietary application. Special rules apply beyond the netting cut-off time.

> **FXNet has proved to be a reliable service on a bilateral basis.**

The SWIFT Accord netting service provides a simple capability, using confirmations, that would be generated anyway. FXNet can be regarded as a step beyond this. While other, more ambitious, initiatives have come and gone, FXNet has proved to be a reliable service on a bilateral basis.

Netting +

Since early 1996 a number of active FX banks have pursued a further extension of netting concepts called Netting +. This procedure involves the continuous use of tom/next swaps to achieve a still greater reduction in bilateral netting exposure. Under this system, on the day prior to the value date the participants enter into a series of tom/next swaps to offset each of the bilaterally netted non-USD cashflows due on the value date. This leaves a net single amount in USD to be paid/received, which represents the 'profit' or 'loss' on the settled transactions.

The second leg, or next day, part of the swap is in turn netted against the maturing transactions for that day and another tom/next swap is raised, again leaving a net USD amount for payment/receipt. The process is repeated for each settlement date.

Multilateral netting

With bilateral netting arrangements the parties involved retain the default risk on the netted amount. A multilateral netting system is a more ambitious arrangement as there are several participants in the netting process and there is normally a redistribution of default risk, to a greater or lesser extent.

To facilitate multilateral netting it is necessary to have a structure in place with a legal entity at the centre – a clearing house – which, rather like the financial futures clearing houses, becomes the counterparty to all transactions to be cleared. In the event of default, by any member, the clearing house has the legal authority to net out gains and losses on all outstanding transactions, irrespective of value date. Understandably, the agreements and legal documentation necessary are far more onerous than for standard bilateral arrangements.

The two initiatives described below have both been recently acquired by CLS Bank, which will operate a new venture called CLSS (standing for Continuous Linked Settlement Services). This is effectively a new multilateral payments netting facility involving over 60 major financial institutions. The aim will be to eliminate settlement risk initially for FX.

Exchange Clearing House Organization (ECHO)

ECHO, a netting clearing house owned by major international banks, was set up to provide FX netting and settlement services covering the main financial centres. It aimed to reduce credit risks during the life of the outstanding contract, not just at settlement. The basis of the contract with ECHO was one of 'open offer' to users, so that each counterparty effectively dealt with the clearing house and not with each other.

The objective was to serve as a global clearing house for the interbank FX market, but the intention had been eventually to extend the instruments available. The SWIFT Accord system, using MT 300 confirmations, was used as the matching platform for its participating users. ECHO operated through two time zones, with strict cut-off times for trades to be reported.

ECHO would not have absorbed losses itself, in the event of default. It would have allocated them to members who had outstanding trades with the defaulter, depending on whether the individual contracts were in profit or loss after marking to market to calculate a single net present value. Standby facilities were in place to allow remaining net settlements for the day to be completed.

Multinet

Multinet International Bank, based in Chicago, was the US counterpart of ECHO, with a similar concept as ECHO. It has also been absorbed into the CLS initiative.

Continuous linked settlement (CLS)

CLS represents the next stage in an on-going search for the most efficient way of settling transactions after the initial trade is done. It implies that settlement is on-going or continuous throughout the business day and that deals are settled intraday.

Recently, CLS Services (CLSS) has acquired ECHO and Multinet and is working towards establishing a single global multilateral netting scheme for FX, with a revised target start date of late 2001. This means that, apart from FXNet, there is no major cross-border netting capability operating until CLS comes on stream. Many of the issues that faced ECHO and Multinet are being addressed by CLS, as well as other problems such as critical mass, intraday liquidity, who carries the final risk, 'just-in-time-payments' and time zone complications. The CLS initiative and impact it could have on global settlements is outlined in Chapter 11.

WORKED EXAMPLES

Table 6.1 shows eight FX deals between two counterparties done on two different contract dates but for the same maturity (8 June). In this example, the biggest reduction in settlement turnover (and corresponding risk) is achieved in US dollars, where a single payment of USD2 029 500 to Bank X from Bank Y replaces seven payments and receipts totalling USD48 229 500 between the two banks. There are lesser, though significant, savings in GBP, CHF and EUR, whereas there is only one transaction in JPY, which must of course be settled in full.

This typical example of turnover between two active participants in major currency spot and forward FX dealing clearly illustrates the substantial administrative and exposure reduction benefits of payments netting for both counterparties.

Given that the greater part of FX dealing turnover in the main wholesale market involves a comparatively small number of major players, the potential reduction in settlement risk exposure associated with the daily volume of USD1–1.5 trillion by the regular use of payment netting is considerable.

The multilateral CLS payments netting facility, referred to earlier, should have a profoundly beneficial impact in this area when it becomes operational towards the end of 2001.

Simple bilateral payment netting

Table 6.1

Deal date 4 May for value 8 June

Bank X Buys	GBP 3 000 000	from Bank Y against	USD 5 100 000 @ 1.70
Bank X Buys	CHF 12 400 000	from Bank Y against	USD 8 000 000 @ 1.55
Bank X Buys	USD 5 025 000	from Bank Y against	EUR 5 000 000 @ 1.0050
Bank X Buys	USD 5 000 000	from Bank Y against	CHF 7 510 000 @ 1.5020

Deal date 6 June for value 8 June

Bank X Buys	USD 5 104 500	from Bank Y against	GBP 3 000 000 @ 1.7015
Bank X Buys	USD 10 000 000	from Bank Y against	EUR 9 990 010 @ 1.0010
Bank X Buys	JPY 1 105 MIO	from Bank Y against	USD 10 000 000 @ 110.50
Bank X Buys	EUR 5 000 000	from Bank Y against	GBP 3 125 000 @ .62 50

If no further deals are contracted between Bank X and Bank Y for value 8 June, the payments and receipts can be netted out as follows (from the perspective of bank X):

USD	Receipts	Payments	Total
	5 025 000	5 100 000	
	5 000 000	8 000 000	
	5 104 500	10 000000	
	10 000 000		
Gross total	25 129 500	23 100 000	48 229 500

Net movement USD 2 029 500 payment to Bank X from Bank Y

GBP	Receipts	Payments	Total
	3 000 000	3 000 000	
		3 125 000	
Gross total	3 000 000	6 125 000	9 125 000

Net movement GBP 3 125 000 payment to Bank Y from Bank X

CHF	Receipts	Payments	Total
Gross total	12 400 000	7 510 000	19 910 000

Net movement CHF 4 890 000 payment to Bank X from Bank Y

EUR	Receipts	Payments	Total
	5 000 000	5 000 000	
		9 990 010	
Gross total	5 000 000	14 990 010	19 990 010

Net movement EUR 9 990 010 payment to Bank Y from Bank X

JPY	Receipts	Payments	Total
	1 105 000 000		1 105 000 000

Net movement   JPY 1,105,000,000 payment to Bank X from Bank Y

SUMMARY

Key points

- There is a clear distinction between the legal basis for netting and its practical application as bilateral and multilateral procedures
- The main systems available and how they operate
- Examples of netting calculations

In this chapter we looked at netting in its several forms and how important it is in the reduction of settlement risk and the mitigation of the possibility of systemic risk – which are two of the key imperatives for practitioners and regulators of the world's financial markets today.

Reconciliation and cash management

7

Cash positions

Nostro reconciliations

Brokerage

Securities reconciliations

Summary and key points

Reconciliation and cash management

Cash positions

Nostro reconciliations

Brokerage

Securities reconciliations

Summary and key points

This chapter looks at how cash positions are managed, the reconciliation of cash nostros and aspects of brokerage relating to the front, middle and back office. The reconciliation of securities held and collateral management is also covered.

CASH POSITIONS

In the dealing room at one time the positionkeeper played a pivotal role between the dealers and the back office. All trades were passed through this function so that they could be recorded manually against the bank's position limit to monitor if, for example, the key 'open position limit' as well as other limits might be exceeded. Additionally, the keeper would record the transaction against the relative nostro account for value date in the books of the bank, which represented the contra to the actual account held with the agent.

In the larger treasuries the positionkeeper would decide which account the transaction would be passed over and show this accordingly on the deal ticket. Quite often there was more than one account held in a particular currency and each instrument would have its own account. For example, for DEM, FX would be passed over Dresdner Bank Frankfurt, while for money market transactions Deutsche Bank would be used. In some banks this segregation is still maintained today.

This allocation served two primary purposes. Firstly, it acted as a running control on the balance of a nostro, alerting the keeper when funds were running too low or high for a particular value day against agreed internal parameters. Secondly, the recording of the nostro agent on the deal slip gave an authority to the back office to use that account for settlement purposes. While separate accounts helped simplify the control of funds, the system was disadvantageous to the extent that one account could be overdrawn while another could have excess funds. The surplus balance would earn far less interest, if any, than that being charged on the corresponding overdraft if an error occurred in settlement. Thus there is a risk of overdraft interest versus idle balances. The volume of transactions would usually dictate which arrangement was the most cost effective for a particular bank's treasury.

From time to time, the positionkeeper would request an 'agent's transfer' between the accounts of the same currency, depending on the value of transactions starting and/or maturing on a particular date. The back office recorded the chosen account as part of its input process and arranged settlement, after swapping instructions (where their agent was not already known) with the counterparty.

In a modern bank, other business areas such as trade finance, international lending and payments units, initiate transactions that create cash items and need to be taken into account on the bank's position. Procedures will vary, but in the absence of an automatic link between these systems and the bank's treasury system these will need to be added to the position for the dealing room. Even where an automatic link is in place, it is advisable for large transactions to be advised verbally to ensure that cover funds are available to meet the transaction and that the required value date is consistent with the need to make payments within time zone deadlines depending on the currency involved.

It is the responsibility of the areas concerned to ensure that the dealing room is advised of currency transactions and movements in a timely way.

> **It is the responsibility of the areas concerned to ensure that the dealing room is advised of currency transactions and movements in a timely way.**

Each day the start point for the positionkeeper is the agreed and reconciled position from the previous day, and this becomes the opening position for the current day. If this essential discipline is followed it means that any errors occurring must be within the day, making them easier to identify and correct. Additionally, dealers need to cover positions where necessary for the bank's commitments in international currencies, with earlier cut-off times than their own domestic or home currency. Of course, no amount of positionkeeping can counter the deal that has been wrongly entered and therefore fast matching of counterparty or other confirmation remains essential to reduce the costs of correction to a minimum.

One of the open questions with regard to positionkeeping has been where the function should be located: either within or outside the dealing room. In other words, should responsibility lie with the dealers and support staff (to manage their own 'collective' position) or with the back or middle office (under the 'segregation of duties' argument). Different banks take different approaches and there is no hard or fast rule. Of course, dealers should not perform any role in the processing chain beyond the position, but our view is that positionkeeping is a dealing room function and not a back office one. The position can be checked or shadowed in the back or middle office, but this can be counterproductive as the prime positionkeeper then knows that they have back-up and may possibly not take as much care.

Today, the combination of automated trading, standard settlement instructions and automated reconciliation processes for nostro accounts with agents' statements have removed much of the rationale for separation of instrument by account. Nevertheless, the positionkeeper's role is still there, even in an automated and reduced form, as funding of the agent's account as required will still be necessary.

Function of and key reports used by the positionkeeper

The primary role of the positionkeeper is to keep the balance or 'position' of the accounts or nostros in each currency representing the accounts held by the bank's agents. These would be agreed intraday and at the end of the day to the record of transactions that have been recorded in the bank's books, irrespective of value date.

The respective debit and credit entries that go to make up what is known as the open positions show the overall net position by currency of potential value movements for all instruments traded on a particular value date. This report, now usually screen based, gives the positionkeepers the anticipated net balances on a day-by-day basis so that they can judge the flow of the account. (This data is also used by the respective dealer in each currency to run their position.)

When all the individual days are combined into one net figure this is known as the bank's trading position in each currency. The net effect of all currencies consolidated into one and valued at the current spot rate against the home currency of the bank is the net open position. However, because on balance sheet items such as loans, deposits create entries on both sides of the ledger (asset or liability and corresponding nostro) their effect is nullified, leaving the bank's own purchases and sales of currency as the net result.

A net open positions report is produced which can be used as the basis of reporting the bank's position to the relevant central bank of the country concerned, against the limit granted for the bank (*see* Chapter 10 on regulatory reporting.)

Ladder maturity report

This is the opposite report to the open positions report by currency. Instead of building up the position day by day to arrive at a net balance, the ladder maturity report starts with the net open position and runs off day by day to arrive at a zero balance. This allows the dealer and the positionkeeper to see what action is required on any day to square the position.

Future nostro balances report

This report is usually produced up to five or six days ahead to show the anticipated balance on the account as a result of running off existing business. Of course, this changes during the day as new business is booked, and can be viewed as required on screen.

NOSTRO RECONCILIATIONS

This function is vital to the proper running and efficiency of the settlements area. The main purpose of nostro reconciliations is to agree the cash entries that have been passed over the bank's internal nostro or 'shadow' accounts, representing transactions that are starting or maturing on a given value date, with the actual cash movements at the bank's agent account. Thus expected cash movements are compared with actual cash movements.

As with confirmations, it is essential that the function is performed in a timely and efficient way. It is really the 'last line of defence' if an error is to be picked up quickly before your counterparty tells you! Although performed generally after the close of business, the process of reconciliation for matched items can commence intraday before the close of business if fully automated entries and payments are being passed.

In theory, reconciliations should be unnecessary if all other functions have been performed properly, including the actions of the bank's agent. In practice, this is rarely the case and good operations heads will keep a close watch on the work of their reconciliations unit to ensure high performance is maintained. If the unit is not under the direct control of the settlements area, a service level agreement stating by when each currency reconciliation is required should be in place.

Procedure

Pre-automation, it was necessary to perform a 'reconciliation' item-by-item matching on a visual basis. Matching is now typically done on either an in-house system or with a proprietary software application using a technique of 'by exception'. This means that items are reported depending on how well they have been matched to their corresponding item. This allows valuable back office resources to concentrate on investigating queries rather than on clerical tasks. This is a similar approach to that of confirmation matching explained in Chapter 3.

The criteria for matching are also similar with mandatory fields such as value date, currency, amount, credit/debit required to match exactly. If the item does not match it would normally be for one or more reasons. These can be summarized as:

> **Corrective action at an early stage can stop the situation becoming unmanageable and limit losses due to claims by counterparties.**

- pay (credit) entry on nostro but no or wrong funds paid away by agent;

- agent has paid away (debited) funds but no or wrong entry on nostro;

- receive (debit) entry on nostro but no or wrong funds received by agent;

- agent has received (credited) funds but no or wrong entry on nostro.

Non-matched entries must be quickly investigated by experienced back office staff who have been trained to use the system utilities such as 'drilling' down to the problem entry and who understand the various entries that are passed for a particular instrument. The highest value entry should be investigated first, as these have the highest loss potential.

For control purposes the maturity profile of outstanding items should be frequently reviewed. This allows the controlling officer not only to see what is unreconciled by value and counterparty, but also how long items have been outstanding and whether the trend is improving. Corrective action at an early stage can stop the situation becoming unmanageable and limit losses due to claims by counterparties.

Compensation

If the error is in-house then it is necessary to arrange good value payment or other correction at the expense of the bank, or pay compensation to the counterparty on an overdraft interest basis for the number of days involved.

If the error is an agent, counterparty or third party then compensation can be expected on a similar basis. Quite often one error will lead to another and may be committed by both sides to the transaction. Sometimes errors of commission and omission are made by both sides and a negotiation is required as to how much each side will pay, depending on the seriousness of the errors.

Because time is of the essence with regard to claims and counterclaims for errors, it cannot be too strongly emphasized that both confirmations and reconciliations for all currencies should be completed by the day following value day at the latest and this should form a key performance indicator for the relevant units.

Customer Automated Reconciliation Service

The Customer Automated Reconciliation Service (CARS) system from City Networks is a typical software application providing an integrated reconciliation and investigation processing capability for cash nostros. An application for the reconciliation of securities transactions is also available. Essential functionality provides for on-screen, exception processing, including manual matching and linking of related open entries, investigation processing, reporting and SWIFT/telex chaser message generation.

The basis of matching is as indicated above, comparing the nostro entries passed in bank's books with the automatic data feed advice of entries received from the correspondent bank. This would normally be performed daily. CARS is able to process many different message types equating to different SWIFT messages or ASCII file formats. Users are able to schedule events for processing out of normal working hours.

An additional application available is TIPS (Transaction Investigations and Problem Solving) which provides a control mechanism and inquiry function for all categories of investigations. As part of an integrated solution to the problem of matching and reconciliation, links are available to automate the flow of information to and from TRAM (*see* Chapter 3), CARS, TIPS and other applications, thereby streamlining several actions in this part of the processing chain.

CARS reconciliation of entries status screen

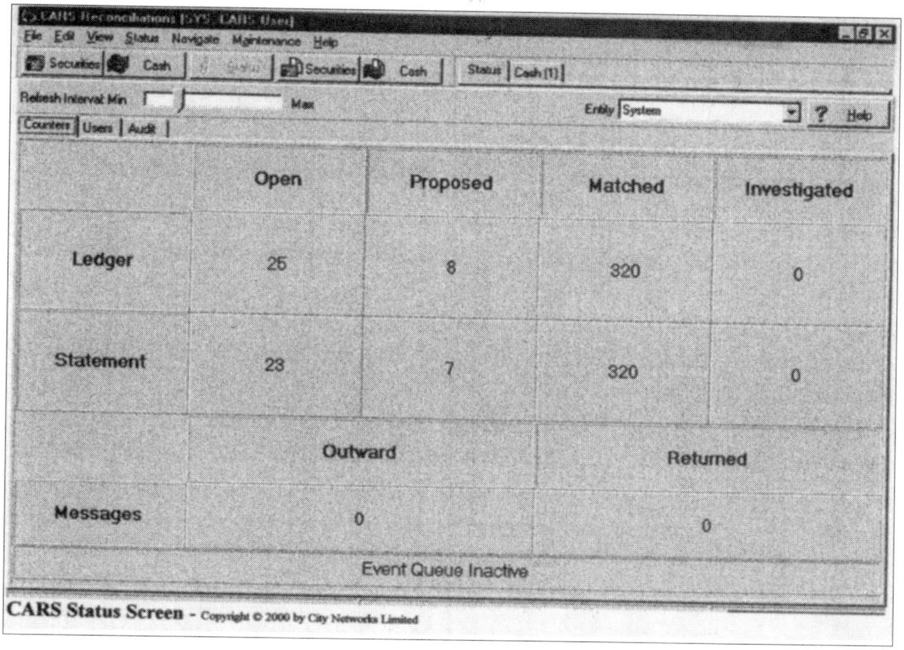

Fig 7.1

	Open	Proposed	Matched	Investigated
Ledger	25	8	320	0
Statement	23	7	320	0

	Outward		Returned	
Messages	0		0	

Event Queue Inactive

CARS Status Screen - Copyright © 2000 by City Networks Limited

Source: City Networks Limited

Internal (or dummy) nostros

Internal accounts are used where entries match internally in the books, such as the rolling up of principal plus interest in a deposit or loan into a new transaction. An internal account is used to keep unnecessary entries away from the cash nostros, thereby keeping these accounts as clean as possible. Another use of this type of account is where it is necessary *exceptionally* to mature a transaction *temporarily* pending another event or action. In this case it would normally be called a suspense account. It goes without saying that these accounts must be reconciled daily to at least the same standard as the cash nostros and signed off by the senior management responsible for the transaction, with satisfactory explanations provided.

Escalation

Full procedures should be in place to escalate unreconciled nostro or corresponding agent entries quickly up through supervisory, management and senior management for items that remain outstanding after normal investigation procedures. If settlement staff, for any reason (such as market rumour), have any doubt regarding the financial ability to settle, the relevant account officers in the risk management and credit units should be informed immediately. Frequent operational problems with a counterparty may also lead to limiting or even stopping the business done, to minimize costs.

BROKERAGE

Brokers form a vital link between banks and other parties that wish to deal in the financial markets. An agreed fee or brokerage is paid on each transaction, which is normally settled at the end of each month, although in the early days of trading derivatives the practice initially was to bill after each transaction. Because of the complexity, value and number of deals and the costs involved, it is important to have a sound system to check and verify brokerage accounts.

As banks and brokers have become more international it has become common to have agreements in place to cover all instruments traded through a particular broker. This in turn allows for a floor discount, which is a reduction in the overall brokerage due, dependent on the total volume of business given to a particular broker. Global agreements are now usual, with the major banks covering all their main trading centres worldwide.

> **It is important that brokers' bills are reconciled promptly at month end prior to payment.**

The rate will vary depending on the type of instrument (for example, FX, money market or derivatives transactions) and will usually be shaded depending on value and other special factors. Throughputs, done as a favour for a broker, will be free of charge.

It is helpful if, when local or global brokerage rates are agreed with brokers, the settlements of operations units are involved, as well as the head of trading (who may be leading the negotiation). In this way, systems and procedures can be changed in good time to meet any new or revised arrangements, which may be quite complex.

Reconciliation

It is important that brokers' bills are reconciled promptly at month end prior to payment. There should be a brokerage module in the treasury system being used that stores the brokerage calculated on each deal input into the system, based on a table of charges for each broker by instrument type. Alternatively, this can be input as an amount to override system calculations. Reports are produced showing brokerage based on calculations using the deal data. This streamlines the otherwise laborious task of collation. These reports are then agreed with the itemized brokers' invoices and any discrepancies investigated. Initially the back office will contact the broker and this will usually result in an agreement over the cause of the difference. Where the difference still exists, the

Fig 7.2

Simplified workflow for reconciliation and approval of broker commissions

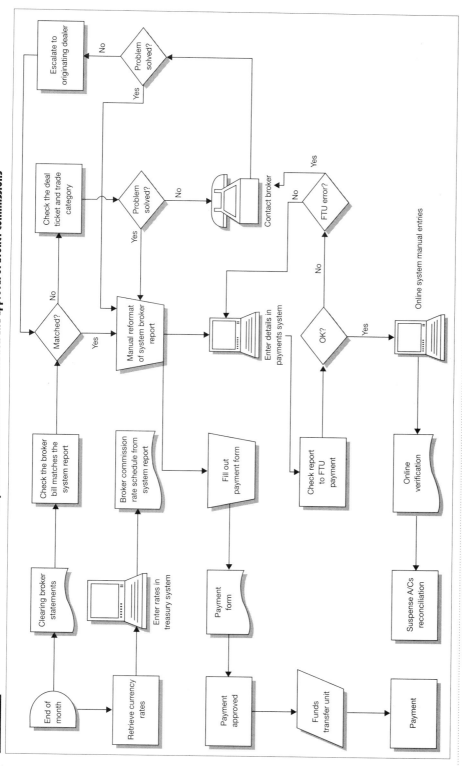

originating dealer should take the responsibility to resolve it, in direct negotiation with the broker concerned and with the co-operation and approval of senior bank official management.

Where differences arise resulting from an acknowledged broker error or misquote, the normal procedure to be followed is for the broker to make good the loss to the bank by payment of a cheque for the appropriate amount.

There is, however, a special reimbursement 'points' system still operated by some London market participants (see London FSA Code Schedule 4) and the Model Code recommendations on this issue are covered in Chapter 10 (17) 'Differences with brokers/use of points'.

Currency conversions will be required where the broker invoices in currency and requires payment in domestic currency. The rate required will be the rate as at the last day of the previous month. From an accounting viewpoint, brokerage is effectively paid one month in arrears and in varying months; this can distort the monthly and yearly management profit and loss figures significantly in high volume/value treasuries. Normal practice is therefore to accrue the brokerage in the month in which it is payable, irrespective of when it is actually paid.

Brokers' statements for futures

With futures business, the broker will normally provide a statement each morning to the derivatives desk. The statement contains details of all transactions conducted for the previous day, such as:

- open positions
- initial and variation margins
- closing prices for open contracts
- commissions charged.

A check should be made for price differences using the derivatives system report. It is quite common for a separate derivatives system to be linked to the bank's main accounting system with a spreadsheet used for reconciliation purposes between the two (i.e. positions and account balances).

A query file should be maintained for all outstanding items, with each query being given a unique reference. This allows a query log to be run from which an outstanding reconciliation report can be produced. This should be reviewed by the unit head at least once a week.

Trading systems

The impact of live trading systems such as Reuters and EBS, bringing together potential counterparties directly, has had a significant impact on the brokers' traditional revenue streams. The brokers, in the old sense, are no longer required in this environment, although it should be noted that they have effectively been replaced by the trading system vendors, which charge a fee as the brokers did.

This has been particularly true in FX and to a lesser extent in the money markets. The switch from OTC to exchange-traded instruments has also impacted what otherwise would have been a rich source of increased revenue for the money brokers. Nevertheless, brokers are still required in the markets and their role continues to bring together potential counterparties.

SECURITIES RECONCILIATIONS

Another aspect of reconciliations performed by the back office is that of agreeing holdings and/or transactions as recorded within the books of the bank against those held by custodians of various types as agent. Typically, this might be a bank custodian service, Euroclear or Clearstream for international holdings, and national custodians for domestic securities. The international custodian houses do not actually hold the securities themselves, but these are held to their order by the national clearing houses.

There are two parts to securities reconciliation. The first is the daily agreement of entries that have passed over the *cash account* in the name of the clearing house in the books of the bank, in a similar way as that done for the cash nostros. The second is the agreement of the *securities held* by the clearing house to their representation in the same books.

Clearing house cash accounts

For reconciliation of the cash accounts, a range of software applications are available to automate the process, allowing more efficient and quicker investigation. However, a real problem with securities reconciliation is failed trades. As explained in Chapter 5 trades are settled in sequence and one fail can mean that a number do not get settled on a particular day, which in turn means a half-reconciled account.

At the start of each day the clearing house provides an expected cash position for the close of the day. Thus the reconciliation of this account forms the first step in the funding of the account. Typically, after automatic reconciliation and initial examination, receivable and payables are summed up to provide a preliminary funding figure. This is then adjusted for:

- failed trades, noting reference numbers to identify ownership within the bank;
- coupons/interest on the account, for which entries have not been passed;
- coupons/interest to be received at bond level.

Based on the above calculations, it is possible to determine the funding necessary to bring the account to the required level of funding. This needs to be advised to the money market desk so that funding impact can be positioned. A SWIFT message for the required funding is generated from the cash nostro as an agent's transfer.

The bank's standard procedures should be in place for chasing open items and noting resolving actions and progressive escalation of unsatisfactory situations. A failed trade log is an essential reference in determining the compensation arrangements at a later date. The criteria for escalation should be based on days past settlement date and value and/or compensation likely to be involved, and the actual level escalated (depending on the size of the organization involved).

> **A failed trade log is an essential reference in determining the compensation arrangements at a later date.**

Where more complicated transactions are involved, such as leveraged deals, issued securities and other investment bank-type activities, the reconciliation may be more involved, covering one or more systems and spreadsheets to provide a true figure for funding. (*See* Chapter 5 for the use of securities as collateral at clearing houses and how this can determine the funding level required based on the value of securities available.)

Securities-held accounts

In these accounts, automatic links provide the details of each security transaction by name and type, together with security ID and value. This is matched to the ledger account balance held and a status accorded as to matched or unmatched on the exception report. Items are reported that have been outstanding for stipulated periods of time in a similar way to the cash accounts. Banks with ageing treasury systems may find that an additional system is needed to cope with the differing instrument types required until the main treasury system can be upgraded. A three-way agreement is then required of the main system, showing the bank's general ledger, the supplementary system showing the individual holdings, and the records at the clearing house.

Open and matched items are identified separately, with the usual audit log and full reconciliation reports. Escalation rules will apply, depending on the length of time outstanding of the discrepancy and value involved.

Securities CARS

This system, provided by City Networks, is adaptable separately for securities holdings and cash transactions, as distinguished above. The reconciliation and investigation package is fully functional with on-screen exception processing facilities and GUI interface. The system may be expected to reduce operational costs and lessen the exposure to losses. The system can be used in conjunction with other modules of CARS, described above.

The system can process the following SWIFT format message types such as:

- MT 571 statement of holdings
- MT 572 statement of transactions
- MT n99 chaser message.

Key features include a standard balance data feed for automatic population of both balances, and outstandings on initial set-up, multiple account processing and interrogation. It is also possible to status view at account level any items outstanding and to schedule events for processing outside normal working hours.

CARS securities reconciliation exception processing screen

Fig 7.3

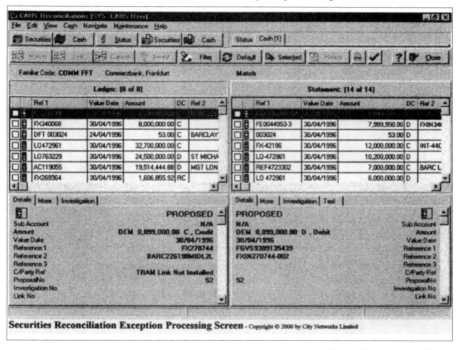

Source: City Networks Limited

SUMMARY

The role of position in the dealing room remains vital to ensure the efficient use of funds even in an automated environment. Reconciliation functions for the cash nostros, brokerage and securities reconciliations are important links in the processing chain. If well organized, they will improve and maintain effective treasury operations.

Key points

- Effective use of technology to automate separate routine operations is a half-way house to STP
- Will automated trading platforms mean niche-only brokers in the future?
- Securities business requires cash and holdings reconciliation

Settlement of derivatives and money market instruments

This chapter covers additional aspects for processing and settlement of different types of derivative and money market instruments, including workflow and calculations.

In the first part of this book we looked at the general requirements to process FX, on balance sheet money market loans, deposits and other instruments and derivatives. This essentially consisted of input, verification and confirmation, settlement and lastly reconciliation. All treasury transactions must go through this procedure in one form or another.

However, derivative settlements have their own idiosyncrasies and we examine these by designing a standard template for a generic trade administration cycle for these types of financial instrument. We then look at the individual workflows for FRAs, swaps, futures, options and repos. Additionally, the necessary calculations for a simple loan/deposit, CD, bond purchase and banker's acceptance are given to complete the picture.

BASIC FEATURES AND GENERIC PROCESSING CYCLE FOR DERIVATIVES

Features of derivative instruments

We must begin by distinguishing between over-the-counter (OTC) and exchange-traded (EXT) derivative instruments. OTC instruments are traded on a bilateral basis and are not listed on a recognized exchange. In the OTC market, transactions can be for any amount mutually agreed and settlement is for the difference between the counterparties (*see* list of treasury products in Chapter 2). Internationally, there has been some movement towards establishing clearing houses to settle OTC derivative transactions. EXT instruments are traded on a recognized exchange for set amounts and may be delivered in some cases.

Basic examples of OTC derivative instruments are forward rate agreements (FRAs), interest rate and cross-currency swaps (swaps), caps/collars/floors (OTC options) and repos.

Examples of EXT instruments include futures and EXT options. The basic derivative building blocks, which are used extensively, for hedging, speculative and arbitrage purposes are (FRAs), financial (interest and currency) futures, and interest and currency options.

It is worth noting that the essential element that makes these instruments different is that they are usually based on the concept of a contract for difference – the trade makes reference to a notional amount upon which the settlement values are determined. However, this notional amount is not normally exchanged between the counterparties and this feature effectively means that derivative trades are generally 'off-balance-sheet' transactions.

Generic processing cycle for derivatives

As we have seen throughout this book, settlement and administration processes are driven by systems, product attributes and regulatory requirements, both internal and external. This is also true of derivatives processing. Each is now addressed in turn.

The first constraint on any trade cycle is the computer system upon which it is recorded. Most systems are based on a relational database, which is surrounded by a set of product-related functions. These functions drive the workflow of the trade cycle and determine the level of manual intervention that is required. System-specific tasks are often included in trade workflow diagrams because the 'day's work' is so system dependent.

> **Regulatory requirements, are not usually flexible so consequently must be factored into workflow equations.**

The second factor that influences trade flow is the product or instrument attributes – the date it 'fixes' or is paid, the day basis for calculation etc. Most derivative systems are moulded around trade-specific functionality. Product lines within the derivatives industry evolve rapidly and consequently place a great deal of strain on back offices, which have to react quickly to product development without compromising accuracy and control.

Regulatory requirements, either from internal audit, compliance departments or external regulators, such as the FSA, dictate the level of manual intervention or system control that is required in the trade cycle. The requirements are not usually flexible and must be rigidly complied with, so consequently must be factored into workflow equations.

Figure 8.1 shows how each of the trade cycle elements is linked. The trader now normally performs trade entry into the trade administratioin system by direct entry, the back office merely has to accept the trade into the trade database.

Once validated by the back office, the trade is considered beyond the trader's reach as far as amendment is concerned. Any subsequent trade amendments or cancellations need back-office approval before being actioned. The first deal check that is usually performed is to validate the deal against any external record. If a trade is made over Reuters or telex then a paper trail is available. Voice-only trades are not checked at this stage.

After accepting the trade, both back offices exchange confirmations to evidence the trade, with the exception of some of the simplest products. The confirmation is almost always a telex or fax, followed by a hardcopy-printed confirmation. Derivative instruments are usually dealt with in reference to a

Fig 8.1

Simplified workflow for generic trade

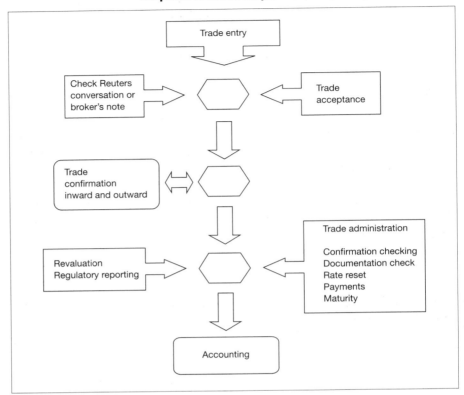

standard set of terms and conditions issued by the International Swap Dealers Association (ISDA). ISDA documentation takes the form of a master agreement negotiated between the both counterparts' legal areas. Subsequent trade confirmations make reference to this documentation (*see* Chapter 10).

ISDA has made great efforts to standardize documentary terms and trade conditions, to simplify the trade confirmation process for complex instruments and to facilitate standard confirmation templates through SWIFT. However, the number of possible variations of transaction terms, even within a simple swap, has meant that electronic trade confirmation and matching systems for derivatives have not blossomed in the same way as in the FX market. The cost of trade administration therefore remains high.

Once the confirmation of the trade has been sent, the inward confirmation is matched against the bank's own records. Care must be taken at this stage to make sure that all the relevant financial and settlement information agrees with the record trade. The deal is now considered part of the trade database and drops into the trade administration domain, ready for future settlement.

WORKFLOWS AND CALCULATIONS FOR DIFFERENT DERIVATIVE TYPES

Forward rate agreements

Definition

There are probably more varied definitions of the FRA than any other financial instrument. The reason for this may have more to do with its simplicity rather than complexity. Many trainers and publications incorrectly refer to an FRA as a 'bet'. Although its design and settlement process resemble a kind of wager, it is nonetheless traded as a legally binding financial transaction.

An FRA is an over-the-counter contract, usually between two financial institutions, to settle the difference in interest for a notional amount in a given currency between the contracted rate and the eventual settlement rate for a fixed period commencing in the future.

In money market financial terminology: an FRA is essentially a fixed rate forward/forward non-deliverable deposit/loan transaction, cash settled with an agreed market reference rate calculation process at commencement of the forward/forward period.

Development

Neither the concept nor the practice of setting an interest rate in advance for a deposit or loan transaction that would commence at sometime in the future was anything new to the money markets when FRAs first came on-stream in the early 1980s. Indeed, it was not at all rare for dealers to trade or quote what were called forward/forward deposits in the London money and eurocurrency markets of the 1960s and there was substantial business in forward/forward certificates of deposit in the early 1970s. However, these transactions never developed or grew to the level of a liquid market as such. The new instrument that paved the way for the emergence of FRAs was the 90-day Eurodollar financial futures contract launched at the Chicago Mercantile Exchange in 1981 (covered in more detail later).

Following the spectacular success of the Chicago and later London (LIFFE) short-term futures contracts, it became obvious that sooner or later an over-the-counter version would emerge that would not be confined to set IMM or futures market dates. As the cash settlement concept (*see* below) gained in respectability, the first FRAs came on-stream in London towards the end of 1983. Soon after, the British Bankers Association (BBA) took on the role of co-ordinating the rate-fixing process and in 1985 published FRABBAS, the first formal guidelines or standard terms and conditions for principals trading in the FRA market. These soon became the normal basis for FRA deals transacted globally in most Eurocurrencies.

Structure

The counterparties in an FRA transaction are:

- the seller, who will be compensated by the buyer if interest rates fall;
- the buyer, who will be compensated by the seller if interest rates rise.

Other factors are as follows:

- the amount – any amount agreed by the contract parties;
- contract date – the date on which the transaction is agreed;
- commencement date – the first or near date of the FRA period;
- maturity date – the final or far date of the FRA period;
- contract rate – the interest rate at which the FRA is bought and sold;
- settlement rate – the reference rate, usually set by the BBA, who appraise the market rate (usually LIBOR, London Interbank Offered Rate) by which the contract is cash settled.

Uses of FRAs

Forward rate agreements can be used for three main purposes: hedging, arbitrage and speculation in interest rates.

At the outset, it is more practical to illustrate the use of FRAs with a simple example of speculation because:

- the instrument resembles a wager or bet;
- a high percentage of FRA transactions are speculative;
- a speculative example enables the student to acquire an early understanding of the product.

Example

A treasurer or dealer at Bank A feels confident that short-term interest rates in US dollars are due to escalate within the next three months. In the FRA market, 3/6 FRAs are trading at 6.⅛–6.⅟₁₆. The dealer at Bank A therefore purchases USD10 000 000 three months against six months FRA in the market at 6.⅛% from Bank B.

Scenario 1

The dealer's forecast proves correct: interest rates rise and three months later the contract is cash settled with reference to BBA LIBOR at 8.⅝%. (For the sake of clarity, let us assume a 90-day run.)

Accordingly, as rates have risen, the seller, Bank B, is obliged to pay the buyer, Bank A, an amount equal to the rate differential on the principal amount for the FRA period (which is the speculative profit on the transaction):

8.⅝ less 6.⅛ = 2.½% p.a. on USD10 000 000 for 90 days = USD62 500

However, as is normal procedure, the settlement amount is discounted to reflect NPV (net present value), the formulae and calculations for which are as follows:

$$\frac{(L-R) \text{ or } (R-L) \times D \times A}{(D \times L) + (B \times 100)}$$

L = LIBOR (BBA settlement rate)
R = Contract reference rate
A = Contract amount
D = Days in contract period
B = Day basis (360 or 365)

In the above scenario:

$$\frac{(8.625-6.125 \times 90 \times 10\ 000\ 000)}{(90 \times 8.625) + (360 \times 100)}$$

$$= \text{USD61 180 79}$$

Scenario 2

Contrary to the dealer's expectations, USD interest rates have eased in the intervening period and the contract is cash-settled three months later at 4.⅞%. In this case, the dealer at Bank A has lost 1.¼% p.a. (6.⅛ less 4.⅞) which must be paid to Bank B:

$$\frac{(6.25-4.875) \times 90 \times 10\ 000\ 000}{(90 \times 4.875) + 36\ 000}$$

$$= \text{USD30 873 73}$$

Workflow

Although the simplest derivative is probably the FRA, the actions required to manage an FRA are largely the same for all other over-the-counter instruments (for example, swap, cap/floor). An example of the events and actions involved are given in Table 8.1.

Events and actions required to manage an FRA

Table 8.1

Example of FRA	
Counterpart	A Bank PLC
Trade date	12 March 1999
Fixing date	10 June 1999
Start date	12 June 1999
Maturity date	12 December 1999
Notional amount	USD10 000 000
Contract rate	5.25%
Benchmark settlement rate	5%

Event	Action
Trade date	The trade is recorded in the trade database and confirmed with the trade counterpart.
Each day until fixing date	The trade will be revalued and known as 'marked to market'. This allows the profit and loss of the trade to be recorded in the bank's general ledger.
Fixing day	On the trade fixing date (usually two business days prior to the start date, with the notable exception of sterling) the fixing rate is determined by the back office. In this case the period of the trade is six months (June to December) although the trade date was March; this is the forward element from which the instrument gets its name. The six-months rate on the fixing date (10 June) is applied to the trade and the difference between the benchmark rate and the fixing rate is used to calculate the trade settlement amount.
Settlement date	Cash is paid in settlement of the contract.

Swaps

Definition

An interest rate swap is an exchange of cashflows between counterparties, based on a notional trade amount for a fixed period of time.

Structure and use

The example in Table 8.2 is for an interest rate (vanilla) swap. Counterparty A may wish to receive three-monthly floating rate interest but has some asset that pays a fixed amount of interest annually, whilst Counterparty B wishes to receive a fixed amount of interest and has floating funds; these opposite needs are 'swapped' through the trade.

Simplified workflow for an FRA

Fig 8.2

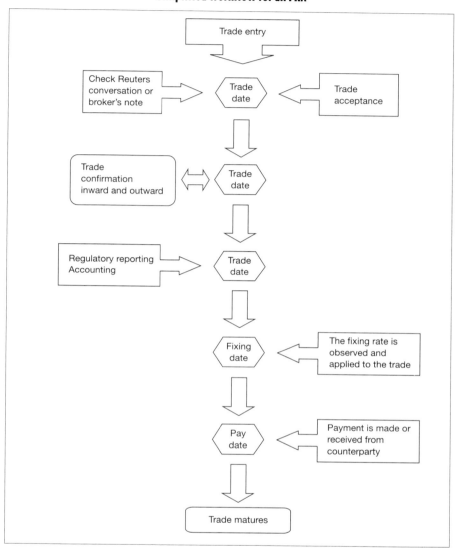

Each floating period of the swap is treated like an FRA, with the notable exception that the cash payment is made at the end of each period and not discounted. The fixed side is known at the outset of the trade and usually coincides with one of the floating payment dates. this being the case, the cashflows are netted for convenience.

Table 8.2

Events and actions required to manage a swap

Event	Action
Trade date	The trade is recorded in the trade database and confirmed with the trade counterpart.
Each day until maturity date	The trade will be revalued and known as 'marked to market'. This allows the profit and loss of the trade to be recorded in the bank's general ledger. Interest rate swaps are usually for a maturity of one to ten years, with a fixed payment every year and either three or six months floating against a market index (e.g. Libor). The nature of swaps means that they are highly flexible and virtually any payment schedule can be constructed.
Fixing date	The fixing rules for a swap are the same as for the FRA. The rules determining the fixing are prearranged in the swap contract and confirmation, covering such areas as the day basis, period and reference rate of the interest calculation.
Settlement date	The settlement date for each floating period is the start date of the next floating period. Swap flows are usually made in arrears – at the maturity date of the single floating side or on the fixed payment date.

Points to note

For an interest rate swap there is no actual exchange of principal between the counterparties. For currency swaps an exchange of principal will normally occur.

Financial futures

History and development

There are two kinds of futures exchanges:

- *Commodity futures*, which have been in existence since the mid-19th century;
- *Financial futures*, which have been in existence since 1972.

As both were invented and launched in Chicago, where two of the largest futures markets in the world are situated, the Midwest American city is the obvious place to start.

Simplified workflow for a swap

Fig 8.3

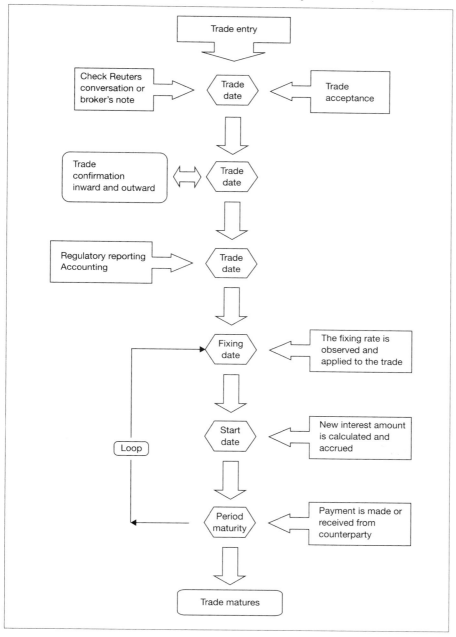

Commodity futures

The historic need for commodity futures was clearly in evidence in Chicago long before the Chicago Board of Trade (CBOT) was set up in 1848. Generations of Midwest farmers had to endure plummeting autumn prices, reflecting the seasonal over-supply, as they brought their annual grain harvest for sale to the town market. They were often obliged to sell at the prevailing low price, knowing full well that by the spring, as supplies predictably dwindled, prices would rally.

The first futures contracts facilitated the delivery of wheat at an agreed price. This opened the way for other commodities such as oil, precious metals (gold and copper), soya beans and cotton. A rival market, the Chicago Mercantile Exchange (CME), was established in 1919, reflecting the successful growth of the business, which had the unique advantage of enabling producers of the traded contract commodity to hedge their price risks cheaply and efficiently, thus guaranteeing a future price for their product. Similarly, users of the commodity enjoyed a corresponding hedging facility for the produce that they needed to buy.

Financial futures

Financial futures were conceived, developed and launched at the CME in 1972, as a logical extension of the commodity futures philosophy. Money, according to Milton Friedman, the famous Chicago economist, was just another commodity. The initial products were currency (FX) contracts, followed in 1975/6 with interest-rate contracts in treasury bills and bonds at the CME and CBOT.

Perhaps the most exciting innovation was the 90-days Eurodollar contract, which was launched at the CME in December 1981. Up to that time, financial futures had been an American phenomenon, attracting scant attention from the international money and exchange market centres in London, Tokyo and Frankfurt (although New York had earlier launched a rival exchange, NYFE, with little success). There was an attitude of indifference towards financial futures exchanges in the much more liquid and well-developed euro and forward exchange markets, later commonly referred to as the 'cash markets'. The general view was that whilst commodity futures had an important role in risk transfer and hedging, there was really no need for financial futures. Money was not just another commodity and the forward cash markets were already globally developed and professionally conducted. In any event, Chicago was neither an international money nor banking centre, so why bother?

> The new Eurodollar contract was a resounding success and drew instant and widespread international attention and participation.

However, the new Eurodollar contract was a resounding success and drew instant and widespread international attention and participation. The novel non-delivery cash settlement feature of the product, described in detail below, rendered it similar to a wager-type instrument with potentially serious legal implications. As this problem was gradually resolved, the off balance sheet aspect of the instrument virtually assured its international success as an interest rate hedge, arbitrage and speculative tool.

As the business grew in the 1980s, stock market (equity index) and options on futures were added, enhancing the range of financial risk transfer products, traded in the main futures exchanges.

The success of currency futures

The original financial futures currency contracts launched in 1972 were successful for two main reasons.

Firstly, and as will be illustrated later, the commodity futures style of strict margin payments controlled by a daily mark to market of all contracts, virtually eliminated the marginal or replacement credit risk that exists in the corresponding forward cash market transactions. This advantage effectively opened up the business to a wider field of participants, many of whom would neither have the financial muscle, in terms of the balance sheet footings, nor the net worth to trade actively or warrant dealing limits in the mostly financial institutional forward exchange market.

Secondly, the timing of the launch of financial futures coincided fortuitously with the demise of the US dollar fixed exchange rate regimes (Bretton Woods and Smithsonian), which finally collapsed in March 1973, heralding a new era of wider exchange rate volatility and immediately highlighting the importance of forward/future hedge instruments, markets and strategies.

However, despite the marked local success of the currency futures in Chicago, with substantial support and an active customer base throughout the USA, the business never really assumed an international dimension and the turnover remained but a small percentage of the main exchange market.

Interest rate futures

The futures t'bills and bonds in 1975/6 attracted more attention as interest rate hedge strategies, with gradual overseas participation. The liquidity in these contracts grew impressively as the outside world sat up and took notice of a new concept in financial trading and risk transfer. But it was the arrival of the Eurodollar and other short-term interest rate contracts that really marked a watershed in the evolution of the euro, capital and forward FX markets, effectively paving the way for the emergence of other off balance sheet products and instruments such as FRAs, which would later be known as 'derivatives'.

The new futures markets

By 1980 the main international currency and banking centres were already examining the viability of establishing a financial futures exchange. Study groups and working parties were set up, involving bankers, brokers and other financial institutions. London was the first to move and by 1981 the Bank of England gradually let it be known that, with the appropriate prudential constraints, it would not be averse to the setting up of a market in London.

This was interpreted as a green light for the steering committee to move into top gear. Despite some objections and a lack of enthusiasm amongst certain institutions, the London International Financial Futures Exchange (LIFFE) opened at 10 am on 30 September 1982. Singapore and Tokyo followed and by the early 1990s most major international currency and banking centres boasted a financial futures exchange to complement their existing cash markets.

Definition

In common with many recent financial instruments and strategies, definitions vary enormously. Some are comprehensive and detailed but rather long and at times constitute a short descriptive essay. Others are brief and to the point, easy to understand but fail to convey the shape and structure of the product.

For the purpose of this book on the back office, the version favoured is that used by the London Steering Committee in defining the business for a study paper, prior to the launch of the London market in 1982:

A futures contract is a binding agreement to buy or sell through an established exchange, at a definite date and at a specified price, a standard quantity of a commodity of predetermined quality on fixed conditions of delivery. In the case of financial futures, the commodity would be currency or financial paper.

At first, the definition may seem rather long-winded, but it does cover the essential parameters of the business. If we examine it phrase by phrase, and where appropriate compare it with the cash or OTC markets, it should be possible to highlight the fundamentals.

- '... a binding agreement: the contract must be a legally binding financial transaction, as is the case in the traditional FX and money markets.

- '... to buy or sell': all futures contracts are purchase/sale format whether the underlying risk transaction is a commodity exchange, a currency exchange or an interest rate period or instrument. In the cash markets, FX, bonds, bills and other financial paper are buy/sell style, but deposit and loan contracts are written in 'borrow' and 'lend' or 'take' and 'place' agreements.

- '... through an established exchange': all futures business takes place at a centralized or established exchange such as the CME in Chicago or LIFFE in London. The OTC markets such as FX are remote global markets in several centres, where the business is executed by the phone or a dealing communication system, such as Reuters, with no organized 'market place' as such. The need for an established or centralized futures market place of business is illustrated later.

- **'... at a definite date':** futures contracts stipulate a definite value date in the future, for either delivery or cash settlement of the transaction.
- **'... at a specified price':** the contracted price is agreed at the time of the deal, similar to the cash markets.
- **'... a standard quantity':** all futures contracts are for fixed or standardized amounts, such as USD1 million or GBP0.5 million in the short-term interest contracts. Deals must therefore be for one or multiples of these contracts. The OTC or interbank cash market deals can be contracted for any amount agreed by the counterparties.
- **'... of a commodity of predetermined quality':** this requirement applies more to commodity futures. When physical delivery takes place (usually less than 3 per cent of transactions) the commodity delivered must conform in quality to that stipulated in the contract conditions. For example, potatoes delivered must be of a stipulated variety with a specified maximum of 'faults'; wheat delivered must be of correct origin, with a set percentage maximum of heat damage or moisture content. In financial futures 'quality' is not entirely out of place, to the extent that in certain interest rate-related contracts the deliverable financial paper, such as CDs, bills and bonds, must conform to the correct debt level (usually US or UK government or prime name) – or 'quality'.
- **'... fixed condition of delivery':** this is a particular reference to commodities, where conditions and place of delivery are important stipulations.
- **'... currency or financial paper':** this is true, but of course not applicable to the 'cash settlement' contracts.

Important features of financial futures markets

Clearing house

A the core of every futures exchange is the clearing house, which controls the clearing and administration of the business. More importantly, and as is illustrated later, it becomes the counterparty to every trade. For this reason it must be a financially stable, well capitalized institution. Mindful of this, the appointed LIFFE clearing house was purchased by the five largest banks in the UK (a development encouraged by the Bank of England), prior to the commencement of the London market.

> **The clearing house must be a financially stable, well capitalized institution.**

The present clearing house for LIFFE is called the London Clearing House (LCH). The LCH is now owned by London Derivatives Exchanges and their members.

In addition to its broad-based ownership, LCH has a guarantee backing of substantial funds to cover residual risks of membership default. Given the strict margin daily payment system, it would be difficult to envisage a default situation that could test the financial stability of the clearing house.

The structure of the clearing house does vary between exchanges. The CME clearing house is owned by all of its members.

Trading

Traditionally, futures have been traded by 'open outcry' auction on a centrally located floor area called a 'pit' where buyers and sellers have to shout their prices and transactions in a clearly audible voice. The essential transparency of this 'public' system is unique to the futures business and means that all prices and trades can be witnessed by all participants in the pit.

The area in and around the trading floor of a busy futures exchange can be crowded, noisy and, at times, near chaotic. To help facilitate the flow of business, the open outcry trading jargon is supported by a formal hand-signal system, which is used both in the pit and between the telephone booths of the members and the pit brokers to transmit prices, orders and executions.

In recent years advances in technology have led to the introduction of screen-based trading through a centralized computer that automatically matches the bids and offers of the participants who access the market from remote termini. This method requires no physical presence of trading personnel on the floor and replaces the open outcry procedure. Screen-based futures trading with global electronic linking is gaining in popularity, particularly in futures bond trading, and there is at present a lively debate throughout the industry as to which system will prevail in the long run.

In June 1998 the LIFFE board announced that, following the result of a vote amongst members, electronic dealing would be introduced for all contracts by mid-1999, although a contingency capacity to trade by open outcry remains – unlike the MATIF (Paris) market, which appears to have permanently abandoned open outcry and embraced electronic trading as the sole dealing system.

In the meantime, the main markets in Chicago continue to use both systems for some contracts, but still favour open outcry. In this book we are concerned primarily with short-term interest (STIR) and currency instruments, which are generally traded by this method in Chicago.

Online trading through the internet is also certain to impact the futures exchanges, with the London market appearing to set the pace.

Purpose and uses

The main purpose of futures contracts is to transfer or hedge risk. In financial futures, the risks to be hedged are interest rate or exchange rate related and users of the contracts include banks, exporters/importers, fund managers, and other derivative national and multinational corporate entities.

Another use of futures is arbitrage. This activity is mainly carried out by bank-dealing specialists who exploit pricing anomalies between the futures markets and the corresponding cash and other derivatives market periods or instruments, such as interest rate swaps (IRS) and forward rate agreements (FRAs), which the futures markets complement. This was particularly lucrative in the early life of the new futures instruments, or while the business was 'maturing'. Although arbitrage still accounts for a substantial part of futures turnover, competition has eroded much of the arbitrage incentive, with the result that modern futures-based arbitrage has become cumbersome and complicated, with only tiny price differences to exploit.

From the very outset of the business in Chicago, it was recognized that an important requirement would be the regular participation of short-term risk takers or speculators. The continuous activity of speculators gives the market volume and liquidity, without which genuine hedge customers could not reliably cover or transfer their risk. Unlike the main money and exchange markets, speculation is not considered an embarrassment but actively encouraged and regarded as an important supportive function.

Arbitrage and speculation probably account for over 95 per cent of financial futures turnover, which makes the business highly unusual in that its *raison d'être* or valid justification for its existence only makes up a very small fraction of the activity.

Method of quotation

In the currency contracts, the method of quotation differs from the FX market in that the US dollar is the counter currency rather than the base. In the main FX market the US dollar against the Swiss franc quotation between banks and brokers is expressed as Swiss franc and centimes (Rappen) per dollar: USD/CHF = 1.53 70. In the futures exchange, the Swiss franc (CHF) is quoted in US cents: CHF/USD = 65.06. The two quotations have the same effect and are, in fact, identical reciprocal rates.

When currency contracts were launched in London, the LIFFE committees considered changing to the cash market style in an attempt to encourage the cash market bank dealers to use futures. However, it was felt that the futures system had administrative advantages, such as a consistent tick value (described later), so the futures style prevailed.

For a similar administrative and consistency reasons, the interest rate contracts are quoted at 100.00 minus the interest rate, i.e. 6.25 per cent is quoted as 93.75, or 5.87 per cent is quoted as 94.13.

Standardization of dates

In order to have a neat and efficient system for processing and clearing trades and to facilitate the imposition of strictly enforceable margin payments, it is advantageous to have standardized contracts in dates and amounts. For the main financial futures contracts the four key contract delivery/settlement dates are the third Wednesday of March, June, September and December. This standardization is also more practical for open outcry trading.

Short-term interest rates (STIR) futures

For the purpose of this book we shall concentrate on the two main types of financial futures contracts: short-term interest and currency contracts.

The 90-day Eurodollar interest rate contract launched in 1981 has been the most spectacular and most successful futures instrument traded. The main short-term interest rate (STIR) contracts now traded on the international futures exchange are given in Table 8.3. These contracts are standardized in tenor and amount and run from four specific dates: March, June, September and December (as is the case in most short-term contracts).

Table 8.3

Main STIR contracts

Tenor	Currency	Exchange	Amount
3-month	Eurodollars	CME, SIMEX	USD 1 Mio
3-month	FR Fc (PIBOR)	MATIF (Paris)	FFR 1 Mio
3-month	CHF	LIFFE	CHF 1 Mio
3-month	Sterling	LIFFE	GBP.05 Mio
3-month	Euro (Euribor)	LIFFE	Euro 1 Mio

Margin requirements

One of the most important advantages that the futures market enjoys over the cash or OTC market is the virtual elimination of the replacement credit risk in the transaction.

In the forward market, if either party fails or goes bankrupt before a contract matures, the counterparty may be obliged to re-enter the market and cover the deal again at the new market rate. This could be as much as 20 per cent or more from the original rate, depending on the beaviour of the two currencies in the interim. The resulting potential loss is usually called the replacement risk – not be be confused with delivery risk, often called 'Herstatt risk' and associated with the FX market delivery process.

The replacement risk does not really exist in futures. In addition to clearing house involvement, all transactions are effectively secured by strict payment of 'initial' and 'variation' margin, which ensure that no large credit risk can build up during the unmatured life of the transaction.

Initial margin

Initial margin requirements vary from exchange to exchange and depend largely on the potential volatility of the contract. the amount payable is calculated on the basis of the maximum likely volatility for one day. The flat rate therefore varies from about ¹⁄₁₆ per cent of the contract amount for the three-month interest rate contracts, to 2 per cent for the ten-year treasury bond.

Initial margin can be paid by cash or certain negotiable securities, whereas variation margin must be paid in cash.

Variation margin

Variation margin is calculated by a daily 'mark-to-market' exercise on all futures contracts, whereby margin requirements are settled by a daily revaluation of all contracts based on the closing market rate. All customers are automatically debited for loss-making positions and credited with profits. If the customer's margin account falls below the maintenance level, the futures exchange can and will close out the contract in the market. On days of extreme volatility or movements, the London Clearing House can call for additional variation margin to be paid during a trading day by certain members with positions and has the authority to use its discretion in the matter.

These margin disciplines are the very cornerstone of the essential financial integrity of a futures market. Even at the height of the Barings problem in the Singapore futures market, involving a loss of over US$1 billion, there was never a serious doubt as to the viability of the futures exchange. The strict enforcement of margin payment rules effectively ensured its stability at all times.

SPAN margining

SPAN (standard portfolio analysis of risk) is the risk analysis system favoured by many futures markets in assessing initial margin requirements. Originally developed in Chicago at the CME, it is used primarily to calculate the initial margin necessary for a portfolio of different contracts and contract months.

The London version constructs 16 different scenarios to illustrate how much a contract would gain or lose if underlying contracts or option-implied volatility were to vary. The various risk parameters are set by LCH after consultation with LIFFE and are modified in response to changing market conditions. Table 8.4 examines one active contract in detail.

Function

The primary justification for all futures is to hedge risk. In financial futures a hedge is established by buying or selling futures contracts to cover the instrument or period in the future where the risk of rate change exists. This effectively 'locks in' a cover rate for the risk.

As the futures hedged period or instrument nears maturity, or comes close to being current, the price of the futures moves ever closer to that of the cash,

Table 8.4

A three-month CHF future traded on LIFFE

Amount	CHF1 000 000
Delivery months	March, June, September and December
Delivery day	First business day after the last trading day
Last trading day	11.00 am Two business days prior to the third Wednesday of the delivery month
Quotation	100.00 minus the rate of interest
Minimum price movement	0.01
Tick size and value	(CHF 25)
Trading hours	7.30–16.10
APT trading hours	16.25–17.59

Notes: All contracts are cash settled at the exchange delivery settlement price based on British Bankers Association London Interbank Offered Rate (BBA LIBOR). Settlement price = 100.00 minus BBA LIBOR, rounded to two decimal places.

money or exchange market which it complements until it eventually reflects the cash price. The reason for this essential 'convergence' is that by the time the contract period becomes current or 'spot', the contract must either be 'delivered' or 'cash settled' (revalued at the going cash rate with a profit paid or loss deducted). The 'cash settlement' process is explained in detail later.

The profit or loss on the futures hedge will correspond to an opposite movement in the cash book, so that the netted-out positions of cash and futures will result in overall cover at the locked-in rate at which the risk was hedged. Let us illustrate all of this with an example:

The treasurer of a multinational corporation is advised in December that an asset sale will release US$10 million in March. A corresponding acquisition will require funding in June. In the interim he will have the use of the funds, which he must invest in the Eurodollar market where he has the facility to lend at the interbank bid.

The current bids for three and six-month's Eurodollars are 6.¼ per cent and 6.⅛ per cent respectively. Were he in a position to lend now, he would be pleased to accept the 6 per cent level but the funds will not be available until mid-March and he is concerned that rates may fall.

The current price of the March Eurodollar contract is 93.97/98 which equates to 6.02–6.03 per cent. The treasurer decides to hedge, or 'lock in', the 6.02 per cent yield by purchasing 10 March contract at 93.98.

In the period December to March, the treasurer will receive or pay variation margin, depending on which way the interest rate moves.

Scenario 1

Interest rates fall in line with forecasts. In early March the March contract is trading at 95.50 or 4.½ per cent p.a., reflecting the three-month Eurodollar interest rates. The treasurer's funds become available and he lends them at once for three months at 4.½ per cent, at the same time selling (closing out or reversing) his futures hedge at 95.50 in the market:

	%
Interest on deposit	4.5
Plus accumulated futures/margin profit	
(95.50 less 93.98)	1.52
Total yield	6.02% p.a. (the rate at which the hedge was taken)

Scenario 2

Interest rates rise between December and March, contrary to the treasurer's expectations, and by early March the contract is trading at 91.75, reflecting Eurodollar interest rates at 8.25 per cent p.a. When the US$10 million become available for investment, the treasurer lends them at 8.25 per cent in the market and simultaneously reverses or closes out his futures hedge with the following result:

	%
Interest on deposit	8.25
Less loss on futures hedge (93.98 less 91.75)	2.23
Net yield	6.02

In this case, the futures hedge creates a final loss of 2.23 per cent which must be subtracted from the interest received from the deposit and which will have been gradually debited as margin due on the daily revaluations or mark to market.

By hedging the transaction with the purchase of the futures contract at 93.98, the treasurer effectively 'locked in' or guaranteed the 6.02 per cent return, but in doing so relinquished the chance of an additional or windfall profit from a rise in interest rates, which is common to this type of hedge transaction.

The margin effect on profit and loss

In both the above scenarios, the payment of initial margin and payment of receipt of variation margin has a small, though not negligible, effect on profit or loss. This is determined by the level, the change and timing of the change of interest rates during the life of the hedge.

In Scenario 1 the fall in interest rates and corresponding rise in the futures price will give the hedger the use of the profitable variation margin during part of the life of the hedge, which he can absorb or use in day-to-day cashflow. In Scenario 2 the hedger will be debited for variation margin loss as soon as the futures contract reflects a rise in interest rates. The treasurer will additionally have to fund the margin payments.

Although these effects of interest on marginal interest are small and often swing both ways as the price hedge instrument moves either side of the contracted price during its life, they should not be entirely ignored when considering the business.

Cash settlement

One of the unique features of the futures short-term interest contracts is that they are 'non-deliverable'. This effectively means that any contracts still outstanding at maturity, or when the futures period becomes current or spot, cannot be delivered (unlike commodity or currency futures).

What happens instead is the exchange clearing house prices the contract at 11.00 am on the 'last' day, or the day on which it becomes spot value date, and makes a final cash settlement of the profit or loss due to or from the member with the position. Great care is taken in assessing the settlement rate by reference to a number of prime banks in the Eurocurrency market.

This process was invented in Chicago in December 1981 and originally involved certified quotes from 16 large banks active in the Eurocurrency market. The three highest and lowest quotes (of offer) were eliminated and the rounded rate accepted was calculated from the average of the other ten banks. This painstaking process ensures that the rate is accurate, but above all fair, with no possibility that any party or parties can unduly influence it.

In London, this role is co-ordinated by the BBA, who publishes the LIBOR (London Interbank Offered Rate) for the currency and period concerned, following a similar exercise.

London has become the recognized centre for this exercise in Eurocurrency. Most FRAs are settled daily by reference to the BBA LIBOR. The validity and reliability of the London rate was further recognized in 1996 when the CME abandoned its own process and appointed the BBA LIBOR for settlement of its STIR Eurocurrency futures contracts.

Currency futures

As stated earlier, the currency futures were the very first financial futures contracts traded and were launched in Chicago in 1972 at the CME. Unlike the interest rate products launched a few years later, the currency contracts have not enjoyed the same global success.

In the interest rate, stock index and option products, London, Tokyo, Singapore, and later Paris and Frankfurt, have successfully 'copied' the Chicago phenomenon and enjoyed spectacular growth and liquidity. Chicago, however, remains the only real currency futures centre with substantial volume, particularly in the major convertible currencies.

The main reason for this is that the newer 'futures' locations, unlike Chicago, are also international banking centres and therefore already boast well developed and extremely liquid spot and forward foreign exchange markets.

An analysis of futures currency turnover figures, converted to cash market terms, reveals that the entire CME currency futures market turnover represents approximately only 1 per cent of the corresponding global cash FX market figure.

Currency futures contracts

Although several futures markets trade currency futures, we need look no further than the CME contracts, as the Chicago market is predominant in the business, particularly in the major currencies.

Let us examine one of the more liquid contracts ones: the Swiss franc.

- **Ticker symbol: SF**

   Future symbols, though logical and easily recognizable, differ from the standard cash/FX market, which uses SWIFT codes (in this case CHF).

- **Trading unit: CHF125 000**

   Although substantial amounts can be traded, the standardized amounts for each currency futures is small, as they must be accessible to small risk hedgers as well as big financial institutions. Large amounts can, of course, be accommodated, provided the liquidity is there, by trading multiples of each contract. It is not uncommon to see trades of 10 100 or, in the case of the STIR contracts, 1000 'lots' in one trade. Most currency contract amounts equate to approximately US$100 000.

- **Quotations: US$ per SF**

   This is the reciprocal of the cash market quote, as explained earlier.

- **Minimum price change (tick): 0.0001 = $12.50**

   The 'tick value' is the value of the minimum allowed price movement on a futures contract.

- **Months traded: March, June, Sept, December**

   These are the four standard futures months, except for the Brazilian réal, which trades for all 12 months.

- **Regular trading hours (Chicago time): 720 am–2.00 pm**

   These are the hours of business for trading in the pit by open outcry.

- **Globex trading hours (Chicago time): 2.30 pm–7.05 am Monday–Friday morning.**

   These are the hours of business for automated screen trading through the 'Globex' system.

- **Last day of trading: second business day preceding the third Wednesday**
  This is the last day on which contracts can be traded. All currency contracts outstanding as at close of business on this day must be delivered. Unlike STIR contracts, all currency futures are deliverable. The sole exception to this was the Russian rouble contract (launched in April 1988), which was settled to cash against the Moscow Interbank Currency Exchange (MICEX) fixing.

Exchange-traded options

An exchange-traded options contract is a trade that gives the buyer the right to buy or sell an amount of futures contracts at some date in the future. The cost of this right is called the options premium and is paid to the counterparty in advance. Options contracts, like futures, have standard terms and tick values and are subject to 'initial margining'. As for futures, the exchange effectively acts as agent to both sides of the transaction and therefore is at risk if either side of the deal should fail (as technically both sides deal with the exchange not each other). To protect itself from this risk, an exchange will ask for a deposit or initial payment against each traded lot. This money is refundable when the deal is completed. If an option is exercised, the buyer either receives or gives a futures contract, depending on the nature of the bargain.

> The exchange effectively acts as agent to both sides of the transaction and therefore is at risk if either side of the deal should fail.

Both futures and options contracts are marked to market and the change in their value paid to the counterparty through the futures exchange where they are traded. (This is true for all futures but not all options, as there are subtle differences in management of options depending on the exchange).

The value of each contract is published by the exchange each business day and the counterparties and the exchange determine the amount of money due as variation margin. The settlement for each day's movement is paid the next business day.

Fig 8.4 shows an overview of both futures and exchange-traded options.

Simplified workflow for futures and exchange-traded options

Fig 8.4

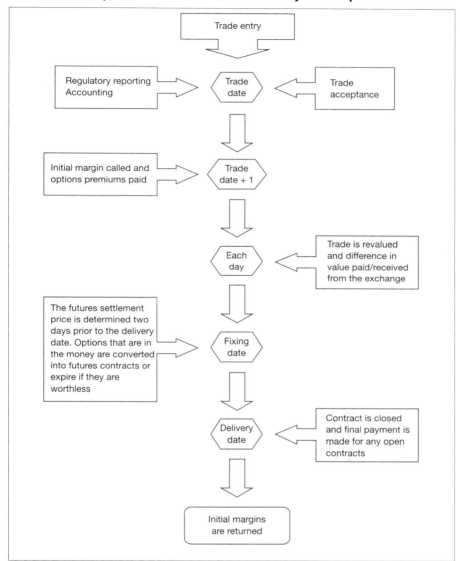

Repurchase agreements (repos and reverse repos)

Definition

A repo is an agreement to sell against cash and subsequently to repurchase against cash, a security at a pre-determined date and price.

A reverse repo is the opposite or 'mirror image' of a repo contract but otherwise behaves in a similar way as the asset is received 'up front' and is resold at maturity. Thus it is a repo as viewed from the perspective of the lender of funds. Another practical way to aid understanding is to regard a repo as a secured deposit while a reverse repo is a secured loan.

A triparty repo is an agreement where the two counterparties agree to use a third party at settlement. A third party (such as Clearstream or Euroclear) acts as agent for each of the counterparties or principals involved arranging the transfer of securities and taking on some of the processing roles such as margining. Although a fee is charged, this can be a cost-effective method of administering repos, particularly where high volumes of transactions are involved.

Structure and use

Repos, in various combinations, are commonly used by governments in open market operations to influence market liquidity, both short and longer term, usually through secondary market dealers.

Additionally, it allows commercial holders of a fixed asset, such as a bond or US treasury, to utilize the holding to raise short-term funds to fund their inventories and to borrow securities as required. This flexibility has encouraged more participants thereby improving liquidity in the markets. Each agreement consists of a sale of stock against cash, with a pre-determined purchase of stock against cash and interest at some time in the future.

The cash amount (loan) and the interest are determined by the market rate of interest plus the credit quality of the asset. The cash value is reduced by a percentage of the face value of the asset, called a 'haircut', the lower the quality the asset, the greater the haircut. This means in effect that the lender retains a portion or percentage of the value of the security against a drop in value when the underlying instrument is marked to market.

The cost of financing is the difference between the amount received by the seller on the first leg of the transaction and the amount paid on the second leg. The complete contract is agreed at the outset of the transaction on trade date.

The types of securities used are typically government bonds or stocks such as gilts and high quality, international, semi-governmental or corporate paper. It should be noted that, unlike a normal lending transaction, both the lender and the borrower have credit risk. This comes about because the lender (of funds) may be unable to resell the bonds at maturity.

As we have seen in the documentation chapter, standard agreements are now usually in place for repo and reverse repo business. This will usually be either the ISMA version for non-USD, cross-border deals or the original PSA document. These documents cover important points relating to the transaction such as ownership of securities, margin maintenance, income payment, substitution of securities and events of default.

Workflow and settlement

While the settlement and administration of the repo contract can be thought of in terms of a stock sale and purchase plus an interest rate deposit for a notional amount, in practice the stock is delivered only against payment, so the three elements are linked.

Settlement of the stock will usually be made via a clearing agent such as Euroclear or Clearstream (*see* Chapter 5).

The timing of settlement depends on many factors including local regulations, whether the asset is currently held or has to be bought in and market practice. A generic trade flow and event table is detailed in Table 8.5 assuming a current stock holding and same-day settlement.

The daily revaluation will determine the value of the stock being held by the lender in the transaction. This collateral must be maintained at an appropriate level to ensure that the loan amount could be repaid if the borrower should default on the contract (see Fig 8.5).

Events and actions required to manage a repo

Table 8.5

Event	Action
Trade date	The trade is recorded in the trade database and confirmed with the trade counterparty. An instruction by the seller to move the stock position to the counterparty's agent is sent against the simultaneous receipt of funds.
Each day until maturity date	The repo contract is revalued against the current market rate. Interest is generally accrued to maturity and entries passed on a daily basis. The collateral quality is checked daily to ensure that the appropriate haircut percentage is maintained. This is to ensure that the lender's security is not eroded by adverse movements in the market. If it is, the lender will call for margin to make up the difference.
Maturity	An instruction is sent to receive stock against the simultaneous payment of funds to the counterparty account.

Substitution by the borrower of securities of equal market value is allowed during the term of the repo. Netting of both securities of the same issue and payments can also be agreed.

It should be noted that with normal secured lending, the ownership of the security, subject to certain rights of the lender, stays with the borrower. In repos the ownership passes to the lender as he is the buyer of the security. However, any coupon on the security such as a bond has to be paid by the lender when received to the borrower. Thus the ownership of the income during the term of the transaction does not *pass* from the buyer to the seller.

Fig 8.5 **Simplified workflow for repos**

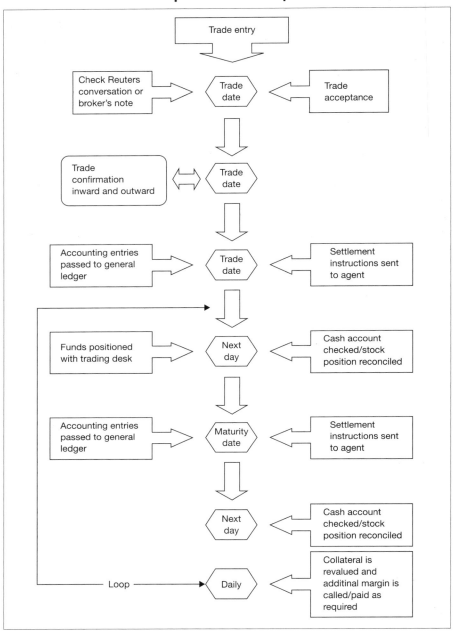

Settlement calculation

We are only concerned here with the mechanics of settlement and not the various ways that repos can be used to raise finance more cheaply than other forms of funding.

Simple interest rates are used to calculate interest over the life of a repo transaction.

Basic example of Repo

ABC Bank deals with Corporate XYZ agreeing a repo transaction of USD10 000 000 for seven days.

The security is a 5 per cent US Treasury bond with a market price of 95.

The dealer's bid rate is 7.5 per cent and there is accrued interest due of 1.5 per cent.

The nominal value of the collateral can be calculated based on the equation:

$L \times 100/(MV + A)$
Where:
L = Amount of loan
MV = Market value of security
A = Accrued interest

Thus
$10\ 000\ 000 \times 100/(95 + 1.5)$
= USD 103 362

The repurchase price is therefore the original sale price plus interest at the dealer's repo rate of 7.5 per cent p.a.
Thus interest is:
$L \times R \times T/360^* \times 100$
*Number of days in year

Where:
L = Amount of loan
R = Dealer's repo rate
T = Term

Thus:
$10\ 000\ 000 \times 7.5 \times 7/36000$
= USD14 583.33
Thus the repayment amount is USD 10 014 583.33 due at maturity.

MONEY MARKET INSTRUMENTS CALCULATIONS

Market conventions

Before looking at instruments based on interest it is necessary to understand the basis of interest calculations.

The first point to consider is the number of days to be used as the numerator and the denominator in an interest rate calculation. For normal money market transactions this is usually the actual number of days being calculated in period (numerator) divided by number of days in the year (denominator).

For bond transactions and other types of paper a monthly basis may be adopted, typically on the number of days in the month or the number of days in the period being calculated.

The most common bases are:

- $\dfrac{\text{Number of days}}{360 \text{ or } 365}$, depending on the currency;

- $\dfrac{\text{Number of days in month}}{360}$, this is used for bond and other paper;

- $\dfrac{30 \text{ days}}{360}$, an alternative method sometimes used in the USA.

While these are the most commonly encountered bases, there are other methods in use, depending on the country issuing the paper. Examples of calculations are given below, using these conventions based on ACI formula where applicable.

Money market loan deposit

Definition

An agreement to lend/borrow between two counterparties of a fixed amount in a specified currency for a fixed term or specified number of day's notice.

Settlement calculation

Bank A places USD5 000 000 with Bank B for three months (91 days) at 5⅞ per cent p.a. The repayments at maturity by Bank B will be principal plus interest, calculated as follows:

$$\frac{\text{Principal amount} \times \text{interest rate} \times \text{number of days}}{\text{Day base}}$$

$$= \frac{5\ 000\ 000 \times 0.05875 \times 91}{360}$$

$$= 74\ 253.47 + \text{Principal } 5\ 000\ 000 = \text{USD5 } 074\ 253\text{--}47$$

Points to note

- Watch for interim interest payment dates during fixed term.
- The loan/deposit may be a floating rate, with the rate repriced at specified dates during term.
- Is the basis of interest calculation 365 days?

Certificate of deposit

Definition

A receipt (usually negotiable) for a time deposit issued for a stated period of time and normally paying a fixed rate of interest (coupon).

Settlement calculation for a secondary market transaction

Bank A is holding a CD face value GBP1 000 000 with an original maturity of 180 days, a coupon of 5.5 per cent and 45 days left to run. Bank A decides to sell the CD in the secondary market which is dealing 5.7–5.8 per cent.

Secondary market proceeds:

$$\frac{\text{Face value} \times (1 + \text{coupon} \times \text{number of days/day base})}{(1 + \text{yield} \times \text{days remaining})}$$

$$= \frac{1\ 000\ 000 \times (1 + 0.055 \times 180/365)}{(1 + 0.058 \times 45/365}$$

$$= \text{GBP1 } 019\ 830.80$$

Points to note

- Is the CD negotiable?
- Check the interest rate wording carefully – there are numerous variations.

Bond purchase

Definition

A fixed income unsecured security, which means that it pays a fixed or floating interest rate over the life of the obligation that is acknowledged in the certificate. A bond may be issued at a premium or discount.

Settlement calculation for a purchase in secondary market then subsequent sale

Purchase

The price of the bond will already have been calculated by the dealer based on current yields using the ACI formula calculations covered elsewhere in the course. Refer also to bond market formula on ACI website. The current or running yield is calculated using the formula:

$$\text{Interest rate coupon} \times 100/\text{Net price} = \text{Current yield}$$

Example:

$$\text{Coupon } 6.0\%, \text{ Net price } 103.0$$
$$6.0 \times 100/103 = 5.82\%$$

In this example interest rates have fallen since issue so the bond is trading above par.

This is the 'running' or current return on the bond for the full period. It will not be the redemption yield or yield to maturity as this assumes that interest will be reinvested at the current yield and takes into account a profit or loss adjustment depending on whether the bond has been purchased at a discount or premium.

Premium/discount

In practice, to enable the accounting and settlement side of the bank to function correctly, it is usual to input both the face value of the bond and the amount to be paid together with the coupon rate and to pass off discount or premium elements to separate accounts either automatically by the system or manually. The system will then calculate daily accruals and post the amortization to date to a profit or loss account. Most treasury systems allow for automatic adjustments as a result of complete or partial sale before maturity without having to delete the item entirely and resubmitting. On sale the discount or premium is passed off to a profit/loss sale of asset account.

Broken interest

Because trade date and interest payment dates rarely coincide, it is necessary to pay out the accrued interest to trade date to the seller of the bond. An accounting adjustment is also necessary to reflect the accrued interest component 'bought' by debiting this amount to a separate 'broken interest' account for control purposes and cleared at next interest payment date against the coupon amount for the full period or prior sale.

Thus extending the above example, assume the value of the face value of the bond was USD1 000 000 and it was purchased two months after coupon payment date. The following simplified accounting would essentially represent the transaction ignoring when entries are passed for the purposes of trade date accounting and the subsequent accruals process from settlement date.

Asset account –Bond dr USD1 000 000
Premium account on bonds dr USD30 000
Broken interest account dr USD10 000*
Nostro account cr USD1 040 000 as the total due to seller to be paid on settlement date.
*Broken interest is calculated as follows:
1 000 000 × 6.0 × 2 × 30/360 × 100
= USD10 000.

Under ISMA rules, Eurobond interest is calculated on a 30-day month irrespective of the actual number of days in the month. This may change to calculate on the actual number of days with the advent of the euro and to bring into line with other money markets.

Interest is paid without deduction of interest withholding tax, but this is currently under consideration within the EU. Actual accounting would vary depending on whether bond bought as a trade or investment.

Although origination and syndication is outside the scope of this book, it is worth noting that the investment house for the original issue can be a valuable source of information for details of a particular issue.

Settlement would normally be three business days after trade date at typically Euroclear or Clearstream between which there is an electronic bridge.

Details of the trade would be advised by SWIFT or Euclid link by each counterparty including their respective securities account numbers. All trades must carry the identification reference (ISIN number) or the original issue.

Sale

Assume that the bond was now sold five months after purchase at 104.0. At settlement date the relevant entries would be (one month's interest outstanding after last coupon date).

Asset account cr USD1 000 000 clearing this account.
Premium account cr USD40 000 (net USD 10 000 to P/L via sale of asset account).
Interest received cr USD5000 (to P/L) on 30-day month basis
Nostro account dr USD1 045 000 in anticipation of receipt of funds on settlement date.

Settlement would normally be three business days after trade date at typically Euroclear or Clearstream. Details of trade would be advised in a similar way as for a purchase above.

Points to note

- Interest is paid without deduction of tax.
- Interest, discount or premium (if applicable) and profit or loss on sale will be accounted for separately.
- Originally issued in bearer form, a band is now usually registered at clearing house.

Floating Rate Notes (FRNs)

Definition

FRNs are usually negotiable bearer notes with coupon interest being set at intervals according to a pre-determined formula.

The nominated agent bank for the issue is responsible for the calculation of the interest rate for a given period after averaging rates provided by reference banks at a given time.

FRNs can only show an interest rate to next repricing date in the dealers, ladder.

Mechanics of settlement work in the same way as Eurobonds.

Points to note

- There may be a cap on the interest rate.
- Accounting is similar to that for the bond.

Discount of a bill or a banker's acceptance

Definition

This is a time draft, which has been accepted by an authorized bank. The bank agrees to pay, should the original drawer of the draft fail to do so. BAs are widely used to finance international trade and can often be a cheaper way of raising finance than straightforward borrowing.

Settlement calculation

A 90-day US dollar bill of exchange for USD5 000 000 is discounted at 5⅞ per cent:

$$\text{Amount of discount} = \text{face value} \times \text{discount rate} \times \frac{\text{days}}{\text{year}}$$

$$= 5\,000\,000 \times 0.95875 \times \frac{90}{360}$$

$$= \text{USD}73\,437.50$$

Secondary market proceeds:

$$\text{Face value} \times (1 - \text{discount rate} \times \frac{\text{days}}{\text{years}}) = \text{face value} - \text{discount amount}$$

$$= \text{USD}4\,926\,562.50$$

Points to note

Bills are calculated on a discount-to-yield basis. Thus only the face value is paid at maturity.

SUMMARY

An understanding should have been gained of the processing flows and settlement of derivatives and calculations involved in money market instruments.

Key points

- The difference between the OTC and EXT instruments
- How derivatives are processed differently from cash instruments
- The calculations for money market instruments

Treasury systems, accounting and risk management

This chapter looks at the linked aspects of systems, accounting and risk management. The right processing and settlement systems for the business is essential as is the correct accounting. The second part of the chapter covers the various types of risks in treasury business and the controls required to understand and manage those risks.

ESSENTIALS OF A TREASURY SYSTEM

Before studying accounting and risk management issues for treasury, it is important to consider what is the best kind of model for the business. While there are many international systems available, several common features can be identified that form part of an 'excellence' model.

Firstly, in a fast moving market, information must be available online, with real-time access to positions, prices, rates and mark-to-market revaluations. This facility illustrates for the dealers the effect of various changes both on their own and on the bank's position. In parallel with this, risk monitoring and management capabilities should be provided to meet middle office requirements.

Secondly, it is critical that interfaces to the bank's payments, risk control, main commercial banking and general ledger systems are facilitated by an open architecture. This modular flexibility will allow a bank to choose where it needs to process the particular mix of instruments to meet its treasury business requirements.

Mainstream treasury models generally offer these capabilities, so the final choice may depend on how the new system will impact on the existing configuration into which it must fit. As most major international banks and their treasury businesses now have a global perspective, they tend to look for global solutions to problems wherever possible. The era of large in-house system-creation is fading as specialized software vendors offer complete quality solutions 'off the shelf' to meet the needs of the banks. Progressively, banks elect to buy rather than build what is required, preferring to put resources into assured interfaces that will integrate quickly with existing systems. This can be done in partnership deals with the vendors. Time is of the essence if competitive advantage is to be grasped.

This does not mean that one-site solutions cannot be satisfactory. A bank can gain competitive advantage with a new product while avoiding the long lead time of a global project (provided quality links are made with the other systems, particularly a bank's general ledger).

Effectively, most banks have a mix of systems at various stages in their life-cycle, quite often on different systems platforms. It is not uncommon for FX/money market business to exists on the oldest system while derivatives instruments are on newer systems, reflecting their more recent introduction.

This can lead to a lack of integration, making the systems environment inflexible whilst inhibiting vital new product development. One way of addressing this problem is to replace existing older systems progressively, under careful project management. However, to accomplish this, adequate resources with appropriate skills must be available.

A summary checklist of essential requirements for a treasury system from a user perspective could be:

- **FX spot and forward dealing input and processing module:**
  – open and exchange risk management by currency
  – real-time rates feed and revaluation capability.

- **Money market dealing and processing module:**
  – loan/deposit input and mismatch analysis capability
  – interest received/paid rates analysis capability
  – interest arbitrage dealing for balance sheet swaps
  – (money market loan/deposit and forward swap).

- **Derivatives dealing and processing module:**
  – FRAs, interest rate and currency swaps
  – interest and currency options
  – repos and reverse repos.

- **Securities dealing and processing module:**
  – purchase and sale of bonds, FRNs and other paper
  – trade date accounting
  – custodian account reconciliation function.

- **Standard front office features:**
  – ability to access to all main trading systems (e.g. Reuters, EBS)
  – screen-based dealers' blotter for new deals
  – screen-based dealers' ladder and position for each currency traded
  – overall open position for trading room management control.

- **Standard back office features:**
  – brokerage reconciliation, confirmations, cash management and nostro reconciliation
  – external interfaces to SWIFT and other message and payment systems
  – internal interfaces to credit risk management, general ledger
  – accounting control reports (*see* below).

- **Standard middle office features:**
  – mark-to-market valuation capability
  – value at risk capability
  – limit monitoring capability by dealer and treasury management
  – profit and loss and balance sheet production
  – capital adequacy calculations
  – treasury accounting module interfacing with the bank's general ledger.

- **Other aspects to be considered:**
  – what hardware is required for the system?

– what compatible operating systems are available?

– what type of security system exists?

– what is the track record of the software company itself?

– do they have the resources to install and train satisfactorily?

– what service level agreement is available?

– what is the record of development and quality of release?

– is there a user group to focus on future issues?

These, together with budget calculations, are some of the key questions that a new business system proposal should address. There are of course other issues to be considered before the go ahead for a new package. The formal documentation process begins with the 'request for information' from the software company, followed by an 'invitation to tender'.

A typical system will have a number of key files or tables on which the basic information is stored. These include:

- **Client file** containing full details of client, bank, corporate or individual. In addition to basic data such as name, location, the base account number and SWIFT code (where applicable), it will also carry indicators representing country of residence, country of head office, business classification and other information.

- **Deals file** containing the details of each live transaction that has been input and verified.

These two main files will be supported by:

- **Currency file** containing country, currency code – usually SWIFT format (i.e. USD, GBP, CHF).

- **Holiday file** containing all weekends and bank holidays for at least two years ahead for all currencies held in the currency file.

- **Exchange rate file** containing middle market exchange rates for all currencies against base currency and usually also the USD and euro where neither of these is the base currency. These rates would be updated intraday with a real-time feed. Base currency is explained below under accounting.

- **Business codes file** containing the codes for each business type used in the client file and the differing business/industry codes used in national jurisdictions' regulatory returns.

- **Business centre code file** containing the codes representing each unit within treasury whose business should be identified separately – this could extend to dealer level.

- **Trade or deal type** containing the code that identifies the type of transaction involved. This code will have many uses throughout the system and leads on to the account code and rules files below.

- **Account types file** carrying the different accounts over which the account rules below can pass entries for the various transaction types.

- **Account rules file** containing the codes that instruct the accounting entries to be passed on the occurrence of an event for each transaction type.

This leads us to the accounting attributes required in a treasury system, which are discussed below.

ACCOUNTING PRINCIPLES

An understanding of the accounting for treasury instruments in banks is useful for all treasury staff and is essential for operations management.

Briefly, the framework is shaped under the Companies Act (1985/9) and various UK and international accounting and financial reporting standards and statements of recommended practice (SORPS) issued by the British Bankers Association (BBA). The Financial Reporting Standard (FRS) 13, covering accounting for derivatives, is particularly important.

> **An understanding of the accounting for treasury instruments in banks is useful for all treasury staff and is essential for operations management.**

One important tenet for treasury accounting is the distinction between investment and dealing transactions and the corollary that income recognition for the latter can be on a mark-to-market basis. This works on the premise that profit and loss as a result of mark-to-market are in effect realized because of the ability of a bank normally to close its dealing positions at any time.

Hedge transactions also require special consideration. Where an interest rate swap has been used to hedge the money market book, it may be treated in the same way as the underlying instrument.

There are also other detailed rules and practices, particularly for securities, relating to the liquidity of the market for the instrument being valued and whether the intent on purchase was to trade or hold as an investment. Some of these issues are outside the scope of this book. However, some of the accounting disclosures recommended under the BBA SORP concerning off balance sheet instruments relating to risk are outlined later in this chapter.

Treasury systems typically have the following accounting features to meet best practice standards:

- double entry to meet conventional accounting standards (part single-entry accounting for outstanding FX forwards has been replaced in modern treasury systems, though not always in the older financial systems that have FX as a supplementary feature);

- multicurrency, to cover a wide range of currencies traded and the valuation of assets and liabilities in those currencies;

- a separate self-balancing ledger up to trial balance for each currency;

- multicompany to cover the situation where more than one company or subsidiary is being accounted for on one system;

- the concept of a common or base currency to which entries in currency are related at a set or current exchange rate (for FX, revaluation is calculated between book value and current value against the base currency);
- to achieve the above, the use of a shadow or trading account that mirrors every conversion from one currency to another (*see* example below) – this approach is also used as a building block to calculate profit and loss on FX business;
- accounting entries passed on an 'event' basis for each transaction type (for example, payment out of principal at start date of loan, repayment in at end date of principal and interest).
- balance sheet income recognition accounted for on an accruals basis with a mark-to-market overlay where this is appropriate (the mechanics of the accrual mechanism in the system may be full reversal each day of the previous days value or incremental over the life of the transaction).

BASIC TREASURY ACCOUNTING AND CONTROLS

Control reports

In a complex treasury system it is important that efficient housekeeping is performed on a day-to-day basis in order to achieve early identification and quick correction of rogue entries. There are several important reports that help to highlight problems. These should be verified by experienced back office and accounting staff and management should make frequent checks to ensure the reports receive prompt attention.

Examples of these reports are:

- **Accounts opened report:** particularly important where the system can automatically open new accounts using the client account base number, currency code and account type. This report should be signed off every day by the account opener who takes responsibility for the account.
- **Outstanding deals v accounts mismatch:** where the accounting automatically generates an entry for all outstanding transactions, a check should be made that this report agrees by currency. A 'difference' is an early warning that a manual (non-automatically generated) entry has been passed to a wrong account or, worse still, there is an error in the account rules file for a particular event for a transaction type.
- **Ledger balance report by currency:** with dual entry this should always self-balance with any rejected items being passed to computer errors for attention. This report should be checked daily.
- **Currency open positions report:** typically a *calculated* position capturing all accounts in a particular currency. The effects of outstanding assets and liabil-

ities will be cancelled out as, for example, the start of a loan passes a debit to the asset account with a credit to the nostro. This leaves an FX trading position, which can be compared to the currency trading account balance. Allowance must also be made for any other currency conversion instrument, such as currency futures, which will also have passed entries over the trading account. Although primarily a dealing report, it also serves as a very useful accounting control document for the back office and accounting supervisors.

Aspects of accounting

Table 9.1 gives an example of basic accounting for an FX trade to show the concept of the trading account. Table 9.2 shows an example of basic accounting for a currency term loan.

Basic accounting for an FX trade

Table 9.1

Details of trade	
Deal date	9 February 2000
Value date	11 February 2000
Sell	GBP5000
Buy	AUD12 500
Exchange rate	2.50
Base rate	1.60
(against sell currency in USD)	

Deal date (contingency entries)	9 February 2000
1 Credit forward sales	GBP5000
Debit trading account	GBP5000
2 Debit forward purchases	AUD12 500
Credit trading account	AUD12 500
3 Credit trading account	(GBP/USD) USD8000
Debit trading account	(AUD/USD) USD8000

Value date	11 February 2000
4 Debit forward sales	GBP5000
Credit nostro	GBP5000
5 Credit forward purchases	AUD12 500
Debit nostro	AUD12 500

Table 9.2 **Basic accounting for a currency term loan**

Details of trade	
Term loan to a foreign bank for USD2000 for 90 days @ X % rate (assuming interest to be USD90)	
At start date	
1 Debit term loan foreign banks	USD2000
Credit nostro or customer account	USD2000
2 Debit accrued interest receivable, term loan foreign banks	USD1
Credit interest received, term loan foreign banks	USD1
(Daily accrual thereafter at USD1 per day)	
At maturity date (start date plus 90 days)	
3 Credit term loan foreign banks	USD2090
Debit nostro or customer account	USD2090
4 Debit term loan foreign banks	USD90
Credit interest received term loan foreign banks	USD90
5 Debit interest received, term loan foreign banks	USD89
Credit accrued interest received, term loan foreign banks	USD89
(Reversing previous days' total accrual entries on maturity date)	

Note: In some bank systems, the daily accruing interest will be in-built to show in the dealing position for that currency. In other systems, total non-base currency interest will be positioned at the start for the dealer to sell off, in which case interest will effectively be accrued in base currency.

Interest arbitrage mechanism for a funding (balance sheet) swap

- Entries are the mirror image of the real transaction, consisting of FX swap, loan and deposit.
- The effect is to square out spot and forward FX, loan and deposit dealers.
- Adjusts ladders for the currencies involved and transfers profit/loss from loan/deposit book to FX book.

FX profit and loss accounting methodologies

Basic approach:

- currency and base currency trading accounts used to revalue nostro and forward book at current rates;
- adjustment is made for cost benefit of forward book using middle market rates for agreed time periods. Most banks use 'market' time periods (for example, one month, two months, three–six months etc.).

Revaluation methods:

- apply mid-market rates to market-related time periods;
- apply bid–offer spread to net positions for agreed time periods;
- take all losses and leave profits on a deal-by-deal basis, whichever is the most conservative.

TYPES OF TREASURY RISK

Volatility of both interest and exchange rates in an increasingly complex environment has made the process of managing the risks involved a critical aspect of treasury management. It is important that the treasury management involved in dealing control have a trading background themselves as this is almost certainly the best way to acquire the necessary level of technical expertise. Whilst too many controls will suppress dealing skills, experience has shown that a breakdown of critical controls will almost invariably result in losses. Strict control over delegated authority within the dealing room is therefore necessary from the head of treasury.

> The segregation of duties and reporting between the front, middle and back offices should be strictly enforced by the head of treasury.

The segregation of duties and reporting between the front, middle and back offices should be strictly enforced by the head of treasury responsible for the total business in order to avoid exposure to the operational risks explained later (page 167). In addition to conventional audits, most banks have in place 'professional standard review' programmes to review the conduct of treasury officers and ensure that local and global supervisory and in-house guidelines are followed.

The main risks to which treasuries are exposed might be conveniently grouped into credit and market:

- *Credit risks:*
  - country risk
  - counterparty risk.
- *Market risks:*
  - open exchange position risk
  - interest rate/maturity mismatch and liquidity risk
  - legal risk.

The logic behind these groupings is that the former are counterparty-related risks to be considered before the deal is entered into, while the latter are generally positional risks associated with running the book. A seperate aspect of credit risk is settlement or delivery risk.

The division and analysis of this subject can involve other terminology and groupings. Given the nature of risk generally, overlap and even duplication are common.

Country risk

This risk arises where borrowers or the counterparty is unable or unwilling to settle outstanding transactions because of domestic country crisis or restrictions. In some ways this can be perceived as an overriding or 'top-level' risk as it is not independent of an individual counterparty. Political and economic factors play a crucial role in the assessment of country risk and these considerations have become increasingly important in a global economy. Guidance notes on the factors involved in assessing country risks are issued by the relevant authorities.

Counterparty risk

Similar to other transactions where credit is involved, the bank is exposed to the risk that a counterparty in an outstanding transaction may not be able to complete. Limits are therefore set on the value of unmatured deals, both in terms of total and intraday-settlement limits. Netting arrangements greatly reduce this risk, provided that the legal agreements are in place (*see* Chapter 6 on netting).

Rating agencies, such as Standard & Poors and Moodys, play a key role in the markets' perception of banks' (including one's own) creditworthiness. It should be noted that most interbank credit lines are 'unadvised' meaning that no specific limit is advised to other parties or any undertaking given that business will be done to an agreed level. However, trading systems such as Reuters and EBS require a limit allocation to be input for a particular counterparty before trading can commence.

The credit unit within the bank will normally be responsible for monitoring and approving credit limits requested by treasury management for dealing business.

Open exchange position risk

This represents the cost of closing out open positions in each currency, whether as a result of FX, or FX derivatives business. A bank assuming that potential fluctuation exposure was 10 per cent on an individual currency open position of $100 million, would calculate the risk as $10 million. Modern concepts of risk control often use a 'maximum permitted loss' figure for any one day, rather than a single-dimensional open amount limit. This has led to the enormous increase in FX limit orders between currency market centres in recent years.

Middle office risk management needs to monitor the limits relating to this risk intraday, based on real-time price feeds. However, this can present logistical problems if several separate systems are being used for different product processing. Reports showing the bank's spot and forward position should be reviewed at least daily and compared with the approved limits in place. A recognized procedure for taking action on excesses should be in place. For a global bank with 24-hour trading, this position will be controlled centrally but dealt out locally, depending on the time zones being trading in.

Interest rate/maturity mismatch (gaps) and related liquidity risk

This arises where interest rates of a given currency will change relative to the maturity mismatches of assets/liabilities of that currency in the books of the bank. There are a number of ways of measuring these risks; the FSA website gives a detailed explanation (http://www.fsa.gov.uk).

Even though a bank may have small open exchange positions, there may be a considerable mismatching of maturing assets and liabilities. This is one factor involved in liquidity risk, where a bank may be unable to meet its commitments as they fall due.

There are two main considerations here: firstly, whether the uncovered position is out of proportion to the bank's ability to cover it at all times; and secondly, whether the on-going liquidity in the market of the currency/instrument concerned realistically justifies uncovered positions of the size contemplated. These issues in turn lead on to consideration of capital adequacy requirements to meet liquidity requirements. Capital adequacy calculation is briefly considered in Chapter 10.

Liquidity maturity ladders by currency should be prepared and analyzed, based on assumptions for each type of transaction. Policy can then be drawn up, taking into account crisis scenarios, and a contingency plan should be in place that sets out appropriate action and responsibilities (*see* Chapter 10 for liquidity reporting to the FSA).

Legal risk

This risk comes from the inability to enforce contracts that are either incomplete or incorrectly completed. A procedure should be in place, usually in the middle office where the documentation unit will be sited, to ensure that completion of documents is pursued. Part of the procedure should be to ensure that counterparties have the necessary authority to transact business. This was highlighted in the local government Hammersmith and Fulham case where derivatives business done with the council was found to be *ultra vires*.

Settlement (delivery) risk

Settlement or delivery risk, often referred to as 'Herstatt risk', (*see* Chapters 1 and 6), is really a separate aspect of credit risk, though somewhat related to what is often termed systemic risk and also to operational risk.

> **An exception report should be seen daily to monitor exposures against set limits in the middle office as part of a risk monitoring role.**

A bank is exposed to the risk that a counterparty in any dealing contract may be unable to complete. But in this context it means that a counterparty may not pay the countercurrency to settle an FX deal, even though delivery of one side of the deal has been made (as in the case of Bankhaus Herstatt in 1974). This risk forms part of *valeur compensée* risk and is represented by the highest aggregate figure of boughts and solds with any one counterparty maturing on any one day.

An exception report should be seen daily to monitor exposures against set limits in the middle office as part of a risk monitoring role.

Risk concepts

Where counterparty credit risk is involved, the value that can be lost in a deposit/loan, or CD transaction in case of default, is usually the face or nominal value of the loan or paper held. However, with FX or derivatives such as FRAs or swaps the replacement credit risk calculation varies considerably, from approximately 2 per cent for a three-month duration FRA to 40 per cent for a five-year currency or interest rate swap.

The modern approach to allocation of credit limits for products is based on a variable weighting for each instrument or product, taking into account the nature of the instrument, tenor, currency and potential volatility.

Where positional risk is involved, a modelling approach that examines what would happen to portfolios on a given shift or change in interest and/or exchange rates is 'value at risk'(VAR), which is designed to measure potential loss on a statistical basis. Thus in simple terms, while mark to market gives the current value of a portfolio, value at risk (which is still evolving) looks beyond this to estimate a value over a defined time horizon.

There are disadvantages to VAR in that some of the assumptions made may be inaccurate. Under VAR, calculations are based on historic events and on the premise that changes in rates will generally have a normal distribution and that there are no sudden shifts in volatility. However, the method does enable risk controllers put some meaningful measure on risk parameters. The essential point to bear in mind is that it must not be the only measure.

More information on risk concepts can be found on the websites listed in the Appendix.

OPERATIONAL RISKS AND CONTROLS

Practically every area of treasury business covered in this book has a degree of operational risk, which has been highlighted and analyzed accordingly in the recommended systems and controls for each section. For our purposes, operational risks are defined as risks that are not directly related to counterparty and/or market exposure. Thus, for example, the breakdown of a control relating to a counterparty limit would be an operational risk, while the exposure caused would be counterparty/market risk. The consequences of operational risk could be the loss of all online trading screens, a rogue trader or ultimately the inability to make for example, USD payments on any particular day.

From the consummation of the trade through to settlement, elements of operational risk will crop up at various stages of the administrative process. The full range of operational risks may involve poor supervision, defective controls, systemic inadequacies or even natural disasters.

It is therefore important that management has a sound knowledge of operational risks and systems. In addition, most banks now have a regulatory compliance register that is updated regularly and seeks to identify possible risks to the bank, what action is to be taken and who is responsible.

While thorough and enforced internal controls are the front-line defence against operational risk, a number of software applications can also be used. These sit over the top of the production system and will be triggered only when an event happens outside the parameters set for that event. As straight-through processing with exception checking only becomes the norm, the role of such 'sleeper' applications is becoming critical in identifying rogue transactions.

The headings and control areas where problems most frequently arise can be summarised as follows:

- the essential segregation of duties and reporting between front, back and middle offices (Chapter 1);
- the important disciplines that govern the timely dispatch and checking of confirmations of trades (Chapter 3);
- the use, where desirable, of standard settlement instructions (SSIs) (Chapters 1 and 6);
- the implementation of payment netting and close-out netting agreements (Chapter 6);
- prompt exception reporting and quick response (Chapter 7);
- strict and timely reconciliation of all positions and nostro accounts (Chapter 7);
- the control of credit/positional limits and allocation and use thereof (this chapter);
- the risk controls recommended for third party payments (Chapter 6);
- well planned and tested contingency arrangements for systemic failure (this chapter).

Many of the above issues and recommended controls are also covered in detail under back office code of conduct in Chapter 10.

Disaster recovery issues

In recent years technological innovation has led to frequent changes in payments systems, clearing and other administrative functions. Therefore it is important that management conducts regular reviews of operational systems in order to keep pace with corresponding changes in control priorities. Disaster recovery (otherwise known as the 'business resumption plan') should be at the forefront of planning. This may range from the provision of a warm or hot back-up site for the main computers or servers through to the replication of a full dealing room and supporting payments and messaging services.

The main requirements are to:

- put in place a logical plan that covers the major factors while being reasonably simple and flexible enough to cover the differing types of failure (this may range from the failure of one machine at one site through to systemic failure of a whole network involving many banks, caused by any number of natural or man-made disasters);

- ensure that all staff are aware of whom to contact in the first instance and what they are required to do;

- make available quickly an essential infrastructure such as communications, dealing and payments capability – a comprehensive, up-to-date contact list of suppliers and vendors is vital;

- inform the market, counterparties etc. of the situation and what is being arranged regarding outstanding deals, payments etc.;

- keep the main disaster recovery steering group compact to minimize confusion;

- update the disaster plan frequently based on regular testing of systems and personnel.

SUMMARY

In this chapter we looked at the fundamentals of treasury systems and how they work. This led on to treasury accounting and various aspects of market and operational risks.

- Treasury systems account types and rules
- Treasury accounting, including the concepts of trading account and base currency
- Open position risk
- Operational risks

10

Compliance, control and documentation

This chapter introduces a range of compliance, control and documentary issues, emphasizing the Model Code relevant to the Settlements Certificate syllabus. Operational risks are covered in Chapter 9.

REGULATORY AND STATUTORY ISSUES

The central bank normally covers the regulatory arrangements for the wholesale markets in each country. In some countries an independent entity, such as the Banking Commission in Germany, grants banking licences in a separate function from the supervisory work of the central bank. The appointed regulatory body will, as a minimum, usually enforce the statutory environment at any point and in some periods anticipate it.

Operations management and staff must have an understanding of the main aspects of the banking regulatory regime for their 'home' country, as well as an awareness of the same issues in the major international centres in which they operate. Additionally, they should have an understanding of the method of monitoring adopted and the returns that are required to be produced for the authorities, particularly in the complex markets in which banks conduct their business today. These points are explored below, using the UK as a model.

UK Supervisory Policy

In the UK wholesale market, supervision is undertaken by the Financial Services Authority (FSA) to which responsibility was transferred in 1998 from the Bank of England. The FSA has set out a comprehensive *Guide to Banking Supervisory Policy* for financial institutions authorized under the Banking Act (1987) and explains the provisions of the Act relating to day-to-day issues. Supervision also takes account of the Basle Concordat principles regarding liquidity, solvency, FX positions and consolidation and relevant EU legislation directives such as cross-border supervisory provisions (*see* the FSA website at http://www.fsa.gov.uk). However, the Bank of England still actually collects the data on behalf of the FSA.

The most important of the other documents that make up the 'framework' under which the FSA regulates the wholesale markets may be summarized as follows:

- list of 'Authorized' money market institutions that 'act in the relevant markets as either principal or broker';
- the Grey Paper that sets out the FSA's approach to the regulation of the wholesale cash and OTC derivatives markets and firms under section 43 of the Financial Services Act;

- the London Code of Conduct covers issues such as the need for prompt settlement instructions and details payment and confirmation guidelines; it therefore becomes a first reference point for resolving treasury issues.

Both the Grey Paper and London Code of Conduct were reissued by the FSA in June 1999, replacing the previous versions issued by the Bank of England in 1995. Subsequent changes are now notified to the market through the issue of statutory instrument or market notices. (Details of the Grey Paper and the London Code of Conduct can be viewed at the FSA website.)

The Bank of England provides a list stipulating the frequency required from each banking institution depending on its classification. Where a foreign branch or subsidiary is reporting to the local supervisor, special rules often apply, with the local supervisor relying on the home supervisor to monitor the overall situation. In practice, this means some of the returns may not be required from the individual branch. Fortunately, as we have seen, the requirements of regulators worldwide are converging as a global approach is adopted. In the case of the UK the supervisory returns given in the list should not be confused with other statistical returns required by the Bank of England Statistical Returns unit.

Liquidity reporting (form LR)

It is important for the confidence in a bank that it can meet its depositors' demands on its resources. Traditional approaches to fulfilling this requirement have included identifiable reserve assets (mandatory liquid assets in various forms), the careful monitoring of cashflows over time periods and the maturity transformation of assets.

The EU Second Banking Directive sets out the requirements to monitor liquidity in the EU. There is a growing trend for supervisors to adopt a maturity mismatch approach, which measures liquidity by measuring the mismatch between inflows and outflows within specified time bands in a structured maturity ladder.

In the UK Schedule 3 of the Banking Act (1987) requires a bank to maintain adequate liquidity if it is to be considered that it is conducting its business in a prudent manner. A revised liquidity reporting (LR) return introduced in 1999 replaced several of the existing returns reporting maturity profiles and other analyses. The new return requires institutions to report on both a cashflow basis (out to one month) and a maturity analysis of assets and liabilities for time periods between one month and five years. By the third quarter of 2001 a cashflow out to six months may be required.

Foreign currency exposure (form S3)

Although every return is important, a key report from a treasury perspective is the open positions report, which needs to be monitored daily. In the UK this return is the S3 (foreign currency exposure report), the main components of which are:

- the net spot position – the sum of all assets (net of provisions) less all liabilities including accrued interest;
- the net forward position – all amounts to be received less all amounts to be paid under forward FX, gold transactions, futures, repos and reverse repos and the principal on currency swaps not included in the spot position
- other adjustments relating to guarantees, profits, future income/expenses, options and other derivatives (certain structural and non-banking positions may be excluded with the prior consent of the FSA).

The amalgamation of the net spot and forward positions above produces the overall open exchange position. Treasury management should agree the open position with the FSA return figure and comment on or explain any notable changes from the previous S3 return.

For S3 purposes, the overall open position limit is set individually for each bank by the FSA. (Outstanding liabilities and holdings of assets are normally reported at book value. For positions held in the trading book the reporting institution reports on a mark-to-market basis unless, otherwise agreed.) The S3 is slowly being phased out in favour of a risk modelling based approach to FX exposure.

Capital requirement

From this data the bank can calculate its overall capital requirement using one of two methods, with adjustments for currency pairs and additional charges for options. This is fully covered in the FSA *Guide to Banking Supervisory Policy* Volume 1 Section 4: FX risk. To give an indication of the process, Table 10 .1 shows how the calculation is made.

Capital adequacy

This area of supervision of the banking industry is evolving rapidly and what follows is a summary of the main issues involved, which the reader may investigate further. The term "capital adequacy" is used to describe the adequacy of a bank's capital in relation to risk, which arises from its assets, dealing operations (including off balance sheet transactions) and other risk associated with its business.

One of the main purposes of equity capital is to enable a bank to bear risk and absorb losses. These risks can include credit, country and transfer, market, interest rate, liquidity, operational and legal risk.

The Basle Accord of 1988 produced by the Committee on Banking Supervision has become the main capital adequacy structure used by banking supervisors and covers aspects of capital, risk weighting of assets and the required capital ratio to meet the mix of a bank's activities. The following issues in particular should be considered.

Calculating the overall capital requirement for FX exposure

Table 10.1

Calculate the net open position in each currency, excluding sterling. Translate each open position into base currency at prevailing spot rates.	
FOR CURRENCIES AND GOLD SUBJECT TO THE BASIC METHOD	
Sum of all net FX **short** positions in reporting currency	W
Sum of all net FX **long** positions in reporting currency	X
Overall net FX open position	Y (the larger of W or X)
Net open position in gold (whether long or short)	G
Capital charge under the basic method	Y+G $\times$ 8%=Z
EXTRA CAPITAL CHARGES FOR OPTIONS	
Options treated using carve out method	A
Options treated using a recognized model (including scenario matrix)	B
TOTAL CAPITAL REQUIREMENT	**Z+A+B**

Source: FSA Guide to Banking Supervisory Policy

- The basic distinction between the banking and trading books of a bank.
- The effect of hedge and matched transactions on capital adequacy calculations.
- Weighting of assets on the balance sheet depending on the type of transaction.
- Definition of capital and how it is classified and allocated against risk assets.

Types of capital and their use

Capital is classified into tiers depending on the quality of different instruments. Thus an example of tier 1 (or core) capital is the ordinary issued share capital of the bank. Tier 2 (supplementary) would be subordinated term debt, certain reserves and general provisions. The classification is further subdivided into upper and lower to allow more accurate grouping. For example, perpetual debt may be upper tier 2 while dated subordinated debt is always lower.

Ancillary capital, called tier 3 is allowable to support the trading book activity only for some banks. This debt has a minimum maturity of two years.

There are limits on the different types of capital. For purposes of calculating a bank's capital for capital ratio purposes the following main rules generally apply:

1 Total tier 2 subordinated term debt cannot exceed 50 per cent of total tier 1 capital.

2 An overall limit is applied to the banking entity (whether consolidated group or an individual bank) so that the total of tier 2 and 3 capital does not normally exceed 100 per cent of tier 1 capital.

3 There are limits on capital used to meet banking book requirements. Thus tier 2 capital used cannot exceed 100 per cent of the tier 1 capital to meet those requirements.

4 There are limits on capital used for trading book requirements. The total Tier 2 and tier 3 subordinated debt used must not exceed 200 per cent of the tier 1 capital used.

Balance sheet risk asset weightings

For practical purposes the Capital Adequacy Directive (CAD) sets out how risk weighting is applied to market risks. Under the CAD there are six risk weighted categories which, in the UK, are set out in the Bank of England's notice and capital adequacy returns. For treasury purposes, the most important of these are on-balance sheet, conversion and treatment of interest and foreign exchange related instruments (together with large exposures and counterparty risk). Once categorized, one of five balance sheet weightings is applied ranging from 0 to 100 per cent as appropriate. Illustrative examples of each weighting are:

- 0 per cent cash and collateralized cash deposits.
- 10 per cent fixed interest securities issued by specified governments with a residual maturity of one year or less.
- 20 per cent certain government fixed interest securities issued with a residual maturity of more than one year.
- 50 per cent certain types of secured lending.
- 100 per cent aggregate net short open foreign exchange position.

Capital requirements in the trading book

The treasury unit is concerned mainly with the trading book of the bank and the CAD defines this inter alia as proprietary positions in 'financial instruments' (generally speaking those transactions which a treasury would undertake), repos/reverse repos, settlement and counterparty risk and positions in loans/deposits where these are hedged trading book positions. Tests can be applied to determine whether a transaction should be classified as banking or trading.

Interest and foreign exchange risks form part of the market risk capital requirement under the CAD under a 'building block' approach. This means that each risk component is treated separately. The FX CAD charge has been explained earlier under FX capital requirement. The CAD interest rate risk charge is the addition of a general interest rate calculation and a specific interest rate calculation for each traded currency.

The general risk calculation is based on the scenario of risk of loss through general movements in interest rates. Two scenarios are allowable called the maturity and the duration methods.

The maturity method allows for individual positions to be allocated to agreed time bands depending on repricing criteria and allowing for different treatment of matched positions. The instruments are risk weighted.

The duration method allows for positions to be calculated using an assumed change in interest rates after adjusting for interest rate sensitivity based on cash flow time profiles. The figures are then matched within bands and the resulting matched and unmatched positions multiplied by appropriate percentages.

Special considerations apply for interest rate and currency derivatives such as swaps, FRAs, futures and options with the amount of risk dependent on several factors: how closely the transactions are matched; how far the contract is from maturity; the volatility of the underlying rate or price; whether the underlying is in the same currency.

The specific rate charge is calculated based on a percentage of 0 to 8 per cent of the market value of the instrument. E.g. certain government instruments are rated at 0 per cent while qualifying debt instruments range from 0.25 per cent to 1.6 per cent depending on residual maturity. There are a number of tests to meet the lower percentage criteria and an instrument failing one of thse would become a non qualifying item at 8 per cent.

Extracts from BIS Core Principles (Basle Accord on Capital Adequacy)

Principle 6 states that banking supervisors must set prudent and appropriate minimum capital adequacy requirements for all banks. Such requirements should reflect the risks that the banks undertake, and must define the components of capital, bearing in mind their ability to absorb losses. At least for internationally active banks, these requirements must not be less than those established in the Basle Capital Accord and its amendments.

In 1988, the member countries of the Basle Committee on Banking Supervision agreed to a method of ensuring a bank's capital adequacy. Many other countries have adopted the Capital Accord or something very close to it. The Accord addresses two important elements of a bank's activities: (1) different levels of credit risk inherent in its balance sheet; (2) off-balance sheet activities, which can represent a significant risk exposure.

The Accord defines what types of capital are acceptable for supervisory purposes and stresses the need for adequate levels of 'core capital' (in the accord this capital is referred to as tier 1 capital) consisting of permanent shareholders' equity and disclosed reserves that are created or maintained by appropriations of retained earnings or other surplus (e.g. share premiums, retained profit, general reserves and reserves required by law).

Disclosed reserves also include general funds that meet the following criteria: (1) allocations to the funds must be made out of post-tax retained earnings or out of pre-tax earnings adjusted for all potential tax liabilities; (2) the funds and movements into or out of them must be disclosed separately in the bank's published accounts; (3) the funds must be available to a bank to meet losses; and (4) losses cannot be charged directly to the funds but must be taken through the profit and loss account.

The Accord also acknowledges other forms of supplementary capital (referred to as tier 2 capital), such as other forms of reserves and hybrid capital instruments that should be included within a system of capital measurement.

The Accord assigns risk weights to on- and off-balance sheet exposures according to broad categories of relative riskiness. The framework of weights has been kept as simple as possible with only five weights being used: 0, 10, 20, 50 and 100 per cent.

The Accord sets minimum capital ratio requirements for internationally active banks of 4 per cent tier 1 capital and 8 per cent total (tier 1 plus tier 2) capital in relations to risk-weighted assets. (Although the Accord applies to internationally active banks, many countries also apply the Accord to their domestic banks.) These requirements are applied to banks on a consolidated basis. (Supervisors should, of course, also give consideration to monitoring the capital adequacy of banks on a non-consolidated basis.) It must be stressed that these ratios are considered a minimum standard and many supervisors require higher ratios or apply stricter definitions of capital or higher risk weights than set out in the Accord. (Bank for International Settlements, Paper no. 30, 'Core Principles for Effective Banking Supervision (Basle Core Principles)', September 1997).

Financial Services Act

The requirements of the Financial Services Act (1986) also mean that dealing and back office staff must be fully aware of the approved in-house procedures to be followed when dealing with counterparties and customers. This extends from 'know your customer' through to ensuring that the customer is identified and classified properly on the treasury system's 'client file' so that the correct type of confirmations will be issued.

While the Act is comprehensive regarding investments, wholesale markets activities generally fall outside the scope of the Act and are supervised separately (as indicated above). However, The FSA definition of investments includes options and futures, as well as stocks and shares, debentures and government and public securities. The 'carrying on of investment business' includes dealing, arranging, managing or giving advice. Thus it is inevitable that banks are involved in the requirements of the Act and therefore a strict 'new account' procedure should be in place for dealers and other staff to follow. Documented evidence of compliance should be held for future reference.

BACK OFFICE CODE OF CONDUCT

In May 2000 at the ACI International Congress in Paris, ACI–The Financial Markets Associated formally announced the publication of the Model Code: a new international code of conduct and practice for the financial markets. The new code is the culmination of an historic initiative, which was launched in 1998 in Sydney and involved close co-operation and regular discussions with the regulatory bodies and central banks in the USA, Europe and Japan, in addition to market committees and practitioners in many centres. The result is one international code that embraces the important provisions of the five previously recognized codes (of London, New York, Tokyo, Singapore and ACI), which had been included in the syllabus for the ACI dealing certificate.

The publication and recognition of the Model Code is therefore a welcome development for examination candidates in the 80 ACI members countries who had been obliged to undertake a rather laborious and time-consuming study of the five different codes.

As in the individual codes, the recommendations of best practice and conduct in the Model Code deal primarily with front office activity. However, many provisions cover back office and there are a number of important issues common to both areas. These have been extracted from the Model Code and are given in the following pages.

1 Back office location and segregation of duties/reporting

The improvement in global communications in recent years has been an important factor in the growing trends amongst financial institutions towards having front and back office in different locations. Many international banks have centralized and consolidated the back office administrative function in or close to head office but covering separate active dealing rooms in several overseas centres. Provided the regulatory authorities involved are in agreement with this arrangement, the Model Code has no objection to such a consolidation of the back office function.

However, there is no flexibility whatever concerning the insistence on the strict segregation of front and back office duties and reporting lines.

The organizational structure of market principals should ensure a strict segregation of duties and reporting lines, as well as independent risk management controls between front and back office staff. Where the middle office has a control or administrative function, a similar segregation of duties and reporting should apply.

> **The organizational structure of market principals should ensure a strict segregation of duties and reporting lines, as well as independent risk management controls between front and back office staff.**

The issue of physical segregation or location of the two offices is a matter for the management of each institution to decide, taking into account essential controls and local regulatory requirements. Whereas some institutions favour the administrative advantage of immediate or close proximity, there is, with modern communication and information technology, a growing trend amongst international banks active in several dealing centres to centralize back office operations in one location near to or in the same centre as head office. This structure will inevitably require the approval of the regulatory authorities in the centres involved.

The incentive and compensation plans for back office and middle office personnel should not be directly related to the financial performance of the traders.

2 Confirmation procedure – written

All transactions have to be confirmed in writing. Although the style and means of despatch have changed considerably in line with modern trends in information technology and communications, there are certain essential disciplines, particularly concerning timing and checking, which must be adhered to.

The issue and checking of confirmations is a back office responsibility, which should be carried out independently from those who initiate deals. Confirmations should be sent out as quickly as possible by both counterparties after a deal has been done, through an efficient and secure means of communication (preferably electronic) and should be addressed to the back office or settlements department of the counterparty. The practice of sending two confirmations (an initial one by fax or other acceptable electronic means), followed by a written confirmation is not recommended because the latter, if posted, might not arrive until after the settlement date and could cause confusion and uncertainty.

The format and content of a confirmation will vary according to the instrument dealt in and reference should be made to any applicable terms and conditions published, in order to ascertain the correct content and format for any particular instrument. As a minimum, however, all confirmations should include the following information:

- date of transaction
- by which means effected (broker, telephone, telex, dealing system, etc.)
- name and location of counterparty

- rate, amount and currency
- type and side of deal
- value date, maturity date and all other relevant dates (e.g. exercise date, etc.)
- standard terms/conditions applicable (e.g. FRABBA, BBAIRS, ISDA, ICOM, etc.)
- all other important, relevant information.

Brokers should confirm all transactions to both counterparties immediately by fax or other acceptable electronic means.

It is vital that principals check confirmations carefully and immediately upon receipt so that discrepancies can be quickly revealed and corrected. If the counterparty confirmation is considered incorrect, the counterparty should immediately be informed (preferably in writing or by electronic means). A new confirmation (or written agreement to a correction) should be requested from and be provided by the bank or counterparty whose original confirmation was incorrect.

It is not uncommon in some derivatives markets, and perfectly acceptable if the two principals involved agree, for only one party to the deal (rather than both) to send out a confirmation. But where this is so, it is imperative not only that the recipient checks it promptly, but that it also in good time responds to the issuer of the confirmation agreeing/querying the terms. It is also essential that the issuer of the confirmation has in place procedures for chasing a response if one is not forthcoming within a few hours of the confirmation being sent.

Many dealing systems produce confirmations automatically. Provided these are verified in the back office, no additional confirmation need be sent.

3 Confirmation procedure – verbal deal checks

In active and volatile markets, it is essential that any errors or differences between counterparties or brokers are highlighted as quickly as possible. As stated in the previous section, the prompt checking of conformations is an important control in this regard. Additionally, where the turnover justifies it, there is a strong cause to have in place an additional or interim 'call back' or verbal deal check system in order to identify and resolve, as soon as possible after the deal is agreed, any discrepancies particularly those involving amounts or value dates.

The practice of intraday oral deal checks is strongly recommended as it can be an important means of helping to reduce the number and size of differences, particularly when dealing through voice brokers or for deals involving foreign counterparties. It can also be useful in the faster moving markets, such as FX or when dealing in other instruments that have very short settlement periods.

It is for each firm to agree with their brokers (or counterparties) whether or not it wishes to instigate this practice and, if so, how many such checks a day it requires. If a single check is thought to be sufficient, it is recommended that this be undertaken towards or at the end of the trading day.

There should always be an acknowledgement between the parties on completion of the check that all deals have been agreed or, if not, that any identified discrepancies are resolved as a matter of urgency. Where the discrepancy involves a dispute resulting in an open risk for either counterparty, the position should be immediately closed out in the market without inference that either party is wrong, pending final resolution of the dispute. Where an error or difference is first highlighted by either party, lack of response should not be construed as an acknowledgment.

Where it is not possible for the broker to send a full confirmation immediately, for example, during the night, the principal should verbally reconfirm with the broker all the completed transactions.

4 Payment and settlement instructions

Errors or misunderstandings in payment and settlement instructions frequently result in expensive overdrafts and interest claims. Prompt, clear and early instructions are a priority. The use, where possible, of Standard Settlement Instructions (SSIs), helps to eliminate costly mistake.

Payment and settlement instructions should be passed as quickly as possible to facilitate prompt settlement. The use of SSIs between counterparties who regularly trade with each other is strongly recommended as their use can make a significant contribution to reducing both the incidence and size of differences arising from mistaken settlement of funds. SSIs should be established either via authenticated SWIFT message or confirmed letter and not by SWIFT broadcast.

Payment and settlement instructions should be passed as quickly as possible to facilitate prompt settlement.

In some FX and currency deposit markets, it is not customary for brokers to pass payment instructions where both counterparties are based in the same country as the broker, but the counterparties themselves must exchange instructions without delay.

Whether dealing direct or through a broker, principals should ensure that alterations to original payment instructions, including the paying agent where this has been specifically requested, should be immediately notified to the counterparty, and where a broker has been used and at least one of the principals is in another country, to the broker also. This notification should be supported by written, telex or similar confirmation of the new instructions, receipt of which should be acknowledged by the counterparty concerned. Failure to inform the broker of a change in instructions could place the liability for any ensuing difference with the principal.

Where the beneficiary of a transaction is a third party, it is management's responsibility to ensure that appropriate authentication controls are in place for the payment to be executed.

Where differences or costs occur resulting from a broker's error on payment instructions, it should be recognized that once payments do go astray, the broker is limited in what action it can directly take to rectify the situation. It is therefore recommended that the broker's liability in the event of such an error should be limited accordingly.

5 Netting

For several years there has been a growing interest in netting as financial institutions with substantial daily foreign exchange settlement requirements have sought to reduce some of the related credit exposure. With the global daily turnover in foreign exchange alone reaching USD1.5 trillion by the end of 1988, the Bank for International Settlements, particularly mindful of the potential settlement risk, has together with the major central banks exerted considerable pressure on the market banks to avail where possible of bilateral and multilateral netting agreements.

While the various forms of netting arrangements may have operational similarities, they can differ significantly in their legal and risk reducing characteristics. Some payment netting systems can achieve a substantial reduction in daily settlement risk whereas other more ambitious forms, such as netting by novation, seek to reduce the credit risk on gross outstanding transactions by legally substituting net obligations in place of gross obligations. Bilateral agreements covering these issues are now commonplace amongst active market participants.

The solution that is most likely to resolve the situation and satisfy the regulatory bodies may well involve the creation of a comprehensive international multilateral netting system with a broadly based clearing house. However, the logistical and legal complexities are considerable and after years of discussions and negotiations between various interested groups ad institutions, no such system is as yet operational although plans are well advanced for a multilateral payments netting service to open towards the end of the year 2001.

In the meantime , the Model Code recommends the use of netting systems to reduce settlement and credit risk.

Market institutions should, where activity justifies it, aim to reduce the settlement and related credit risk on currency transactions by establishing legally viable bilateral currency payment and transaction netting agreements with counterparties. They should also explore the potential for multilateral netting agreements.

It is strongly recommended that all participants be familiar with:

- the New York FX Committee's 1994 paper on 'Reducing Foreign Exchange settlement Risk';
- *The Supervisory Recognition of Netting for Capital Adequacy* Purposes published by the BIS in April 1993;
- the Group of Ten central banks' *Report of the Committee on Interbank Netting Schemes* published in November 1990.

6 New bank holidays/special holidays/market disruption

New bank holidays or non business/clearing days are periodically announced by the authorities in various centres. In order to ensure smooth and efficient functioning of the market, and bearing in mind these holidays are often unforeseen, clear market practice/procedures are in place.

In the event a country or a state declares a new national bank holiday or any other occurrence that would prevent settlement of banking transactions on a specific date in the future, the following procedures should be adopted for adjusting the value date on outstanding currency transactions maturing on that date:

- the new value date will be the first common business day (for both currencies contracted in the case of FX transactions) following the original value date, except where a bank holiday is declared on the last business day of the month, in which case the new value date will be the first common business day (for both currencies in the case of FX transactions) prior to month end ultimo;
- value dates in FX transactions will not be split other than in cases where both parties agree or where special local practice allows for split delivery, such as in certain Islamic countries;
- there will be no adjustment of the exchange rate on outstanding contracts.

7 Money laundering/know your counterparty

The various dimensions or phases of money laundering such as 'placing' or 'layering' are by their nature unlikely to directly involve a wholesale market dealer or broker. However, in cases where banknote trading is a treasury activity, there could be potential for involvement. In any event, both dealers and brokers are strongly urged to be aware of prudent 'know your customer' measures and the FATF (Financial Action Task Force) recommendations on this issue.

All banks are reminded of the need to 'know your customer' and should take all necessary steps to satisfy themselves that their transactions are not being used to facilitate money laundering. As part of an international effort to combat such activities, and in particular drugs-related laundering, the central bank governors of the Group of Ten (G-10) countries endorsed, in November 1988, a statement of best practice entitled the 'Basle Statement of Principles'. The Group of Seven in July 1989 promoted the creation of the Financial Action Task Force (FATF) to reinforce the commitments to combat money laundering.

> **Dealers should be aware of their obligation to report any suspicious transactions to the compliance officer, or to the appointed officer.**

Firms should adopt appropriate procedures consistent with the G-10 governors' statement and the FATF recommendations, and be well aware of their responsibilities in this matter. Only senior management should decide whether to undertake business with institutions dealing on behalf of clients on a discretionary management basis.

Dealers should be aware of their obligation to report any suspicious transactions to the compliance officer, or to the appointed officer who is charged with responsibility for money laundering issues.

Brokers are reminded of their responsibility to make their staff aware of money laundering issues and to be vigilant at all times where suspicious transactions are concerned.

8 Fraud

As dealers are generally precluded from a direct role in any administrative procedures requiring special authentication, such as making payments to a third party, instances of fraud directly involving dealers are rare. Nevertheless, strong administrative controls are recommended to prevent its occurrence.

Attempts at fraud occur regularly and many are meticulously planned. As there are several ways in which an institution can be defrauded, great vigilance is required by management and staff, particularly so when calls are received on an ordinary telephone line (usually in principal-to-principal transactions). As a precautionary measure, it is strongly recommended that the details of all telephone deals that do not include pre-agreed SSIs should be confirmed by telex or similar means by the recipient seeking an answer-back to ensure the deal is genuine.

Particular care should be taken in checking authenticity where the beneficiary is a third party or other than the transaction counterparty. In the event of any suspicious circumstances staff must notify management without delay.

9 Dealing for personal account

The practice of dealing for personal account, either in-house or externally, has several implications, including credit risk and potential conflict of interest. The Model Code advocates clear written management policies and controls.

Where dealing for personal account is allowed, management should ensure that adequate safeguards are established to prevent abuse or insider dealing in any form. These safeguards should also reflect the need to maintain confidentiality with respect to non-public price-sensitive information and to ensure that no action is taken by employees that might adversely affect the interests of the firm's clients or counterparties.

Management should have a clearly defined policy for personal transactions of staff, including investment transactions. Written procedures should be in place to cover these transactions, as well as those on behalf of the dealer's family and other members of personnel, management included. Managers should be aware that a conflict of interest may arise if traders are permitted to deal for themselves in those commodities, instruments or products closely related to the ones in which they deal for their institution and should stipulate clearly which ones, if any, the dealers can trade in for their own account.

Particular care should be exercised where day trading for personal account is concerned. There should be a full disclosure and transparency requirement ensuring that the traders give their full attention to their institution's business without being distracted by personal financial concerns.

Traders should recognize that they, too have a responsibility to identify and avoid conflicts of interest.

10 Authorization and responsibility for dealing activity

The process of appointment or authorization of treasury dealers to trade has become an important and more formal function of control in recent years. This official recognition of individual dealer's roles and authority must be set out in writing by management so that there is no ambiguity as to the transactions, instruments or markets in which the dealer is empowered to trade.

It is the responsibility of management to ensure that all employees are adequately trained and are aware of their own and their firm's responsibilities.

Control of the activities of all personnel engaged in dealing (both dealers and support staff) in both banking and broking firms is the responsibility of the management of such organizations. Management should clearly set out, in writing, the authorizations and responsibilities within which dealing and support staff should operate. These authorizations should also govern relationships with customers and clients and should ensure that any individual who commits the firm to a transaction has the necessary authority to do so. The authorizations might include:

- general dealing policy, including reporting procedures
- persons authorized to deal
- instruments to be dealt in
- limits on open positions, mismatch positions, counterparties, stop-loss limits etc.
- confirmation and settlement procedures
- relationships with brokers/banks
- other relevant guidance, as considered appropriate.

It is the responsibility of management to ensure that all employees are adequately trained and are aware of their own and their firm's responsibilities.

11 Terms and documentation

It is now common for OTC market deals to be subject to some form of legal documentation binding the two parties to certain standard conditions and undertakings. These can comprise either signed Master Agreements exchanged between the two parties or can take the form of Standard Terms.

Legal documentation covering instruments and transactions should be completed and exchanged as soon as possible after a deal is done, and the use, whenever possible, of standard terms and conditions to facilitate this process is recommended. Standard terms and conditions have been issued by various authorities for many instruments. Many of these are listed in Appendix 3.

When using such agreements, any proposed modifications or choices offered in the agreement must be clearly stated before dealing. When trading any of the products mentioned in the appendix, using this code of conduct, dealers and brokers should make it clear whether or not they propose to use standard terms. Where changes are proposed, these should also be made clear. If these changes are substantial, it is recommended that these amendments are negotiated and agreed before the consummation of the deal. For instruments where standard terms do not exist, particular care and attention should be paid to negotiation of terms and documentation.

In more complex transactions like swaps, dealers should regard themselves as bound to deal at the point where the commercial terms of the transaction are agreed. Making swap transactions subject to agreement on documentation is considered bad practice. Every effort should be made to finalize documentation as quickly as possible.

12 Telephone taping

Since the early 1970s the practice of recording dealing telephone conversations in the OTC markets has become so widespread that what was reluctantly considered acceptable and later desirable has now become mandatory. Easy and instant access to tapes promptly and efficiently settles dealing conversation disputes that might otherwise go unresolved for long periods, at times creating an atmosphere of doubt and even distrust. The practice of taping conversations is now almost universal for both front and back office lines. One major central bank warns in its code of conduct that 'failure to tape will normally count against a firm if it seeks to use the arbitration process'.

Experience has shown that recourse to tapes proves invaluable to the speedy resolution of differences. The use of recording equipment in the offices of banks and brokers is strongly recommended. All conversations undertaken by dealers and brokers should be recorded, together with back office telephone lines used by those responsible for confirming deals or passing payment or other instructions.

When installing tape equipment or taking on new clients or counterparties, firms should inform their counterparties and clients that conversations will be recorded. Tapes should be kept for at least two months. Firms engaged in dealing in longer term interest rate swaps, forward rate agreements or similar instruments where errors may only be found on the date that the first movement of funds is due to take place, may consider it prudent to retain tapes relevant to these transactions for longer periods.

Management should ensure that installation and control of the recording equipment complies with local legislation and that access to tapes, whether in use or in store, is strictly controlled so that they cannot be tampered with.

13 Internet/online trading

Internet or online trading is a recent but rapidly growing phenomenon that could have a substantial effect on money, exchange and derivative dealing in the near future. Existing use of the internet for client trading in particular has already highlighted the capacity to open up treasury business to a much wider field of participants than has been possible through any other means of communication. Although still in its embryonic stages, currency dealing through the internet has attracted the attention of a large number of international financial institutions, most of whom are actively developing the product to enhance their commercial treasury business.

Where internet trading facilities are established by a bank for a client, the conditions and controls should be comprehensively stated in the bank rule book. There should be appropriate security in place governing access, authentication and identification of personnel who are authorized to use the facility.

The 'know your customer' and money laundering provisions described later in this chapter are particularly relevant in this area and should be strictly adhered to.

14 Assignments and transfers

In the derivatives markets, assignments are a common occurrence. In order to take account of the credit and other implications of these transactions, the Model Code stipulates the correct practice and control procedures that must be adhered to.

Brokers and principals assigning or transferring a swap to a third party must ensure that:

- principals are aware that they are ultimately responsible for assessing the creditworthiness of a counterparty;
- staff are well trained in the practices of the market place and are aware of the firm's business responsibilities.

Principals who enter into any wholesale market transaction with the intention of shortly afterwards assigning or transferring the deal to a third party should make clear their intention to do so when initially negotiating the deal. It is recommended that the confirmation sent by the principal should specify any intention to assign, and give details of any procedure that will be used.

When a principal is intending to execute such a transfer, they should obtain the consent of the transferee before releasing their name. The transferee should give the principal intending to transfer sufficient information to enable the transaction to be conducted in accordance with the principles of best practice.

15 Dealing with unidentified principals

In recent years, the practice of concluding deals with principals who are unidentified at the outset has been a cause for increasing concern particularly in the area of credit risk. The Model Code advocates early identification and written management policy.

The recent increases in the volume of FX transactions conducted through fund managers/investment dealers has resulted in substantial numbers of deals where the principal counterparties are not known at the time of transaction. Dealers should identify counterparties as soon as possible following a deal.

> **Dealers should identify counterparties as soon as possible following a deal.**

Management at financial institutions engaged in trading on this basis need to be aware of the risks involved, particularly with respect to credit exposure and money laundering, and should have in place a written policy governing such transactions.

16 Dealing at non-current rates

The practice of dealing at non-current rates has been a contentious issue in the foreign exchange markets for over two decades. the Model Code strongly discourages such activity for reasons outlined but concedes that under certain stringent conditions the practice can be acceptable.

Deals at non-market rates should be avoided since such practices may result in concealment of a profit or loss, the perpetration of a fraud, tax evasion or the giving of an unauthorized extension of credit. Where, however, the use of non-current market rates may be necessary (as in the swaps market or in certain transactions with corporate clients), they should only be entered into with the prior express permission of senior management of both counterparties. Management should ensure that proper controls are in place, with clear audit trails, for the monitoring and reporting of such transactions.

Cash flow implications should be taken into account in the pricing. When setting the rates for the swap to extend the maturity, the spot rate should be fixed immediately within the current spread, to reflect current rates at the time the transaction was done.

17 Differences with brokers/use of points

The method by which a broker makes good an amount representing the difference for which a bank may justifiably 'stick' the broker has long been a contentious issue, particularly in the international foreign exchange markets. While the Model Code does not favour payment of differences by the 'points' system, there are strict conditions under which it may be acceptable.

Where a broker quotes a firm or unqualified price in a particular market or instrument for a specified or market amount and is subsequently unable to substantiate the quote when a deal is proposed, the bank proposing the trade is fully entitled to 'hold' or 'stick' the broker to the price quoted. This practice, which should not be a regular occurrence, is sometimes referred to as 'stuffing' the broker. This effectively means that the broker must make good the difference or loss to the proposing bank between the price quoted and the price at which the business is concluded.

Where these differences arise, the following guidelines for compensation should apply:

(a) Differences should be routinely referred to senior management for resolution thereby changing the dispute from an individual trader-broker issue to an inter-institutional issue. All compensation should take the form of a bank cheque or wire transfer in the name of the institution or of adjustment to brokerage bills.

(b) All such transactions should be fully documented by each firm. It is bad practice to refuse a broker's cheque or reduction in the brokerage bill for the amount concerned and to insist on a name at the original price.

On the subject of the settlement of differences by points the Committee for Professionalism reiterates its views as follows:

The Committee for Professionalism recognises that the worldwide foreign exchange markets function smoothly and efficiently with a minimum of official regulation, and is of the opinion that it is in the best interests of all members of our profession to promote and support any market practices which continue this tradition. The CFP has concluded that it does not favour the practice of settlement of differences by points, but recognises that it can be an acceptable practice in those centres where it is clearly subject to proper systems and controls.

MONEY LAUNDERING

Definition

The 'Guidance Notes for the Financial Sector', revised June 1997, published by the Joint Money Laundering Steering Group, defines money laundering as: 'the process by which criminals attempt to conceal the true origin and ownership of the proceeds of their criminal activities. If undertaken successfully, it also allows them to maintain control over those proceeds and, ultimately, to provide a legitimate cover for their source of income.'

An easier definition might be: 'Changing the identity of illegally obtained money so that it appears to have originated from a legitimate source. It usually represents the proceeds of drug trading, organized crime, fraud or terrorism.'

The trail often begins with cash proceeds of street drug sales, switched in stages to high denomination notes – convenient for subsequent smuggling across borders (for example the USA to Mexico). The next steps vary from disposal to numerous bank accounts and facilities designed to frustrate the audit trail, before remittance to the beneficiaries' accounts to other financial centres. This often involves the use of shell companies, forged invoices and a complex web of domestic and international transfers along the way.

According to the Guidance Notes, the activity is not confined to banks, other credit institutions and bureaux de change. Sophisticated laundering may often involve other 'unwitting accomplices' such as:

• accountants

• solicitors

- stockbrokers and securities houses
- insurance companies and insurance brokers
- financial intermediaries
- surveyors and estate agents
- casinos
- restaurants
- dealers in precious metals and bullion
- antique dealers
- car dealers
- dealers in high value commodities and luxury goods.

The three stages

The laundering process is usually accomplished in three stages:

- **Placement**: the physical disposal of the initial proceeds derived from illegal activity. The objective here is to move the money out of cash into non-cash form, such as a bank account or a financial product. This may be done by smuggling the cash physically to another country before depositing it into several bank accounts or by making numerous small cash instalments into different bank accounts.
- **Layering**: separating illicit proceeds from their source by creating complex layers of financial transactions. This is designed to disguise the audit trail and provide anonymity.
- **Integration**: the provision of apparent legitimacy to criminally derived wealth. If the layering process has succeeded, integration schemes place the laundered proceeds back into the economy in such a way that they re-enter the financial system as 'normal' business funds.

Legislation: UK

UK legislation on money laundering imposes an obligation on banks and investment firms and their staff, to report any *knowledge* or *suspicion* that funds are the proceeds of serious criminal conduct to the authorities. Failure to do so may render banks and investment firms and/or their staff liable to penalties, including fines or imprisonment. Disclosure is legally protected against breach of confidentiality claims of customers.

Legislation: EU

As money laundering is an international problem, many countries have enacted legislation to combat the phenomenon. In the EU most member countries have legislation similar to the UK. Many major financial institutions now have an appointed 'money laundering prevention officer' and or a 'money laundering reporting officer'. Some combine both roles by the appointment of one officer. The appropriate departments for these positions can be compliance, internal audit, or operations.

Reporting of suspicious activities

It is difficult to define a suspicious transaction because the various kinds of money laundering strategies are almost limitless. However, where treasury back office or dealers are concerned, there is a certain pattern to the types of trans-actions that could signal the need for caution, some of which are:

- transactions that are inconsistent with a customer's known normal legitimate business or personal activities;
- deals proposed at rates that are so profitable for the bank that they are almost off-market or 'too good to be true';
- settlement instructions to unusual or strange third party beneficiaries;
- customers who wish to exchange large quantities of low denomination notes for those of a higher denomination;
- customers transferring large sums of money to or from overseas locations with instructions for payment in cash;
- customers who constantly pay in or deposit cash to cover requests for bankers' drafts, money transfers or other negotiable and readily marketable money instruments;
- buying and selling of a security with no discernible purpose or in circum-stances that appear unusual;
- customers introduced by an overseas branch, affiliate or other bank based in countries where production of drugs or drug trafficking may be prevalent.

Where an employee has reason to be suspicious for the above and/or other reasons they are duty bound to report such suspicions to the appropriate money laundering officer.

Codes of conduct

The Model Code recommendations on money laundering are quoted in this chapter.

A comprehensive guide to money laundering can be found in the 'Guidance Notes for the Financial Sector', revised June 1997, published by the Joint Money Laundering Steering Group (Pinners Hall, 105–108 Old Broad Street, London EC2N 1EX).

DOCUMENTATION

Traditionally, in the wholesale markets, documentation was unnecessary between banks as FX money market lending and borrowing was based on the 'name' of the counterparty. This placed a heavy responsibility on to the credit department, which was asked to be the early-warning system for the bank as well as scrutinize balance sheets to decide what value of business it was comfortable with.

For corporate customers, basic approved documentation was and is necessary to establish:

- what business is to be done
- who can bind the company when dealing
- up to what value
- who can sign or authorize confirmations.

This quite often requires board resolutions; it is normal for a bank to hold a list of authorized signatories for a customer specifying individual authorities. Depending on the means of communication, an indemnity may be required to safeguard the bank, although a duty of care by the bank is always required.

For both bank and corporate entities, the advent of off balance sheet derivative transactions underlined the necessity for formal documentation, particularly in respect of netting requirements. Initially for interest rate swaps, the documentation was extended as new instruments, such as FRAs, and options, developed.

From the mid-1980s the British Bankers Association (BBA) introduced standardized documentation for various instrument types to enable the market to function efficiently. These are still in use today for some existing business, but have been largely superseded. The documents were:

- BBAIRS (1985 terms): standard terms for the trading of interest rate swaps;
- FRABBA (1985 terms): standard terms for forward rate agreements to be traded;
- LICOM (1985 terms): standard terms for currency options (superseded by ICOM97);
- SAFEBBA (1989 terms): standard terms for synthetic agreements for FX.

Documentation initially was on a bilateral office basis between two counterparties. But a more globally recognized document was needed for wider ranging international use. This requirement was met by the International Swap Dealers Association (ISDA) which developed the ISDA document, beginning in 1987 through to 1992; the latter now covering most treasury instruments.

Present-day arrangements

There are now three main document 'groupings' in the interbank/large corporate marketplace covering the main legal jurisdictions and filling differing requirements. These can be summarized as follows:

1 **International Swap Dealers Association (ISDA) Master Agreement**: covers all treasury instruments (for example, derivatives, FX plus options but not repos). It will normally be one of two types:

- a local currency single-jurisdiction master agreement where both parties are in the same jurisdiction and conduct transactions in the local currency of that jurisdiction;
- a multicurrency cross-border master agreement where transactions/payments involve various currencies between parties in different jurisdictions.

Typically 1992 terms are current, with 1998a supplement. There is also a 1999 review, including credit derivatives. For an example, *see* ISDA's website: http://www.isda.org.uk

2 **Global Master Repurchase Agreement (GMRA)**: representing the combined efforts of the Public Securities Association (PSA) USA and the International Securities Market Association (ISMA) Switzerland. This can be used either as an agreement for repos plus gilts repos (under UK law) or as master repo agreement for treasury instruments (under US law). (*See* PSA's website: http://www.psa.com for an example.)

3 **IFEMA (International Foreign Exchange Master Agreement) 1997**: for FX netting on a payments basis, produced by the Foreign Exchange Committee of the FED in association with the BBA, the Canadian Foreign Exchange Committee and the Tokyo Foreign Exchange Committee.

ICOM (International Currency Options Market) 97: for currency options.

FEOMA 97 (International Foreign Exchange and Options Master Agreement: covers both FX and currency options, with special clauses.

(*See* BBA's website: www.bba.org.com.)
Still in use for existing deals are:

- **FRABBAs for FRAs (1985)**
- **BBAIRs for swaps (1985).**

Whereas LICOM (1985) has been superseded by **ICOM 97**.

As these documents are in general standard usage, with simple variables in the schedule, they are sometimes preferred by corporates for product-specific transactions.

General points

A master agreement, such as the ISDA 1992 document, consists of three basic parts. These can be called the agreement, schedule and confirmation. The master agreement addresses two types of risk: credit risk and delivery risk

- **Credit risk** is covered by setting out as covenants the status of the parties at the outset and in the event of default, the consequences of a breach over the life of the transaction enforcement provisions, including the method of valuation of outstanding transactions.

- **Delivery risk** is covered whereby when payments are due under different transactions or instruments on the same date and in the same currency, it allows the counterparties to net payment flows if they choose to do so in the schedule to the agreement. Of course, one party need not pay the other party if the latter is in a specified state of default: this is known as a conditional clause.

> **The trend is now progressively towards global master agreements between banks and in some cases international corporates.**

The trend is now progressively towards global master agreements between banks and in some cases international corporates. The global agreement facilitates cross-product bilateral netting (whether by payment or close-out), reduces negotiation and vetting of agreements, so resulting in lower costs.

In larger treasuries the head of operations is quite often authorized to sign agreements on behalf of the bank after vetting by the legal unit. It is important therefore that the management of the support area has a working knowledge of the clauses that make up these types of agreements. A summary of the main points and a brief explanation of each is given in Table 10.2.

The main clauses in a master agreement

Table 10.2

Clause/heading	Explanation
Local or cross-border	Covers the situation where both parties are governed by the same or different jurisdictions
Representations	Confirms that each party is legally formed and that the officers have authority to contract etc.
Agreements	Requires each party to supply the appropriate documentation as requested; for example, lists of authorised signatures
Obligations	Indicates the payment netting and settlement definitions that address delivery risk
Default and termination events	Indicates action on the failure to pay, bankruptcy and similar events
Early termination events	Details of procedures required for both parties
Transfer	Limits the ability of each party to transfer any contract or interest without the agreement of the other party
Notices	Refers to the schedule and how the agreement will be governed
Definitions	Explains the major terms of the agreement
Schedules	Enables parties to alter or amend the provisions of the standard master agreement as they wish by amending provisions or adding alternatives
Confirmations	A standard form of confirmation is defined for each type of instrument traded

Source: The Chartered Institute of Bankers

SUMMARY

In this chapter we have looked at compliance and control issues, including regulatory reporting and money laundering. We have also reviewed the Model Code as it relates to operations procedures. Finally, we have reviewed the current position with regard to documentation for treasury instruments.

Key points

- Role of the regulator
- Open positions
- The Model Code
- Money laundering procedures
- Types of documentation

Current and future developments

This chapter considers some current and potential developments in the financial markets, the business fundamentals that drive them and how the industry is responding.

The banking industry has gone through tremendous change during the last few decades. Treasury has been in the forefront of this change, driven by twin aims of improved competitiveness in the trading room and increased efficiency in the back office. Advances in technology, which in turn have initiated role changes (examined earlier in this book and summarized below), have met both of these aims.

Electronic trading platforms for dealers and automation of routine procedures in the back office have transformed the way treasury business is conducted and the roles performed by dealers, middle office and back office alike. The relationship between these areas has also changed, along with the recognition that all functions are interdependent and maximum profitability only comes from focus on the total business.

Throughout this book we have remarked on the pace of change in the support areas, as technology progressively allows mundane checking functions to be transformed into automatic matching and exception reporting, so allowing people to be used in more productive and interesting roles. But this is only the beginning with the technology revolution now upon us, we enter the 'real' electronic age.

GLOBAL TRADING: GLOBAL PROCESSING?

To understand the impact of technology on the treasury support functions, we first have to review the changes taking place on the trading floors of the major banks of the world. As we have seen in previous chapters, the advent of trading execution platforms, such as Reuters 2000 and EBS, heralded a profound change in working practices in treasury dealing rooms.

The lucrative arbitrage incentives that for a time existed between cash, FX forwards, FRA swaps and futures while the new market instruments settled down have now all but disappeared, since they 'matured' under the weight of enormous arbitrage activity. Even the opportunities between bonds and equities, often involving more complex and imperfect strategies, have to a great extent been arbitraged out of existence.

On the other hand, dealers now have many more high performance tools to ply their trade – such as multiple data sources, charting software and techniques to a standard not available even ten years ago. The latter however, constitute more of a technical support for the analysis of strategic and dealing risk positions rather than the highly lucrative nil-risk *per se* arbitrage of the 1980s.

One interesting result of the new software tools is that the dealers no longer simply use their skills to execute the trade but are now required effectively to input as well. They now have a vested interest in ensuring the accuracy of input so that the can instantly access online positions, ladders, and run 'what if' scenarios.

The trading platforms have also acted as a catalyst in consolidating diverse financial centres into a *de facto* global market, forcing banks and other participants to trade 'around the clock'. Different approaches have been adopted to do this, which can often involve moving the 'book' and positions from one major centre to another. These may include Tokyo or Sydney, followed by Frankfurt or London and on to New York, following the time zones. Alternatively, one site can be designated as the global point for a particular product, which may be traded 24 hours a day by that centre.

> **Many banks, outside the top flight, still remain generally local in processing terms.**

However, while trading may be moving to a global environment, the processing and settlements functions have been slow to follow, promoting regional rather than global aspirations. Many banks, outside the top flight, still remain generally local in processing terms.

There are various reasons for the drive towards centralized processing and for the slowness of change. These may be summarized as below.

The reasons (and benefits) for centralized processing

- The logic systems of being able to cut costs by processing centrally is compelling. Clearly, if the system are in place and the products are generic, one centre is likely to be more efficient than a dozen scattered around the world all doing the same thing. This centre is likely to be located in the country of the bank's head office: sometimes referred to as a bank going or coming 'home' with that part of its business.

- There is better risk management if all trading, processing, settlement, reconciliation and monitoring are in one place. Credit lines can also be more easily managed.

- Screen-based trading makes the introduction of linked straight-through processing (STP) more practical, achievable and even easier in one place. Coupled with continuous linked settlement (CLS) via real-time gross payments systems (RTGS), this will improve management of intraday liquidity requirements.

- A more benign statutory environment in local jurisdiction may be attained, which may allow local books of the bank to be maintained outside the country of origination.

- It is possible for the local regulators in the host or home country to rely on the regulator for some of the banking supervisory requirements.
- Benefits gained are in streamlining operations, improving control and reducing costs.
- The increasing impact of the internet, providing a platform for real-time trading capability, forces banks to think globally throughout their entire operation.

The problems

- Fragmented legacy systems, which do not allow for efficient processing or settlement beyond national borders.
- Difficulties in meeting payment deadlines in each time zone when the originating unit is remote.
- Impact on staff when 24-hour shifts are imposed, upsetting personal arrangements and normal lifestyles.
- Language difficulties that may inhibit the resolving of errors and queries quickly.

Despite these obstacles, the business rationale will exists to move progressively to regional and eventually global processing and settlement.

We can now look in more detail at some of the responses to these 'drivers', such as STP, RTGS and CLS.

STRAIGHT-THROUGH PROCESSING (STP)

What do we mean by straight-through processing (STP)? Although there is no standard definition, the main aims are to reduce costs and enhance risk management control by automating most of the steps in the processing chain, relying on exception reporting only. This would indicate a definition that included 'end-to-end automation in all interrelated processes from input through to final settlement'.

Another approach is to regard complete automation of a part of component of the processing chain as STP, rather than encompassing all processing activity. STP was for a time on the 'back burner' in the banking industry while resources were focused on preparing for Y2K millennium bug. As this problem has receded, STP should now command much more attention, while the drive to reduce costs and the advent of CLS should further underline its advantages.

Increased efficiency is the initial aim of STP. However, the potential for improved risk management is equally important. STP means fast processing – improving the environment and quality of the database for value at risk measurement before settlement.

The optimal solution is a single database of outstanding trades that can be accessed for risk management purposes on a global basis. Thus the requirement becomes that of 24-hour access. This can be an insurmountable problem for old legacy systems that require an 'overnight' update. A further problem is closing local jurisdiction books, to satisfy local regulators, while maintaining a global set of records offering an overall view of the bank's books.

Costs

One of the main business drivers towards the introduction of STP is the requirement to reduce costs, both in overall terms and on a cost per transaction for each type of instrument. As transactions tend to become more complex, the measurement of these can be more difficult, but the end results in improving the ability to run the business can be very worthwhile. The main point to remember is that the actual basic processing costs may only be the tip of the iceberg and additional tracking of costs will be required to provide the full picture. These will involve such issues as additional accounting, evaluation and management of all the risks involved, and separate profit and loss calculations while the value of the individual instruments making up the total transactions fluctuate independently.

> The optimal solution is a single database of outstanding trades that can be accessed for risk management purposes on a global basis.

Essential elements for STP

STP for FX and money market transactions is a reality. Typically, the essential elements include some or all of the following, on a global or regional basis:

- automated trading platforms and/or input capability with linked field-by-field checking; leading through to
- transaction recall for efficient exception checking by back office using full workflow support techniques;
- automated matching of brokers' confirmations with exception reporting, probably using proprietary specialized software application (PSSA);
- automated matching of counterparty confirmations with exception reporting, probably using PSSA;
- automatic payment generation module, incorporating
  - standard settlement instructions and SWIFT BIC directories
  - special checks (for example, for high value/third party payments)
  - outgoing and incoming message repair;
- automatic cash management and cash nostro reconciliation using PSSA;

- real-time consolidated reporting of positions, credit limits, risk management aspects and profitability analysis.

For many banks it would be understatement to say that the above are still some way from implementation. Nevertheless, a number of major banks have achieved this for all or part of their processing chain.

Derivatives processing are an altogether different story. Quite often the derivatives system has been bolted on to existing cash markets systems and the links back into the bank's main general ledger and other systems are often fragile, requiring significant manual intervention. Further, the transactions, beyond straight vanilla types, are more complex, often forming part of a larger overall arbitrage or linked strategy. This requires special manual intervention by experienced staff on input for such things as message suppression and for accounting and risk management. This increases costs of processing and reduces the net return on trading.

STP for vanilla (uncomplicated) derivatives is one aim of the Global Straight-Through Processing Association, particularly as the infrastructure required for cash, derivatives and other financial markets converge. As part of this we are seeing the emergence of initiatives to create clearing houses for OTC derivatives, parallel to exchange-traded transactions. The first step in this is the standardization and automation of confirmation sending and matching. In a similar way, more automation, including STP, is needed if the securities market is to achieve a further reduction in settlement from the T+3 norm to T+1 or even T=0.

REAL-TIME GROSS SETTLEMENT SYSTEMS (RTGS)

We looked at how RTGS works in some detail in Chapter 4. Here we are more concerned with how RTGS will fit into future developments in a global trading and settlements environment.

The main business drivers can be summarized as the need for increased efficiency at the lowest possible cost, consistent with meeting industry best practice and regulatory requirements. These in turn drive centralization of dealing and support functions in a global market place. The centralization of payments systems form part of this efficiency drive; RTGS reduces the need for intraday liquidity, thus providing banks with a double benefit.

TARGET (see Chapter 4) provides a good example of this in practice. The volume of payments in the euro is high, with good liquidity in the system. This allows for efficient liquidity management, compared to net payment settlement systems where liquidity is effectively caught within the system until the end of the day. As the reality of STP is attained by more institutions, this concept will become effective.

CONTINUOUS LINKED SETTLEMENT (CLS)

This is potentially a very important development in treasury settlements and brings into question whether, over time, other forms of payments netting would still be required. CLS was established in 1997 and by 1998 had the backing of a consortium of 60 major FX trading banks with the aim of eliminating settlement risk, initially on FX transactions.

As explained in an earlier chapter, banks are currently at risk if one side of a FX deal has been settled before the receipt of the countercurrency. CLS Bank will act as a settlement intermediary for each member bank or the main world trading currencies across five time zones, using as the basic mechanism a duplicate MT 300 confirmation, which will be transmitted to CLS. This, after aggregation with other confirmations, forms the basis of settlement through the RTGS system for each currency involved. However CLS will not guarantee settlement of the deals it handles. It is designed only to be a payment versus payment system to protect against 'Herstatt type' settlement/delivery risk.

> **Banks are currently at risk if one side of a FX deal has been settled before the recept of the countercurrency.**

The FX netting operations of ECHONet and Multinet have been closed in anticipation of CLS commencement. However, this has been postponed from its original start date of October 2000 to the third quarter of 2001. Apart from FXNet, this leaves a significant risk gap in the operation of banks' settlement systems, which the market needs to address quickly.

One issue to be resolved is the narrow settlement window in the European time zone of only five hours, which could constrain correspondent bank operations, since payments will still be required to be made depending on where the operations are located.

Another important point is that the system must attract sufficient critical mass to be a success in the medium term.

CLS is an important development because it will provide the capability for the first global payments system which could provide the springboard over time for all users of the net, not just banks.

SWIFT recognizes that for the future it must transform itself from a payments co-operative run by the banks into an institution holding centre stage on the internet acting as the guardian of message standards, security and levels of service.

A useful illustration of how CLS should work is reproduced from the CLS website in Figs 11.1 to 11.6 by kind permission of CLS.

Fig 11.1

A day in the life of CLS Bank International (all time reference in CET summer time)

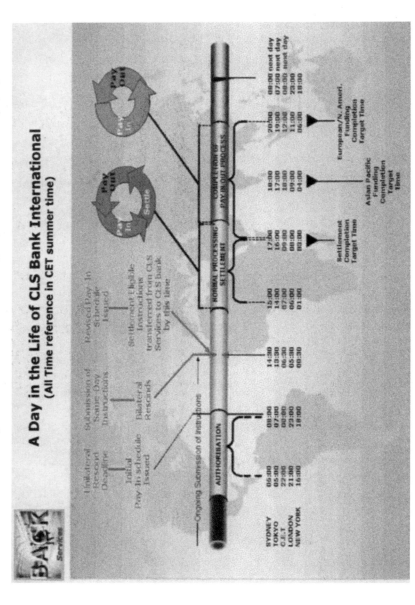

Source: CLS Services Ltd

The settlement process

Fig 11.2

The Settlement Process

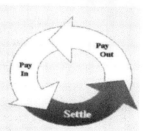

Prior to the start of settlement processing, a settlement processing queue is formed containing all Settlement Eligible Instructions for that Value Date. Each such Instruction will be placed on the settlement processing queue in accordance with its assigned sequence number. Thus, the settlement processing queue consists of all Instructions (including those resulting from the splitting process) that were classified as Settlement Eligible Instructions prior to the calculation of the initial Pay-in Schedule in random order, followed by all Same Day Instructions (including those resulting from the splitting process) classified as Settlement Eligible Instruction after the calculation of initial Pay-In Schedule in sequential order.

The settlement process involves the settlement of Settlement Eligible Instructions in the settlement processing queue that satisfy three risk management tes[t] CLS Bank will only settle Settlement Eligible Instructions if, after giving the effect of settlement to the Accounts of the relevant Settlement Members, the two affected Accounts would each comply with the following risk management tests:

(1) any Short Position in respect of each eligible currency must not exceed the Short Position Limit which is set for a Settlement Member in each eligible currency; such Short Position Limits are based on committed liquidity facilities in that currency that are available to CLS Bank for th[e] settlement day;

(2) the Aggregate Short Position in the Settlement Member's Account, calculated as an equivalent U.S. Dollar value, must not exceed the Aggregate Short Position Limit which is set fo[r] that Settlement Member; and

(3) each Settlement Member's Adjusted Account Balance must be greater than or equal to zero

Upon determining that the Accounts of the two Settlement Members satisfy each of the risk management tests, CLS Bank will simultaneously debit and credit their respective Accounts wit[h] eligible currency in the amounts specified in the Settlement Eligible Instructions which have jus[t] been tested, and final legal settlement of Instructions will occur. If any of these tests are not satisfied, no debits or credits will be made when the tests are completed; however, such Settlement Eligible Instructions will remain on the settlement processing queue and will be re-

▶

Fig 11.2 cont.

applied to all Settlement Eligible Instructions on the settlement processing queue until the applicable eligible currency closing time has passed or all Settlement Eligible Instructions have been settled.

To facilitate the settlement of Instructions, CLS Bank's settlement process will continuously during the settlement day (i) receive payments of specified currencies from its Settlement Members, (ii) settle Settlement Eligible Instructions, and (iii) disburse funds in specified eligible currencies to its Settlement Members.

In order to be in a position to fulfill its obligations to pay-out long balances to eligible Settlemer Members in a particular eligible currency on a same-day basis, CLS Bank must complete its operations in that currency before the Approved Payment System for that particular currency closes. If all Instructions are not settled by the Settlement Completion Target Time, CLS Bank will stop attempting to settle those Instructions involving an eligible currency for which the Approved Payment System closing time approaches . At a time prior to the relevant Approved Payment System close, each affected Member will be automatically notified by the CLS System its Instructions in the closing currency that will not settle in CLS Bank on that Value Date. According to the proposed Operational Timeline, Settlement Members will be notified of the Instructions involving Asian Pacific currencies that will not be settled in CLS Bank at 10:25 C.E. Since more time remains before the other Approved Payment Systems close, CLS Bank intends to attempt settling Instructions not involving Asian Pacific currencies past the Settlement Completion Target Time.

If Settlement Eligible Instructions remain on the settlement processing queue after CLS Bank h finished attempting to settle such Instructions, such Instructions will be removed from the quer and no longer processed for settlement. Each affected Member will be notified of the final statu of its Instructions. Each affected Member will then have to decide whether (i) to resubmit such unsettled Instruction(s) to CLS Bank for settlement processing the next business day, or (ii) settle the related fx transaction(s) outside CLS Bank and manage its settlement exposure unde the terms of its master agreement governing fx transactions.

If expected pay-ins have not been received, CLS Bank will need to follow its failure managemer procedures, which may include calling on its committed liquidity facilities to pay-out Long Positions to eligible Settlement Members.

Source: CLS Services Ltd

CLS participants

Fig 11.3

CLS Participants

Member Types	Other Participants
CLS Bank will offer two types of membership to the qualifying shareholders of CLS Services - membership as either a Settlement Member or User Member (collectively, the "Members").	**Third Parties**
Settlement Members	All other entities may access the Service only having Members, as principals, submit Instructions on their behalf. However, the ter on which Members will act on behalf of customers will be governed through private arrangements with the Members. Such arrangements will not directly involve CLS Bar and these other entities will not have any relationship with CLS Bank.
Each Member of CLS Bank may submit Instructions directly for settlement processing by the Service and receive information on the status of Instructions submitted by it directly from CLS Bank.	
Each Settlement Member will have a single multi-currency Account with CLS Bank.	
Each Designated Settlement Member authorizing an Instruction submitted by a User Member will act as principal in respect of the settlement of each such Instruction through its Account, as well as the obligations to make payments necessary to settle such Instruction, whether for itself or as a Designated Settlement Member for one or more User Members.	 **Nostro Agents**
User Members	
A User Member will not have an account with CLS Bank and must instead be sponsored by a Settlement Member (a "Designated Settlement Member") that will act on its behalf.	**Central Banks & Approved Payment Systems**
Each Instruction submitted by a User Member must be authorized by a Designated Settlement Member (either manually and/or automatically under a set of limits established by the Designated Settlement Member), after which such Instruction will then be eligible for settlement through the Account of the Designated Settlement Member.	

Source: CLS Services Ltd

Fig 11.4

Central banks and approved payment systems

 Central Banks & Approved Payment Systems

Australian Dollar (AUD)

CLS Bank will be a member and direct participant of the Reserve Bank Information and Transfer System (RITS), the AUD RTGS system, which is operated by the Reserve Bank of Australia (RBA). CLS Bank will have an exchange settlement account (ESA) with the RBA. As CLS Bank will not have any offices located in Australia, it will participate in RITS on a "remote access" basis.

CLS Bank will become a member of the High Value Clearing System (HVCS) operated by the Australian Payments and Clearing Association (APCA), of which CLS Bank will also become a member, in order to access RITS. CLS Bank will exchange payment and reconciliation message via the S.W.I.F.T. FIN Network.

In order to support the inclusion of AUD in the CLS Service, the RBA is proposing to extend the operating hours of RITS in order that it overlaps with the CLS Bank funding and settlement processing schedule.

Canadian Dollar (CAD)

CLS Bank will not participate directly in the Large Value Transfer System (LVTS), the CAD payment system, which is operated by the Canadian Payments Association (CPA). CLS Bank will instead use the "nostro services" of the Bank of Canada (i.e., the Bank of Canada will participat in LVTS on CLS Bank's behalf), with which it will exchange payment and reconciliation message via the S.W.I.F.T. FIN Network. CLS Bank will have a central bank account with the Bank of Canada.

In order to support the inclusion of CAD in the CLS Service, the CPA is proposing to provide an earlier opening of LVTS in order that it overlaps with the CLS Bank funding and settlement processing schedule. Its opening time will change to 01:00 E.S.T. from its current time of 08:0(E.S.T.

Euro (EUR)

CLS Bank will not participate directly in the Trans European Automated Real Time Gross Settlement Express Transfer system (TARGET), the inter-linking system which connects all of tl relevant national RTGS systems of the Member States of the European Union. CLS Bank will instead be a customer of the European Payment Mechanism (EPM), the payment system operat by the European Central Bank and connected to TARGET, with which it will exchange payment and reconciliation messages via the S.W.I.F.T. FIN Network. CLS Bank will have a central bank account with the European Central Bank.

Japanese Yen (JPY)

CLS Bank will access the Bank of Japan Network (BOJNET), the JPY RTGS system, through the Foreign Exchange Yen Clearing System (FXYCS), which is operated by the Tokyo Bankers Association (TBA), of which CLS Bank will have a "special" relationship short of full membership CLS Bank will have a central bank account with the Bank of Japan. As CLS Bank will not have a branch office located in Japan, it will participate in BOJNET, through FXYCS, on a "remote acces basis.

Fig 11.4 cont.

In order to support the inclusion of JPY in the CLS Service, the Bank of Japan is extend the operating hours of BOJNET in order that it overlaps with the CLS Ban settlement processing schedule. Its closing time will be extended to 19:00 JST fi time of 17:00 J.S.T., with the capacity to extend to 20:00 J.S.T. should CLS Ban

Pound Sterling (GBP)

CLS Bank will not participate directly in the Clearing House Automated Payment the GBP RTGS system, which is operated by the Association of Payment and Cle (APACS). CLS Bank will instead use the "nostro services" of the Bank of England Banking Office (i.e., the Bank of England will participate in CHAPS on CLS Bank's which it will exchange payment and reconciliation messages through the S.W.I.F CLS Bank will have a central bank account with the Bank of England.

Swiss Franc (CHF)

CLS Bank will be a member and direct participant of the Swiss Interbank Clearin the CHF RTGS system, which is operated by Telekurs AG on behalf of the Swiss CLS Bank will have a clearing account in SIC itself and a central bank account w National Bank. As CLS Bank will not have any offices located in Switzerland, it w SIC on a "remote access" basis.

CLS Bank will become a member of Telekurs AG. **United States Dollar (USD)**

CLS Bank will be a member and direct participant of Fedwire, the USD RTGS system, which is operated by the Federal Reserve Bank. CLS Bank will have a central bank account with the Federal Reserve Bank of New York.

Source: CLS Services Ltd

CLS Bank impact on the markets

Fig 11.5

CLS Bank Impact on the Markets

Pre CLS Bank	Within CLS Bank
• Separate Payments Separate Time Zone • Many Payments for Gross Settlements • Value Day Gross Funding • Nostro in each currency • S.W.I.F.T. Fin • Up to 3 days exposure	• PVP, Simultaneous Settlement of Instructions • Few payments for Net Funding • Funding (precise Timing/Intra Day) • Multi Currency Service • SWIFTNet (IP Protocol)/S.W.I.F.T. FIN • Real time settlement confirmation

Source: CLS Services Ltd

Fig 11.6

Shareholders of CLS Services Ltd.

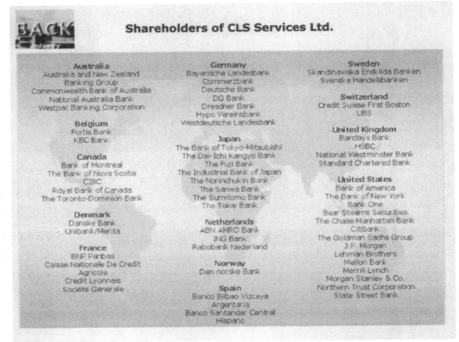

Shareholders of CLS Services Ltd.

Australia	**Germany**	**Sweden**
Australia and New Zealand Banking Group	Bayerische Landesbank	Skandinaviska Enskilda Banken
Commonwealth Bank of Australia	Commerzbank	Svenska Handelsbanken
National Australia Bank	Deutsche Bank	
Westpac Banking Corporation	DG Bank	**Switzerland**
	Dresdner Bank	Credit Suisse First Boston
Belgium	Hypo Vereinsbank	UBS
Fortis Bank	Westdeutsche Landesbank	
KBC Bank		**United Kingdom**
	Japan	Barclays Bank
Canada	The Bank of Tokyo-Mitsubishi	HSBC
Bank of Montreal	The Dai-Ichi Kangyo Bank	National Westminster Bank
The Bank of Nova Scotia	The Fuji Bank	Standard Chartered Bank
CIBC	The Industrial Bank of Japan	
Royal Bank of Canada	The Norinchukin Bank	**United States**
The Toronto-Dominion Bank	The Sanwa Bank	Bank of America
	The Sumitomo Bank	The Bank of New York
Denmark	The Tokai Bank	Bank One
Danske Bank		Bear Stearns Securities
Unibank/Merita	**Netherlands**	The Chase Manhattan Bank
	ABN AMRO Bank	Citibank
	ING Bank	The Goldman Sachs Group
France	Rabobank Nederland	J.P. Morgan
BNP Paribas		Lehman Brothers
Caisse Nationale De Credit Agricole	**Norway**	Mellon Bank
Credit Lyonnais	Den norske Bank	Merrill Lynch
Société Generale		Morgan Stanley & Co.
	Spain	Northern Trust Corporation
	Banco Bilbao Vizcaya Argentaria	State Street Bank
	Banco Santander Central Hispano	

Source: CLS Services Ltd

GLOBAL CUSTODY DEVELOPMENTS

This section should be read in conjunction with Chapter 5 on securities settlement and payments systems (where the functions of international and natonal custodian clearing houses were explained).

There are several concurrent developments in securities processing and settlement, aimed at simplifying settlement and shorter lead time to settlement. In terms of simplification the most important developments are:

- Proposed Euroclear 'hub and spoke' structure, this arrangement would place Euroclear as the international centre of national depositories with the existing link to Clearstream.

- Proposed Clearstream link-up with Deutsche Termin Börse (DTB) to form a new entity. This was to be joined by Sicovam the French clearer. This proposal is now in doubt and a link-up with Euroclear has been agreed in principle.

- Proposals to 'cluster' depositories to form a pan-European group of national depositories.

- On the settlement side, SIBOS in 1999 intensified the discussion regarding the settlement time for securities – currently normally trade date plus three business (working days), or T+3. Current proposals included T+1 or even T+0. These seem some way off bearing in mind current system constraints and the systems efforts required to reach T+3 from the old T+5 in 1997.

CONCLUSION

The pace of change is now unrelenting. Today's cutting edge may be outdated by tomorrow and this is as true of the back office operations as it is elsewhere. Financial markets appear to be converging on ambitious and complex systemic crossroads in the pursuit of efficiency and innovation. It seems likely, for example, that trading focus on the internet will intensify, possibly creating new administrative dilemmas.

Whatever evolves in the area of treasury processing, administration and control over the next few years, it would be naïve to expect a smooth transitional passage. While the regulator's nightmare of systemic chaos or total payments 'gridlock' may recede, some major risk-related phenomena are sure to surface. There may well be serious difficulties or even crises to overcome before superior technology is able to create a more settled and efficient environment.

Financial markets appear to be converging on ambitious and complex systemic crossroads in the pursuit of efficiency and innovation.

In the meantime, the main challenges for treasury back office management will be to keep pace with, analyze and selectively implement and manage the changes.

SUMMARY

In this chapter we have looked at some of the future developments and issues relevant to the office operations area of treasury. The main drivers involved include shortening settlement times as processing is progressively automated and centralized.

Key points

- Telecommunications developments have enabled regional and global processing
- All financial markets moving towards immediate settlement on a STP basis
- CLS, although delayed, will set the benchmark for settlement industry in all instruments

Market terminology

From the instant a deal is consummated there is an immediate back office interest in the transaction. Whether the trade is typed on a dealing system, electronic broker or done on the telephone directly with the counterparty or through a voice broker, the early stages of the administration process quickly involves a member of back office staff. This close order of activity brings the officer into contact with dealing room technical jargon.

A knowledge of this jargon will often be acquired through direct and frequent contact with the dealers. Either way, a working knowledge of dealing terminology in the various money, exchange and derivatives markets is essential in order to understand and process the transactions.

The growth of new markets instruments and products, such as financial futures and derivatives, has brought with it a corresponding proliferation of technical terms. This is true of both dealing (for example, 'out of the money', 'delta hedge' 'synthetic forward') and processing (for example, 'cash settlement' and 'euribor').

There are many glossaries in existence that purport to define financial terminology. Although many are extensive, most are incomplete, especially where new instruments and dealing terminology are concerned. For the purpose of this guide, which has been officially endorsed by ACI–The Financial Markets Association we quote the unique section on market terminology in the new Model Code. Although it is not meant to be an exhaustive glossary on financial products, the following section defines and explains the various markets' terminology, instruments and strategies. It is an important reference document for both dealing and back office management and staff.

INTRODUCTION

In most markets, whether exchange traded or OTC, the process of agreeing trades or deals generally conforms to a pattern. Over time, a recognized, acceptable market jargon or specialized terminology usually evolves. The faster and more volatile the market, the greater the need for concise standardized language, so that the business can be transacted or negotiated quickly and clearly with as few words as possible. This is particularly true of 'voice' or 'open outcry' markets such as voice-broked and telephonically transacted FX and open outcry 'auction' style futures. In the case of the latter, the process is complemented by an official hand-signal language, sometimes referred to as 'tic-tac'.

To ensure the efficiency and integrity of the market, it is vital that the market terminology that evolves has a sound technical basis and is professionally and universally recognized. The language may be brief or concise but there must be no room for ambiguity or misunderstanding as to what is being conveyed.

Spot FX

The FX market is a good example of an OTC market where a useful professional dealing language exists, enjoying widespread recognition. The basic spot dealing terminology clearly illustrates its advantages with liberal use of the complementary terms 'mine' and 'yours'.

The simple term 'mine' when used in response to a spot quotation, effectively means: ' I *buy* from you the base currency and sell you the counter currency for spot delivery in the amount for which the quote was made at the rate at which the base currency is offered in your quote.'

If the spot dollar/yen was quoted 121.15–121.20 in 10, the above spot deal proposal would be to buy USD10 million at 121.20.

The logic that underwrites this standardization is the market understanding that *unless otherwise specified*, the dealer always 'talks' or refers to the base currency and deals in millions. If the quote was made without reference to a specific amount, the proposition '5 yours' would mean I *sell* 5 million of the base currency (USD) for spot delivery at 121.15.

Forward FX

Similarly, in most markets, on a forward points (or premium/discount) quotation of, say, 70–60 for three months USD/CHF in 10, the proposition 'mine' would mean : 'I sell for spot delivery and *buy* three months forward delivery USD10 million at a premium on forward CHF or discount on forward USD of 0.60 CHF centimes.'

Again, the market understanding similar to the spot parameters applies, with the additional proviso that in all forward or exchange swap transactions, the primary reference is to (or the dealer 'talks') the forward date.

However, the latter understanding to 'talk the forward date' may not be universal and for this reason the Model Code recommends that FX swap dealing propositions should include one other element such as the price ('at 60') in order to underline which 'side' and eliminate any possibility of misunderstanding.

In recent years, the increase in arbitrage activity between markets, such as futures (centralized) and money, FX or cash (OTC), has gradually given rise to common or cross-market terminology that does not always convey identical meaning. For this reason, care should be exercised when using abbreviated terminology in diverse markets.

Interest rate swaps

The much younger interest rate swap (IRS) market uses a similarly evolved convention when stipulating exchanges of interest between counterparties.

'Plain vanilla' fixed versus floating interest rate swap deals are quoted and agreed using the fixed rate of interest as the primary variable of negotiation of the trade. The multidimensional and flexible nature of the product, however, means that there are a number of different permutations in terms of fixed and floating rate payment frequencies, day counts and rate references possible for any one swap.

For most currencies, a standard structure has emerged under which the majority of business is transacted. IRS market convention effectively uses redundancy to 'default' to the 'norm' meaning that at the time of quotation/consummation it is not necessary to stipulate the exact structure of each potential transaction.

Unless otherwise specified, where the norm is understood, a 'payer of five year euro at 4.12' will, for the five-year duration of the deal, pay annually a fixed rate of interest of 4.12 per cent on a 30/360 day count and against that receive a floating rate of six-month euribor on an actual/360 day count, reset semi-annually and paid in arrears.

Where potential ambiguities arise, as in the cross-currency basis swap market, the exact terms of the transaction should be specified at the outset, in order to avoid misunderstanding between counterparties or brokers.

Interest rate options

The interest rate option markets for caps, collars, floors and swaptions contain vast numbers of possible permutations of option, style, period, structure and strike price, as well as various underlying interest rate products on which the option may be written. Despite this, as in the interest rate swap market, the majority of business is concentrated into standard structures, which have become the market norm and require no qualification beyond the basic parameters.

Therefore, the writer of a USD three-year European style 6 per cent payer's option on a five-year annual money market (actual/360) swap against three-month Libor at a premium of 95 per cent of the notional principal, on a net cash settlement structure, will in fact be represented in the market as: 'a seller of three years five years, 6 per cent payer's at 95'. If the option was American style, the underlying swap against six-month Libor or the option to be exercised into a swap, as opposed to its present valued cash equivalent, would all require qualification.

As the standard structures differ from currency to currency, are largely unwritten and will sometimes change as markets evolve and mature, it is recommended practice in potentially ambiguous cases to specify the precise terms at the time of quotation or negotiation.

Finally, in all dealing conversations, it is strongly recommended that where there is any doubt, it is best to err on the side of caution and clarify what is being proposed rather than risk using any terminology that could be misinterpreted.

Selected market language and terminology is explained in the following pages of the Model Code in order to clarify certain situations that arise in the course of quotation and consummation of OTC deals and to serve as a useful guide for market participants. This section is not meant to be a comprehensive glossary of every term and instrument, rather an illustration of general market interpretation of the terminology and products contained herein.

1 QUOTATIONS AND TRANSACTIONS IN THE FOREIGN EXCHANGE (FX) AND MONEY MARKETS (MM)

Mine/I buy[1]/I take   Proposal to deal.

FX (spot) or FX forward outright: I take/I buy the base currency at the offered rate in the quotation for the amount quoted or proposed.

FX (forward FX swap):   I sell spot delivery and *buy forward* the base currency at the forward offered rate for the amount quoted or proposed.[2]

MM: I borrow at the offered rate for the amount quoted or proposed.

Yours/I sell[1]/I give   Proposal to deal.

FX (spot) or FX forward outright: I give/I sell the base currency at the bid rate in the quotation for the amount quoted or proposed.

FX (forward FX swap):   I buy spot delivery and *sell forward* the base currency at the forward bid rate for the amount quoted or proposed.[2] In typed dealing conversations, some traders further abbreviate 'buy' and 'sell' with 'B' and 'S' respectively, but this practice is not universal.

MM: I lend at the bid rate for the amount quoted or proposed.

Given   A deal has been proposed and agreed at the bid price quoted.

Taken   A deal has been proposed and agreed at the offered price quoted.

Join ... at/Support ... at   A commitment to putting an additional bid or offer at a current bid or offer price already quoted by the broker. In response to a broker's quote ' 5.⅛–5.¼' a dealer may say ' I shall join you on the bid side at 5.⅛ for 10' meaning ' I also bid 5.⅛ for 10 million'.

Off   Cancellation of existing bids or offers.

Bid/Buy[1]/Pay

FX (spot) or FX forward outright: A statement of a rate at which the dealer will buy the base currency.

FX (forward FX swap): The dealer will sell spot and buy the forward base currency.[2]

MM: The dealer will borrow.

Sell[1]/Offer

FX (spot) or FX forward outright: A statement of a rate at which the dealer will sell the base currency.

FX (forward FX swap): The dealer will buy spot and sell the fwd base currency.[2]

MM: The dealer will lend.

Under reference A qualification stating that the rate quoted (in the market) may no longer be valid and requires confirmation before any trades can be agreed.

Either way/Choice/Your choice Same price for both bid and offer.

Done Deal agreed as proposed.

Firm/Firm price The rate quoted is valid and can be traded on.

For indication/Indication/For information/For level Indicative quotation only – should be validated/confirmed before trades are proposed.

Checking The availability of a credit limit is being checked before the deal can be agreed.

Your risk The quoting dealer cautions the receiver of the quote (perhaps through the broker) that the price may have to be requoted at the receiver's risk.

My risk An acknowledgement by the dealer receiving the quote that the rate may have to be requoted at the receiver's risk

Points/Pips[1] The smallest unit of an exchange rate. Typically:

USD/JPY = One hundredth of a Yen

EUR/USD = One hundredth of a US cent

GBP/USD = One hundredth of a US cent

USD/CHF = One hundredth of a Swiss centime (Rappen)

Basis points One hundredth of 1 per cent in an interest rate.

Premium The difference between the spot and forward FX rates expressed in points, when the rate for the forward date is more expensive than the rate for the near date. (The term when used in options is completely different.)

Discount The difference between the spot and forward FX rates expressed in points, when the rate for the forward date is cheaper than the rate for the near date.

Par The spot and forward exchange rates for a specific period are the same.

Outright price   Any FX price for delivery on any date that is not part of an FX swap transaction. Although it is not usually referred to as such, a spot exchange rate quotation is a *de facto* outright price for delivery on the spot date. All other outright prices are calculated with a spot base, adjusted by the premium/discount swap 'points' for the appropriate period from the spot date.

Notes
1   Denotes terminology used only in the foreign exchange.
2   See the section on forward exchange on page 217.

2 DEALING PERIODS, DELIVERY DATES, AND MATURITY DATES IN THE FX, MM AND DERIVATIVES MARKETS

Spot   Generally, two banking days from 'today'. Exceptions include the Canadian dollar (CAD) and the Hong Kong dollar (HKD).

Regular dates/periods/Fixed dates   One week, one month, two months, three months, six months and one year usually from spot or occasionally from today in domestic money markets.

IMM dates   The four dates for which financial futures contracts are traded at the International Monetary Market (IMM) Division of the Chicago Mercantile Exchange. These are the third Wednesday of March, June, September and December.

Odd/Broken/Cock dates   Dates other than the regular dates.

Short dates   Maturity dates of less than one month.

Overnight   Value today against tomorrow (or next business day).

Tom next   Value tomorrow (next business day) against the following business day (spot).

Spot next   Value spot against the following business day.

One week   Value spot against one week from the spot date in foreign exchange; value today against one week from today in domestic money markets.

Tom week/One week over tomorrow   Value tomorrow (or next business day) against one week from that date.

Turn of the month   Value last business day of the month against first business day of the next month.

Spot against end month/End of the month   Value spot against the last business day of the month.

Turn of the year   Value last business day of the year against the first business day of the next year.

Forward-forward/(fwd/fwd)   Value any forward date against any other forward date. Can apply to both MM and FX instruments.

3 CURRENCY OPTIONS TRANSACTIONS

American (style) option   An option that can be exercised on any business day up to and including the expiration day.

ARO (average rate option)   Options that refer to the average rate of the underlying exchange rate that existed during the life of the option. This average will be used to determine the intrinsic value of the option by comparison with the predetermined fixed strike. If the option is a call option, and the average rate exceeds the strike, the buyer will receive a cashflow (i.e. the difference between the average rate and the strike). For a put option, the average must be below the strike.

At the money   An option is at the money when the price of the underlying instrument is very close to or equal to the option's strike price.

Buyer (holder)   The party that purchases an option by the payment of a premium and who has the right but not the obligation to buy (call) or sell (put) the currency.

Call option   The right to purchase a specified amount of a specified currency against another currency by a certain date at a certain price.

Compound   A compound option is an option on an option: the buyer has the right to buy a plain vanilla call or put option at a pre-determined date and at a pre-determined rate. The strike of the plain vanilla option is also pre-determined.

Cut-off time/Expiration time   The time at which the right to exercise expires on the expiration date. In general, for interbank transactions in the European and American markets it is 10.00 am New York time or 3.00 pm Tokyo time.

Delivery date   The date on which delivery of the two currencies involved is conducted, based on the exercise of an option. Normally, it is two business days after the expiration date.

Delta   Also known as the hedge ratio, the ratio of change in the option price compared with the change in the price of the underlying instrument, when all other conditions are fixed.

Delta hedge   An FX transaction that squares up the potential FX position created when an option transaction is concluded. The amount to be hedged is calculated by multiplying the notional amount of the option by the delta.

Digital   A digital option is a transaction where a specified amount will be paid if the spot rate is above the strike at expiry for calls (or below the strike for puts). The intervening path of spot between the trade date and expiry is irrelevant: the determining factor is whether or not the spot is above or below the strike at the time of expiry.

Double knockin   A double knockin option is a standard type of option that automatically appears if one of the formerly specified exchange rates (or an exceeding level) is dealt in the spot market before expiration. The double knockin then becomes a standard (plain vanilla) option.

Double knockout   A double knockout option is a standard type of option that automatically disappears if one of the formerly specified exchange rates (or an exceeding level) is dealt in the spot market before expiration.

Double one touch   A transaction where a specified amount will be paid on the delivery date only if spot has dealt (exceeding) one of the two exchange rates previously specified before expiration.

European (style) option   An option that can only be exercised on the option's expiration date.

Exercise   To make use of the right which is possessed by a party to an option contract, e.g., the right to buy. Upon receipt of notification of intention to exercise the right, the seller of the option is obligated to deal with the option buyer in accordance with the terms agreed.

Expiration date   The date on which the right of the buyer of an option to exercise the option shall lapse.

Historical volatility   The standard deviation is the logarithm of the relative price of the underlying instrument expressed as an annual rate. Calculations are based on market movements.

Implied volatility   The volatility of an option derived from its remaining characteristics which are known; i.e. strike price, premium, expiration date, interest rates and style.

In the money   An option is in the money when the price of the underlying instrument is lower than the strike price of the put option or the price of the underlying instrument is higher than the strike price of the call option.

Intrinsic value   The amount by which an option is in the money (on a mark-to-market basis).

Knockin   A knockin option is a standard type of option which automatically appears if a formally specified exchange rate or an exceeding level is dealt in the spot market before expiration. Knockin option reaches the instrike point when the spot rate moves towards 'out of the money'.

Reverse knockin option (or 'kickin option') reaches the instrike point when the spot rate moves towards 'in the money.'

Knockout   A knockout option is a standard type of option that automatically disappears if a formally specified exchange rate or an exceeding level is dealt in the spot market before expiration. In the knockout option, the spot rate moves towards 'out of the money' in order to reach the outstrike. A reverse knockout option (or 'kickout option') reaches the outstrike point when the spot rate moves towards 'in the money'.

No touch   A transaction where a specified amount will be paid on the delivery date only if the spot rate is not dealt at the touchstrike or an exceeding exchange rate level previously specified before expiration. No touch is also called 'lock out'.

One touch   A transaction where a specified amount will be paid only if the spot rate is dealt at the touchstrike or an exceeding exchange rate previously specified before expiration. One touch is also called 'lock in' or 'touch digital'. There are also types where the specified amount will be paid two days after the deal has matured.

Out of the money   An option is out of the money when the price of the underlying instrument is higher than the strike price of the put option, or the price of the underlying instrument is lower than the strike price of the call option.

Premium/Option cost   The price of an option, paid by the option buyer and received by the option seller. Payment and receipt of a premium normally takes place two business days after the transaction date.

Put option   The right to sell a specified amount of a specified currency against another currency by a certain date at a certain price.

Range binary   A transaction (also called a 'double no touch') where a specific amount will be paid only if spot is not dealt at, or at levels exceeding the predefined two exchange rates before expiration.

Risk reversal   A combination of a long (short) call option and a short (long) put option with, as a rule, same style, notional value, same expiration date and same absolute value of the delta.

Seller (writer)   The party that sells an option and receives a premium and is obliged to perform if and when the holder exercises the option.

Straddle   A combination of the purchase of both a call and a put or the sale of both a call and a put with identical characteristics (such as style, expiration dates and same notional amounts and the same strike price).

Strangle   A combination of the purchase of both a call and a put or the sale of both a call and a put with different strike prices but with identical other characteristics (such as style, expiry dates and notional amounts).

Strike price/Exercise price   The contracted rate that will apply should the option be exercised.

Synthetic forward   A combination of a long (short) call option and short (long) put option with the same face value, same expiration date, same style, and where the strike price is equal to the forward price.

Time value The portion of an option's value that equals the option current premium minus the intrinsic value.

Volatility A quantification of the standard deviation of the exchange rate for an over-the-counter option market. Volatility rates are quoted at levels that take into account the dealer's expectation of future market movements.

4 INTEREST RATE DERIVATIVE PRODUCTS

Forward rate agreement (FRA)

An FRA is an over-the-counter contract, usually between two financial institutions, to settle the difference in interest for a notional amount in a given currency between the contracted rate and the eventual settlement rate for a fixed period commencing in the future.

In money market financial terminology, an FRA is essentially a fixed rate forward/forward non-deliverable deposit/loan (placement) transaction, cash settled with an agreed market reference rate calculation process at commencement of the forward/forward period.

FRA buyer The FRA counterparty who will be compensated by the seller if the eventual settlement rate exceeds the contracted rate or who will pay the seller the corresponding difference if the settlement rate is less than the contracted rate.

FRA seller The FRA counterparty who will be compensated by the buyer if the settlement rate is less than the contracted rate or who will pay the buyer the corresponding difference if the settlement rate exceeds the contracted rate.

Interest rate swaps (IRS)

An interest rate swap is a contract between two participants or counterparties in which interest payments are made based on the notional principal amount, which itself is never paid or received. The fixed rate payment in the swap (often called the fixed rate coupon) is made by the fixed rate payer to the floating rate payer. Similarly, the floating rate payment in the swap is made by the floating rate payer (or variable rate payer) to the fixed rate payer. Both fixed and floating interest are calculated from the swap's effective date. The trade date is the date on which the counterparties commit to the swap.

Fixed rate payer Pays fixed in the swap; receiving floating in the swap (generally), has established the price sensitivities of a longer term fixed rate liability and a floating rate asset.

Floating rate payer Pays floating in the swap; receiving fixed in the swap (generally); has established the price sensitivities of a longer term fixed rate asset and a floating rate liability.

Currency swaps   A contract similar to a parallel or back-to-back loan. In a currency swap the counterparties do not lend currencies to each other but sell them to each other with a concomitant agreement to reverse the exchange of currencies at a fixed date in the future at the same price. The interest rates for the two currencies are not reflected in the two exchanges but are paid separately.

Interest rate options

Interest rate cap   An agreement between the seller (or provider) of a cap and a borrower, under which the seller pays to the buyer (in return for payment of an up-front fee or premium payable value spot) an amount equal to the extent to which a previously specified market rate exceeds the agreed cap rate during an agreed period of time. This protects the borrower against a rise in rates without locking the borrower into a fixed rate commitment.

Interest rate floor   An agreement between the seller (or provider) of the floor and an investor, under which the seller pays to the buyer (in return for payment of an up-front fee or premium payable value spot) an amount equal to the extent to which a previously specified market rate falls below the agreed 'floor' rate during an agreed period of time. This protects the investor against a fall in rates without locking the investor into a fixed rate commitment.

Interest rate collar   A combination of a cap and a floor agreement designed to limit a borrower's floating rate costs to between maximum and minimum pre-agreed rates. In return for a fee/premium, the seller of the collar pays to the buyer an amount equal to the extent to which a previously specified market rate exceeds the agreed cap rate during an agreed period of time. If the market rate falls below the floor rate, the borrower pays to the buyer an amount equal to the extent of the difference during an agreed period of time. When the market rate is between the cap and floor rates, the borrower pays the market rate. The buyer of a collar, therefore, has their borrowing cost confined to a band (or collar) ranging from the floor to the cap. An investor may also use a collar to provide a return between two agreed interest rates.

Swaption   An option granted by the seller that gives the buyer the right to enter into an underlying interest rate swap transaction, or in some cases to be paid a cash settlement amount in respect of the underlying interest rate swap transaction, at or with reference to a pre-determined settlement rate.

5 MISCELLANEOUS TERMINOLOGY

Cash settlement   The means by which non-deliverable financial instruments usually derivatives such as FRAs, are settled with reference to a pre-specified market settlement rate such as BBA LIBOR and euribor.

Euribor   The interest reference rate specifically for the euro calculated daily by a panel of 57 banks of which 47 are from EC countries.

LIBID   London Interbank Bid Rate. Unlike LIBOR, it is not an officially published settlement or reference rate, rather a non-specific reference to the going 'prime' interbank bid rate in the London market at any one time.

LIBOR   London Interbank Offered Rate, calculated daily from the rates of 16 London banks. It is widely used as a reference rate for loan agreements and more recently as the cash settlement reference rate of non-deliverable financial instruments in the major currencies.

Non-deliverable forwards (NDFs)   Forward exchange contracts where the counterparties have agreed in advance to non-delivery with cash settlement instead, at maturity, by reference to the prevailing spot rate as quoted by a pre-determined source.

Repos   A repurchase agreement between two parties whereby one party sells the other a security, at a specified price, in exchange for cash, with a commitment to repurchase the security at the same price and repay the cash plus interest at the agreed rate at a specified later date.

Appendix

USEFUL WEBSITES

Many financial associations, regulatory bodies and other financial institutions now have readily accessible websites which contain much useful information on several topics covered in this book. The list of websites, which can be visited either for basic information or further reading is being added to regularly.

From the websites that we have reviewed we have selected the following, which we would particularly recommend.

ACI–The Financial Markets Association   www.aciforex.com

Bank of England   www.bankofengland.co.uk

Bank for International Settlements   www.bis.org

British Bankers Association (BBA)   www.bba.org.com

The Chartered Institute of Bankers (CIB)   www.cib.org.uk

Federal Reserve Bank   www.federalreserve.gov

Financial Services Authority (FSA)   www.fsa.gov.uk

International Swap Dealers Association (ISDA)   www.isda.org.uk

Public Securities Association (PSA)   www.psa.com

INDEX